The Dental Team in the European Union

Sondra Z. Koff

The Dental Team in the European Union

Sondra Z. Koff
Department of Political Science
Binghamton University
Binghamton, NY, USA

ISBN 978-3-030-72234-0 ISBN 978-3-030-72232-6 (eBook)
https://doi.org/10.1007/978-3-030-72232-6

This Springer imprint is published by the registered company Springer Nature Switzerland AG
The registered company address is: Gewerbestrasse 11, 6330 Cham, Switzerland

For Steve
This time something different
Always with love

European Union Member States and Year of Entry and Exit

AUSTRIA-1995
BELGIUM-1952
BULGARIA-2007
CROATIA-2013
CYPRUS-2004
CZECH REPUBLIC-2004
DENMARK-1973
ESTONIA-2004
FINLAND-1995
FRANCE-1952
GERMANY-1952
GREECE-1981
HUNGARY-2004
IRELAND-1973
ITALY-1952
LATVIA-2004
LITHUANIA-2004
LUXEMBOURG-1952
MALTA-2004
THE NETHERLANDS-1952
POLAND-2004
PORTUGAL-1986
ROMANIA-2007
SLOVAKIA-2004
SLOVENIA-2004
SPAIN-1986
SWEDEN-1995
UNITED KINGDOM-1973
  WITHDRAWAL-2020

Acknowledgments

I am appreciative of the help with computer technology offered by my son, Dino, and his daughter, Abigail.

Abbreviations

A Level	Advanced Level
AMR	Antimicrobial Resistance
CJEU	Court of Justice of the European Union
CPD	Continuing Professional Development
DCPs	Dental Care Professionals
ECTS	European Credit Transfer System
EEA	European Economic Area
EP	European Parliament
EU	European Union
HIV/AIDS	Human Immunodeficiency Virus/Acquired Immunodeficiency Syndrome
OMC	Open Method of Coordination
SDGs	Sustainable Development Goals
VAT	Value-Added Tax

Contents

1 Introduction 1
Oral Health 1
Europeanization 2
Formation of the European Union 3
Professionalization 7
Professional Training and Recognition: The Legal Instruments 9
References 17

2 The First Stage of Professionalization: Education 21
Dentist: Undergraduate Education 21
Dentists: Specialization 30
Dental Hygienists and Dually Qualified Dental Hygienists-Therapists 34
Dental Technicians 37
Clinical Dental Technicians 39
Dental Assistants/Dental Nurses 40
Orthodontic Therapists 41
Treatment Coordinators 42
Student Attitudes and Behavior 42
The Learning Environment 43
Faculty 44
Curricula 45
Interprofessional Education 46
Outreach 48
Teaching Methods 49
Conclusion 50
References 51

3 Dental Care Professionals: Regulation 61
Dentists 61
Auxiliaries 65
Dental Hygienists 65

Dental Assistants/Dental Nurses/Chair-Side Assistants 66
Dental Technicians 67
Continuing Professional Development 68
Codes of Ethics 75
Patient Complaints and Fitness to Practice 77
Conclusion 82
References 83

4 **Member States: Healthcare Provision** 89
The Healthcare Delivery System: Its Finances 89
Public Healthcare Programs 94
Secondary Sources of Healthcare Coverage 96
Conclusion 99
References 100

5 **The Dental Squad** 105
Dentists 105
Dental Hygienists and Dental Hygienists-Therapists 112
Chair-Side Assistants/Dental Nurses 116
Dental Technicians and Clinical Dental Technicians 117
Staff Health Precautions 119
Cross-Border Care and Indemnity Insurance 120
Direct Access 121
Skill Mix and Human Resources Planning 122
Teamwork 122
Unmet Oral Healthcare Needs 123
Conclusion 125
References 125

6 **The Workplace** 133
Advertising, Consumers' Rights, and Electronic Commerce 133
Work Time 134
Equality, Non-discrimination, and Pay 136
Social Rights 137
The Right to Information and Consultation 138
Work-Life Balance 139
DCPs' Occupational Health Hazards and Disorders 140
Safety and Health at Work 143
Water for Use in Dental Practices 146
Infections and Infection Control 148
Waste Management 152
Liability for Defective Products 154
Medical Devices 155
Cosmetic Products 156
Medicinal Products 157
Conclusion 161
References 163

7 Subjects for Discussion in the Professions 171
Teeth Whitening 171
Dental Amalgam 173
Domestic Violence, Maltreatment, Child Abuse, and Neglect 176
Lifestyle 178
Physical Activity 181
Climate Change 183
Sustainable Development Goals (SDGs) 186
Tobacco 188
Alcohol 191
Conclusion 194
References 195

8 The European Union and the Dental Team 201
The EU, Oral Healthcare Providers, and Patients 201
The EU and Group Consultation 201
The Dental-Medical Divide and Its Integration 202
The Future 203
References 204

Index 205

About the Author

Sondra Z. Koff, PhD, has teaching experience in comparative politics and healthcare policy at Binghamton University (Binghamton, New York) at the undergraduate and graduate levels. She was a member of the Political Science Department until her retirement as professor emerita. She has conducted research as a North Atlantic Treaty Organization, Gladys Krieble Delmas Foundation, and a Fulbright scholar. In addition, she has published in her areas of specialization in the United States and abroad. She reviews healthcare articles for professional journals. Also, she has practical experience in the healthcare sector with a variety of boards as a public member at the local, state, regional, and national levels and often in a leadership capacity.

Chapter 1
Introduction

Oral Health

Oral health has a definite relationship with general health, although, unfortunately, it is not always viewed in this framework. Research has demonstrated that an individual's oral and systemic health are coupled (Better Oral Health European Platform 2015, n.d.; Robinson 2008; Sharma et al. 2016). Oral health is not concerned solely with teeth. Much more is involved. As defined by the FDI World Dental Federation, it "is multi-faceted and includes the ability to speak, smile, smell, taste, touch, chew, swallow and convey a range of emotions through facial expressions with confidence and without pain, discomfort and disease of the craniofacial complex" (FDI 2016). Other elements related to this statement hold that oral health is a part of general health as well as physical and mental well-being. Furthermore, it is impacted by people's and communities' values and attitudes. It mirrors the psychological, social, and physiological traits important to the quality of life. Moreover, the individual's experiences, perceptions, expectations, and ability to adjust to various situations exert influence on it (FDI 2016). Given this definition and these attributes, oral health is multi-dimensional.

The oral cavity is central to several daily activities, and thus, its health sways many facets of an individual's quality of life (Martu 2008; Petersen et al. 2005). The three principal types of oral diseases, dental caries (tooth decay), periodontal maladies (gum diseases), and oral cancer, as well as others, have the potential to cause discomfort and suffering and to impinge on people's diet, manner of chewing, how they taste food, and their speech, physical and psychological capacities, productivity, ability to function, and social and overall well-being, which is also related to personal traits. Stomatologic disorders upset routine activities (Amariei and Nuca 2006; Sheiham 2005; Silva et al. 2015). Furthermore, primarily because of common risk factors, some oral diseases may impact a number of systemic conditions. They have been associated with chronic diseases, including diabetes, Alzheimer's

S. Z. Koff, *The Dental Team in the European Union*,
https://doi.org/10.1007/978-3-030-72232-6_1

disease, rheumatoid arthritis, chronic obstructive pulmonary disease, and HIV/AIDS. Adverse pregnancy outcomes have also been linked with oral health. Many of these ailments have oral manifestations. In addition, it has been asserted that oral maladies are among the most prevalent noncommunicable diseases in modern societies (Jordan et al. 2014; Scannapieco and Cantos 2016).

Due to their economic consequences, oral maladies impinge on society and its health system as well as the individual. Often, these disorders have been more costly to treat than others, such as cancer, heart disease, stroke, and dementia. Moreover, it has been demonstrated that the most expensive part of the body to treat is its mirror, the mouth (Better Oral Health: European Platform 2015, n.d.; Hollister and Weintraub 1993; Patel 2012; Pipitone and Eaton 2013; Sheiham 2005; Silva et al. 2015). Oral health is important not only for the individual's quality of life but also for that of any community (Amariei and Nuca 2006; Papaioannou et al. 2011). Failure to address it today could be more costly tomorrow in terms of multifaceted damage.

Europeanization

Upheavals have taken place in the European landscape and have transformed mental and territorial boundaries. The importance of geographical borders and nationally confined arenas of policy-making has diminished. Focus has shifted from nation states toward European networks and decision-making bodies. International integration in a growing number of sectors has stood up to the territorially bound nature of much domestic policy. Technological and economic interdependence and interpenetration have become prominent features of the European continent. New institutions have been born, and many policy-making responsibilities have been transferred. As a result of Europeanization, formal international, but not complex, integration has given rise to European organizations, one of which was the European Economic Community, which eventually became known as the European Union (EU). This is an institution that has significantly influenced how the challenges of oral health care and its providers are faced. In this case, there was a major shift of political power upward to EU institutions. In addition, other networks of intergovernmental cooperation, with various memberships and agendas, were born, creating diverse units with overlapping boundaries and competences parallel to the construction of a common European economic and social space.

It is the EU that has had much significance for healthcare providers and how they meet the requirements of their profession and how they practice it. It will be seen that the importance of the organization derives from its powers outside of health care, but which reflect on the sector. As for my other research, the aim of this project is to present a portrait of healthcare professionals, in this case, dental care professionals (DCPs), including dentists, dental hygienists, dental therapists, dental technicians, clinical dental technicians, dental assistants/dental nurses, and orthodontic therapists, in the Member States of the EU and to demonstrate how they are affected by EU policies as they practice their profession. Another objective is to acquaint DCPs and other healthcare providers, both present and future, with a notion of EU operations and their importance. At the same time, I hope to introduce social scientists interested in comparative healthcare policy to the realities and challenges encountered by DCPs. Even though more studies have been undertaken on professions other than medicine and nursing, there is a scarcity of cross-national comparative research on the dental team. Such studies would be of use to a wide audience, including policy-makers at various levels of government. I hope to help remedy this shortcoming with this work.

Formation of the European Union

The European Economic Community resulted from the Treaty Establishing the European Economic Community (1957), known as the Treaty of Rome, the first in a series concerning the organization, signed by Germany, France, Italy, Holland, Belgium, and Luxembourg, the six original Member States. From this date, the number of associates grew to 28, and with the results of the EU membership referendum in the United Kingdom on 23 June 2016, it has shrunk to 27. The United Kingdom is cited throughout this work because research for it was begun before the noted referendum and its formal exit on 31 January 2020.

Adhesion to the 1957 accord, whose goals were increased employment and social protection along with an enhanced quality of life, economic and social cohesion, and closer links between the Member States (Treaty Establishing the European Economic Community 1957, Article 2), was open to any European nation that accepted its provisions and agreed to respect them. Focus in the treaty was on abolition of trade barriers in the area. Economic integration was the primary purpose. More specifically, barriers to movement for workers, goods, services, and capital were to be eliminated (Treaty Establishing the European Economic Community 1957, Articles 48–73). Moreover, Member States agreed to guarantee the economic and social advancement of their countries via betterment in living and working conditions. Thus, a Community objective came to be an increase in the standard of living. The treaty laid ground for the creation of a social policy. It promoted collaboration between the Member States in its development (Treaty Establishing the European Economic Community 1957, Articles 17–122) and contained specific provisions concerning equal remuneration for males and females, paid holiday schemes, health and safety at work, and the like. However, little was done at that time to implement these and other provisions of a similar nature. The basic attitude that prevailed was that removal of the noted barriers would generate social progress throughout the Community. For all practical purposes, social policy remained a responsibility of the Member States (Anderson 2015; Barnard and Deakin 2012; Falkner et al. 2009; Shanks 1977).

Nations adhering to the accord, the Member States, renounced some of their sovereignty focused on specific aspects of the treaty, which was transformed to an organizational structure characterized by supranational and intergovernmental features to act in the common interest. The treaty provided for the backbone of the EU's central governance with its creation of an executive body, the Commission; the Council of Ministers (hereafter referred to as the Council), consisting of ministerial delegates from each Member State; the European Parliamentary Assembly, a legislative body, now known as the European Parliament (EP); and the European Court of Justice, thereafter, the Court of Justice of the European Union (CJEU) (Treaty Establishing the European Economic Community 1957, Articles 4, 137–188).

The Single European Act (1986) followed the Treaty of Rome. It provided a timetable for realization of the single market. The date was set as 31 December 1992. In addition, it refashioned the voting system in the Council for most measures central to the achievement of the single market. The EP's role in the legislative process was enhanced as well. In addition, the Community was granted a broader policy remit. Explicit policy competences referenced in the Act related to health and safety at work, environmental and consumer protection, and social security coordination. Also, reflecting a concept of collaboration between social partners, it encouraged the social dialogue process between management and labor at the European level. The preamble of the document enlarged the existing notion of social policy by noting the objective of promoting social justice (Anderson 2015; Falkner et al. 2009; Minogiannis 2003).

The Maastricht Treaty (1992) builds on the Single European Act and furthered developed the EU's social dimension. At this time, the notion of European citizenship was introduced which relates to the aforementioned movement of persons. The accord continued previous transformations in the operation of the institution as well. The Council's new voting procedure was extended to new measures reflecting different subject matter. In addition, the EP's powers were enlarged again. The name of the organization was changed to the European Community, demonstrating the desire for a closer political union and signaling the incorporation of some noneconomic subject matter into its policy remit. Competences were assigned to the institutions in the areas of social security and protection of workers, collective interest representation, co-determination, employment of third-country nationals, general working conditions, the work environment, worker information and consultation, education and vocational training, and gender equality in reference to labor market opportunities and treatment at work. The list of subject matter is long.

Of importance to oral and systemic health is the assignment of public health as a Community competency (The Maastricht Treaty 1992, Articles 129, 129A). Activity was to be related to disease prevention and primarily "the major health scourges." In addition, Community responsibilities were to include industry, culture, and transport, all of which relate to systemic and oral health.

Of note is the mention of subsidiarity, which dictates that policy should be made in structures as close as possible to the populace, meaning that the EU does not act unless it is more effective than authorities at the local, regional, or national levels. The term is interpreted as "a general presumption of precedence of lower level over higher level governance, and ultimately a principle of laissez-faire with respect to whatever lower units may do" (Quote of Wolfgang Streeck, by Minogiannis 2003,

p. 58). As policy has developed in this framework, it has meant that responsibility for healthcare services falls to the Member States.

The next steps in the development of the EU are to be found in the Treaty of Amsterdam (1997). The document was to serve new efforts in the creation of a united Europe and to complete implementation of free movement (Treaty of Amsterdam 1997, Article 1). A significant item in the accord is mention of respect for basic social rights (Treaty of Amsterdam 1997, Article 136) which were to bind the Member States. Social policies were generally reinforced, and they assumed a prime role. This agreement expanded the EU's scope of action against discrimination on grounds of sex, race, ethnic origin, religious beliefs, age, disability, and sexual orientation. Moreover, it reinforced many of the postulates of its predecessor. For example, a high level of health protection was to be guaranteed in all EU policies and activities (Treaty of Amsterdam 1997, Articles 3y, 152). The EU's competence in the equal opportunity sector was enlarged, and the organization was assigned the task of social protection and of coordinating the Member States' employment policies. Of note is the inclusion of a separate employment section in the accord. It demonstrated top-level attempts to seek higher rates of employment as well as better employment conditions (Anderson 2015; Nugent 2010).

The European Community changed its name to the European Union when the Lisbon Treaty (2007) was drawn up. This document recognized the role of good health as a factor of economic development. The health sector shines in terms of dynamism in the accord whose attractiveness relates to the fact that its social dimension is linked to economic strategy (Guimarães and Freire 2007; Vural 2011). Public health objectives remain the same as previously, but actions to conquer major health scourges are multiplied. In addition, Member States are encouraged to establish appropriate guidelines and indicators pertaining to the topic and to exchange best practices (Lisbon Treaty 2007, Article 152).

The treaty reaffirms the principle of subsidiarity in public health and fully recognizes the Member States' responsibility pertaining to the "management of health services and medical care and the allocation of the resources assigned to them" (Lisbon Treaty 2007, Article 152). The cited article specifically states that "Union action shall complement national policies..." There are other references to public health in the treaty. Article 9 asserts that the EU in carrying out its responsibilities shall recognize requirements related to a superior education, training, and protection of human health. Also, prohibitions or restrictions on the movement of goods are justified on grounds of protecting the health and life of humans, animals, and plants (Lisbon Treaty 2007, Article 36). Environmental policy is to have as one of its objectives the protection of human health (Lisbon Treaty 2007, Article 191). The treaty also included mention of other sectors impacting health.

The EU was structured from this series of accords to become the largest market in the world manifesting free movement of people, goods, services, and capital. National healthcare practitioners in general, ones in a specific profession, and policy-makers must continue to confront two challenges. First of all, they must fully recognize how EU law and policy-making resulting from the noted treaties impact the work they do, and secondly, they should recognize when and how to engage with the organs created by them. Such contact provides benefits in terms of funding opportunities and knowledge exchange (Irwin 2010). It is noteworthy that many pilot projects, as well as other types, have been funded by the EU.

Although the subsidiary principle has been reaffirmed time and time again as it relates to health care, and the EU does not have direct healthcare responsibilities, it will be evident in this study that EU legislation which has had the most influence on health and the delivery of health care and, particularly, DCPs, as they practice their professions, is not health-specific. The intersectoral nature of health policy is evident in the EU's role in health and health care (Irwin 2010). Most accounts of the line of action speak of a minimal direct role. Indirectly, the EU has greatly impacted the delivery of oral and systemic healthcare services via policies in another sector wielding great influence on it. Such a situation is referred to as the spillover effect. Policies in one sector impact practices in another. The principles and policies of the EU's internal market have invaded the territory of national health policy, having a strong impact and issuing challenges to the national stage of systemic and oral healthcare delivery, even though the EU has no real authority in health care (Martinsen and Blomqvist 2009).

EU law contains two divisions: primary law and secondary law. Primary law refers to the noted treaties that developed the EU's structure and responsibilities. It is these documents that serve as the basis for all EU action. The origin of secondary law lies in the principles and goals established in the treaties, and this law includes the legislative and other instruments that the EU utilizes to register its output.

A common device of secondary law is the directive. This mechanism establishes objectives to be accomplished. Authorities in the Member States then transpose the document into national law and decide how to realize the stated goals in a manner appropriate to their circumstances. The directive contains an established cut-off date for implementation which is expected to be met by the individual Member States. Another instrument, the regulation, like the directive, is applicable to all Member States and must be observed in full. However, national implementing measures are not necessary because this mechanism immediately or within prescribed time limits comes into force. This instrument is usually affiliated with the assignment of rights and obligations. A decision, another type of mechanism, is issued to some or all Member States, individuals, or organizations, and, as in the case of the regulation, it has immediate force of law. Directives, regulations, and decisions are tools that are binding in nature. On the other hand, recommendations and opinions are non-binding documents. They announce desirable objectives, but do not possess the force of law. However, this does not mean they completely lack legal effect (Mossialos and McKee 2002; Nugent 2010; Wismar et al. 2002).

Member States are responsible for correct and timely implementation of binding EU legislation as well as its treaties. For this purpose, the Commission serves as their surveillant. If a Member State does not integrate a directive into national law and/or fails to communicate to the Commission the measures it has taken, it may take action against the unit and begin formal infringement proceedings and, eventually, refer the Member State to the CJEU (Monitoring the application of Union law 2015).

For example, the Commission has initiated a legal case against the Czech Republic because its national legislation was not congruent with Council Directives 86/378/EEC and 96/97/EC related to equal treatment for both sexes in reference to occupational social security schemes. In addition, Poland received notice from the Commission that it had incorrectly implemented EU legislation (Council Directive 2000/78/EC) related to various types of discrimination. Italy and the United Kingdom were cited for not reporting efforts concerning implementation of Directive 2006/54/EC on the matter of gender discrimination in employment and occupation (Midday Express 2010).

A newer method of policy development is the Open Method of Coordination (OMC) which is essentially a bottom-up approach. Using this procedure, Member States come to agreement on non-binding common goals. In a series of meetings devoted to planning and review of a subject, they share national experiences and practices on the matter with the hope of creating a European framework of analysis and voluntary action. Basically, OMC is a peer review process, involving dialogue, reflection, and experimentation. As opposed to other instances, Member States are not subject to legal action, if they do not achieve policy objectives.

The major disadvantage of OMC is its voluntary nature. However, on the other hand, in terms of advantages, policy respects subsidiarity and national differences in circumstances. Also, governments might be enticed to accept policies developed via the OMC as opposed to those made with the aforementioned binding mechanisms. Activities related to the OMC receive support and assistance from the EU. Furthermore, the organization observes and checks Member States' actions in this regard (Daly 2006; Nugent 2010). It is noteworthy that EU output resulting from instruments related to primary or secondary law concerns not only the Member States but also other nations in the European Economic Area (EEA) which includes the Member States and Liechtenstein, Iceland, and Norway. The latter three nation states have agreed to honor EU laws so as to take advantage of free trade agreements.

Professionalization

At one time, barbers often undertook dental procedures. During the nineteenth century, however, dentistry was transformed from a trade to a profession. There is no consensus as to a concrete definition of profession. Professionalization has been described as:

> a process by which an organized occupation usually but not always by the virtue of making a claim to special esoteric competence and to concern for the quality of its work and its benefits to society, obtains the exclusive right to perform a particular kind of work, control training for and access to it, and control the right of determining and evaluating the way the work is performed. (Freidson 1973, p. 22)

The professionalization process includes a series of interrelated elements aimed at assigning an occupation a number of attributes viewed as the central components of professionalism (Johnson 1972). Given the nature of this process, professions feature similar characteristics: specialist knowledge, admission credentials, regulated activities, and a common set of values (Susskind and Susskind 2015).

A basic central ingredient of the professionalization process is the acquisition of specialized skill and training. Higher education institutions are the major structures which make this possible. Generalized knowledge based on systematic theory and technical competence are acquired through a protracted period of formal training. This element represents the cognitive dimension of professional attributes. The acquired body of knowledge and special techniques are utilized in professional activities. These scarce resources of special knowledge and skills are then to be translated into social recognition and economic rewards (Larson 1977; Santiago and Carvalho 2015; Theodore 1971). The normative dimension of professional attributes relates to the professionals' service orientation. The service ideal holds great importance for a profession. Its occupational niche revolves around problems of universal social concern which relate to a sector that touches all people, but in which only a few are proficient or well-advanced. Consequently, professionals monopolize resources compatible with certain social needs. Their basic commitment lies with the interest of the community. Thus, such a position accounts for the status and prestige assigned to them (Jackson 1970; Susskind and Susskind 2015).

It is generally acknowledged that the formation of professional organizations is part of the professionalization process. Having relatively few functions when initially born, they seek to protect their members from undue advances from a variety of external sources, such as government, the public, and other professions, and they exhibit concern for professional standards and training. Professional associations also define and enforce rules of professional conduct. Often, they are the source for a profession's formal code of ethics which, in the case of the dental squad, regulates professionals' relations with patients, colleagues, and other professions. Part of the code is formal in that it is written and, often, a part may be informal or unwritten, but it usually carries the weight of the formal prescriptions. The specifics of codes vary according to the profession involved. The normative dimension of professional attributes includes ethical codes which are used to justify the practice of self-regulation (Greenwood 1966; Larson 1977).

The professionalization process links two constituents that often develop independently: a quantity of abstract knowledge adaptable to practical application and a market. Professions have utilized diverse resources in their attempts to achieve market control for their expertise (Larson 1977). As presented here, the professionalization process passes through a series of stages commencing with training procedures and terminating with the elaboration of a formal code of ethics. It is noteworthy that as this process unrolls, it is significantly affected by the political, social, and economic environment in which it takes place. Professionalization has a political, social, and economic significance.

Professional Training and Recognition: The Legal Instruments

Modern dental education's seeds were planted in the United States in 1840, when the first dental school was founded in Baltimore, Maryland. In Europe, independent curricula for dentistry were developed in the United Kingdom in 1859 and in Finland in 1880. The development of European dental education has been extremely fragmented (Allen 2005). It has been divided by diverse traditions which stood at the base of training systems: stomatology and odontology. In the latter, the student is educated in a single autonomous discipline—dentistry. In the former, the trainee first completes medical education and then undertakes clinical dental training. Stomatology is considered a specialty of medicine. This model was prevalent in most of the Central and Eastern European Member States, as well as in Austria, France, Italy, Portugal, and Spain. Dental education has undergone extensive change, and the odontological model has now been accepted throughout the EU/EEA. In fact, the legal instruments related to professional training and recognition are now based on this model. However, given this division, there was much variance in oral healthcare systems throughout the Member States, due to differences in training requirements resulting from these models (Scott 2003).

These original circumstances made realization of a single market and, specifically, cross-national mobility difficult in that a professional qualification recognized in one Member State might not always be accepted in another. Obviously, the enshrined goals of free movement, the right of establishment, and freedom to provide services were hindered. The Treaty of Rome exerted great influence on the healthcare professions.

Oral healthcare delivery is influenced by a multitude of important factors, one of which is the education of dental practitioners. Dental training in the EU is governed by EU law, expressed in directives. The EU attempted to harmonize different professional training via the use of directives, some of which pertained to dentistry. These initial documents are known as sectoral directives as they applied to individual professions, including pharmacy, general care nursing, medicine, dentistry, architecture, veterinary surgery, and others, all, except one, of which represented a healthcare sector.

Focus in Council Directive 78/686/EEC was on mutual recognition of diplomas and other documents. It was provided that each Member State was to recognize a dentist's credentials earned in another Member State. The same held for specialists in oral surgery and orthodontics. If, for some reason, a Member State's qualifications did not fulfill the established training requisites, the practitioner had to offer proof of having applied them in her/his practice for at least three consecutive years of the last 5. Specialists found in the same circumstances had to prove having been involved in specialized practice for a specific period of time as well. After evaluating the content and duration of specialist training, if found to be deficient, the professional practitioner was to be notified of any additional training required and the subjects to be included in it. These items were left to the judgment of the individual Member States because the EU had no specific requirements to offer. It was also noted that the host Member State might request evidence of good character and physical and mental health.

Authorities were given 3 months to respond to a formal request for recognition. If granted, the individual, in providing services, was to have the same rights and obligations as citizens of the host Member State. Furthermore, host Member States were to make available to the recognized practitioner information related to health and social security legislation and professional ethics. Also, they were responsible for ensuring that her/his language ability was sufficient to meet the demands of professional practice.

Council Directive 78/687/EEC of 25 July 1978 was concerned with the specific training requirements for dentists. It focused on the achievement of mutual recognition of qualifications and the coordination of training requirements. It specified the required formal qualifications for completion of at least a 5-year full-time training program which was to include theoretical and practical instruction in a university or equivalent institution. The document contained a curriculum listing the specific subjects to be taught to dentistry trainees. Information related to specialization was provided as well. Unfortunately, given the diverse interpretations assigned to the training directive by the Member States, convergence was frequently left to be desired. Also, compliance by individual schools was poor. When EU membership was expanded in 2004, only two of the ten new Member States (Cyprus and Malta) had dentistry training systems congruent with the aforementioned directive's requirements (Allen 2005; Scott 2003).

At the same time, the Advisory Committee for Training of Dental Practitioners was established within the Commission (Council Decision 78/688/EEC of 25 July 1978). Its purpose was to "help ensure a comparably demanding standard in the training of dental practitioners..." (Council Decision 78/688/EEC of 25 July 1978, Article 2(1)) and to advise the Commission on further curricular development. Its role was applicable to practitioners in specialized dentistry as well and also to other relevant matters. It consisted of three representatives from each Member State, representing the practicing profession, a relevant university faculty, and competent authorities. Member States nominated candidates, and appointment was by the Council. Notwithstanding its useful output, the unit ceased to function in 2000.

The Association for Dental Education in Europe has been a leader in the pursuit of superior standards in dental training throughout the continent. Its DentEd Thematic Network Project focused on harmonization and convergence of European curricula. The goal was to be achieved through voluntary self-assessment, communication, and peer evaluation based on peer visitation arrangements and the sharing of best practices and innovations. The EU Directorate for Education and Culture financially supported such an effort (Shanley et al. 2002). However, Scott (2003) writes: "the outcome reinforces the contention that the … Dental Directives [were] insufficient for the EU to guarantee acceptable standards of oral health care from all its dental graduates for all its citizens" (p. 76). Research has demonstrated that these efforts and cited directives failed to garner comparability of basic educational and training standards in dentistry throughout the Member States. Such a conclusion bore negative consequences and posed a problem for the objective of free movement.

In 1999, 29 European Ministers of Education met in Bologna, Italy, to discuss formation and operation of a European Higher Education Area. The result of the gathering was the Bologna Process or the Bologna Agreement for Harmonization of Higher Education in Europe, approved by the nations of the authorities in attendance. Since that time, many more countries have supported the document and signatories now number 48 nations plus the European Commission. The need for achieving coherence with internal diversity was recognized as it relates to the European Higher Education Area. Focus was on harmonization of European systems of higher education (Murtomaa 2009).

A principal goal of the Accord was to adopt a structure of academic degrees that would be comparable. This objective was to be aided by the introduction of the diploma supplement, a document attached to a diploma from all higher education institutions that describes the context, content, and status of the program completed. The diploma supplement was also to facilitate transfer of grades. In fact, it has been judged as very useful in the mutual recognition of academic and professional qualifications (European Commission Directorate-General Internal Market and Services 2011; Zabalegui et al. 2006).

The degree system to be adopted by the signatories consists of two cycles: undergraduate and graduate. Before proceeding to the second cycle which should lead to a master's degree or doctorate, the first which is to last a minimum of 3 years must be completed. The cycle model is based on 3-5-8 years of study: 3 years to complete a bachelor's degree, 5 years from the start of higher education to finish a master's degree, and 8 years total for a doctorate. Cycles were developed so as to be able to react to social and scientific transformations.

A major innovation found in the Declaration is the establishment of a system of credits, the European Credit Transfer System (ECTS). These credits represent numerical values assigned to courses that portray the workload required by students. The determined values are not limited to classroom hours, but include all types of efforts on the part of students to achieve course objectives. A normal undergraduate academic year consists of 30 ECTS credits per semester, and for postgraduate students, a 12-month academic year garners 90 such credits. This system promotes student mobility and enlarges students' access to study opportunities. Moreover, it also aids faculty, researchers, and administrators in the promotion and recognition of their mobility and achievements without prejudicing their statutory rights (European higher education area and Bologna process (n.d.)).

In addition, the approach to the evaluation of academic programs was modified. Instead of an input-based approach that compares training programs and courses on the basis of their duration, an output-based approach was tailored. This method analyzes courses in terms of knowledge, skills, and competences to be achieved, rather than in terms of their duration. It has been noted that implementation of learning outcomes has taken place at a very slow pace (European Commission Directorate-General Internal Market and Services 2011).

At the same time, European collaboration was encouraged in the promotion of quality assurance and compatibility. The Declaration advocates the development of comparable criteria and methodologies in order to be able to assure equivalent quality throughout continental educational systems. It was envisioned that these items could be of use to other nations as well. The European dimension of higher education is promoted throughout the document. The goal was to achieve a convergence of higher education systems via coordination of academic and research programs. The end result, it was hoped, would be the existence of diverse national educational systems which would share frameworks for the bachelor's, master's, and doctoral levels of education (Davies 2008; Zabalegui et al. 2006).

In 2001, at a gathering, European Ministers of Education, whose nation states had approved the Declaration, added three more goals to the document. These relate to the promotion of continuing professional development (CPD), involvement of students in the functioning of their institutions of higher education, and enhancement of the attractiveness and competitiveness of the European Higher Education Area.

Denoting significant educational transformation in Europe, the Bologna Declaration was received with great enthusiasm by a multitude of institutions, including universities, learned societies, thematic networks, and professional associations. Much effort, in particular by the dental profession, was directed toward European convergence in higher education (Sanz et al. 2006). It is generally acknowledged that the Bologna Declaration has had an impact beyond the borders of the European continent.

The next chronological step in the development of professional qualifications and their recognition was the passage of Directive 2005/36/EC of the European Parliament and the Council of 7 September 2005. The aforementioned sectoral directives, for the most part, were aimed at mutual recognition. However, they did not accomplish what they were supposed to because the concept was not facilitated. The established evaluation process was too cumbersome. Thus, it was deemed necessary to consolidate the 15 directives related to diverse professional qualifications into a single document. Once again, stress was on similar objectives: creating a more flexible labor market, liberalizing the right of establishment and the provision of services, stimulating automatic recognition of qualifications in a framework of mutual trust, and streamlining the administrative process (Kyrieri n.d.).

Three diverse systems for recognition of qualifications are set forth. Automatic recognition is related to professions with harmonized minimum training conditions. Such recognition is extended to dentists (Directive 2005/36/EC, Articles 34–37), general care nurses, doctors of medicine, pharmacists, veterinary surgeons, midwives, and architects. A general system of recognition relates to other regulated professions, such as teachers, translators, and real estate agents (Directive 2005/36/EC, Articles 10–15). Then, there is a recognition system based on professional experience that applies to carpenters, beauticians, upholsterers, and the like (Directive 2005/36/EC, Articles 16–20). Third-country nationals can take advantage of equal treatment in reference to professional qualification.

The directive specifies educational requirements, including knowledge and skills, related to mutual recognition of diplomas, certificates, and other documents concerning the formal qualifications of dentists and other professionals. The document also sets forth principles of basic and specialist dental training, pursuit of professional activities of dentists, and acquired rights specific to the profession. Annex V lists the diplomas and titles automatically recognized throughout the EU for each Member State and all professions concerned with the exception of medical and dental specialties. Furthermore, as stated in other legislation, there is a listing of detailed rules for pursuing the profession which includes possession of a knowledge of the needed language or languages. CPD is championed in line with the subsidiarity principle. Responsibility for it was assigned to the individual Member States.

The European Qualification Framework was developed as an aid to the interpretation and understanding of national requirements related to education, training, and qualifications. Set on the aforementioned output-based approach, its objective is to relate European nation states' national qualifications systems to the established framework and, thus, make national requirements more readable across the continent. Once again, mobility between countries is a central goal. The framework initiative was agreed to in 2008 and is closely related to the European Higher Education Area.

Directive 2005/36/EC came into force in 2007 and was due for review in 5 years. The Commission initiated the consultation and evaluation process with various stakeholders in 2011. It was propelled politically by the desire to refashion the single market which had been tainted by the Eurozone's economic crisis. The goals were to increase cross-border service delivery and professional mobility once again as well as to decrease professional protectionism.

Several amendments were incorporated into Directive 2013/55/EU which updated the original professional qualifications directive mentioned above. Most significant is the transformation made in the mutual recognition process with the introduction of the European Professional Card. This document is an electronic certificate testifying that the holder has completed the requisites to provide services in a host Member State on either a temporary or permanent basis (Directive 2013/55/EU, Article 3(k)). Its use is intended to simplify and speed up the recognition process and to contribute to cost and operational efficiencies to the advantage of both professionals and competent authorities. Furthermore, the card is to be supported by the Internal Market Information System, an EU electronic mechanism for administrative communications between national, regional, and local authorities in the EEA (Directive 2013/55/EU, Recitals (4), (5)).

It is also provided that if major differences in qualifications are recognized, competent authorities may impose compensatory measures on an applicant for professional recognition, meaning completion of an aptitude test or adaptation period. Another modification involving recognition which was championed by the Council of European Dentists concerns partial access. This concept relates to cases in which differences in professional activity are so great in the host Member State when compared to the home Member State of the applicant as to require completely new professional education and training. It is provided that if so requested, the host Member State's authorities should consider granting partial access to the person making application for professional recognition (Directive 2013/55/EU, Article 4f; Recital (7)). Professional associations and trade unions in the healthcare sector have assigned major importance to these measures that were to facilitate cross-national mobility.

The CJEU referred to the principle of partial access to a profession in 2006 in the *Collegios de ingenieros* (*Engineering Colleges*) case. The court stated partial access must be granted provided two conditions are satisfied: (1) the differences between the fields of activity are so great that they cannot be modified by compensatory measures and (2) there are no valid public interest reasons to prohibit partial access. This type of recognition by public authorities has rarely been used. Rather, a negative decision concerning professional access has been preferred (European Commission Directorate-General Internal Market and Services 2011).

Another modification relates to the control of language skills which is reinforced. On this subject, there was recognition of the need to clarify the role of competent authorities and employers in the interest of patient safety. It is stated that any controls should be reasonable and respect the principle of proportionality. Professionals are expected to be competent in the official language of the host Member State or one administrative language of the area, provided it is an official language of the EU. Language control may only occur after professional recognition has been granted (Directive 2013/55/EU, Article 53, Recital (26)).

In the United Kingdom, the Royal College of Surgeons, citing the number of patient complaints based on communication skills, was obviously not pleased with the implementation of this provision. It announced that testing of the clinical English language capacity of dentists coming from the EEA to work in the United Kingdom was insufficient. It proposed that after agreement on the Brexit (the name given to the United Kingdom's exit from the EU) negotiations is achieved, the matter should be pursued.

Cross-border mobility is made even easier with the introduction of a new route to automatic recognition of professional qualifications. This is represented by an opportunity given to the Commission to develop common training frameworks and common training tests. The former refers to "a common set of minimum knowledge, skills and competences necessary for the pursuit of a specific profession" (Directive 2013/55/EU, Article 49a/1). This framework is to be designed in line with the aforementioned European Qualifications Framework, and it is not to replace national training programs unless a Member State decides to do so via national law. Moreover, it is mentioned that common training principles should be applicable to specialties as well (Directive 2013/55/EU, Recitals (22), (31)). A common training test is " a standardised aptitude test available across participating Member States and reserved to holders of a particular professional qualification" (Directive 2013/55/EU, Article 49b/1). Passing this test in a Member State allows the professional to practice her/his profession throughout the EU.

Noting that dentists already benefit from automatic recognition throughout the EU, the Council of European Dentists, an organization representing 340,000 practitioners across Europe and having as an objective promotion of the profession in the EU, opposes common training principles in dentistry, primarily, because of the potential hazards related to the profession. The association indicated that patient safety, the quality of dental education, and treatment in the practice of dentistry are subject to risks. Also, it noted that the common training framework has not been tested and, as a precautionary measure, professions with patient safety concerns should not be involved in its introduction. It feared that economic factors held more influence on development of the concept than the quality of dental education and care. Moreover, it also claimed the directive fails to note the method to make common training principles and scientific and technical progress congruent over time (Council of European Dentists 2015). In short, the existing mechanism for automatic recognition was deemed more than adequate.

The mobility of health professionals, in some cases, has been high due to the concept of automatic recognition. Between 2007 and 2010, 6600 dentists were granted automatic recognition. However, there is major variation in recognition rates between the EU Member States that results from factors, such as the availability of resources devoted to management of the volume of requests, the number of requests, and the complex nature of regulation. In 60.83% of the requests for recognition of a qualification, the response has been positive. The EU average for positive recognition of a qualification with compensatory measures is 76.37%. Also, there is much variation in the total number of decisions issued by a country. Between 2012 and 2014, the number ranged from 34,671 in the United Kingdom to 12 in Malta. As a rule, the larger the country, usually the higher the number of decisions (The EU Single Market: Regulated professions database 2018).

Each Member State, according to the amended directive, is to create an assistance center responsible for furnishing the public and other such centers throughout the EU, information relating to the recognition of professional qualifications, national legislation governing the various professions, social policies, and ethical codes (Directive 2013/55/EU, Article 57b).

Recently, discussion has focused on a proposal for a directive of the EP and of the Council on a proportionality test in the Member States before the adoption of new professional regulations. The latest aforementioned professional qualifications directive requires Member States to evaluate the proportionality of their regulations. However, it fails to offer standards or a general framework to be utilized in this effort to avoid the adoption of disproportionate measures. Thus, the proposal aimed to provide a framework for the evaluation of proportionality before the adoption of a new professional regulation. Proportionality is a primary tenet of the Member States' national constitutions and laws as well as of EU law. It requires Member States to seek an appropriate balance between the freedoms afforded by EU treaties, such as free movement, and Member States' latitude of choice to protect a public interest, such as public health (Council of European Dentists 2017).

It was asserted that utilization of an EU-wide assessment mechanism would enhance the single market for professional services, the actual provision of services, as well as professional mobility. Present-day practices were alleged to have negative consequences on entrance to a profession, mobility, and economic performance. Moreover, it was demonstrated that consultation with stakeholders produced broad positive consensus for a new professional directive focused on proportionality tests. Furthermore, the process would be reviewed and evaluated within 5 years of its adoption (European Commission 2017a, b).

It is noteworthy that European healthcare providers, specifically, dentists, doctors, and pharmacists, expressed opposition to the utilization of proportionality tests for professional regulation. They argued that the notion ignored public interest and it also represented a hazard to the quality and safety of patient care (PGEU response to the consultation on proportionality in the regulation of professions 2019). The Council of European Dentists and the Federation of European Dental Competent Authorities and Regulators both denounced the proposal. The former association claimed it undermined the subsidiarity principle. It believed that Member States would be deprived of their privilege to regulate professions. In addition, it asserted that professional regulation does not hinder economic performance. Both organizations suggested that health professions be excluded from the requirements of the proposed directive (Council of European Dentists 2017).

In spite of this opposition, Directive (EU) 2018/958 became law on 28 June 2018. It contained criteria to be utilized by the Member States when conducting proportionality tests before adoption of new professional regulations, including those related to healthcare professionals. A common framework is now involved in an analysis of the desired ends to be achieved and the means utilized. Furthermore, Member States are to notify the Commission of the measures adopted in proportionality tests.

Dentists at one time practiced their profession in isolation, meaning singly. However, times have changed for many practitioners, signaling that professions are not static. Increased knowledge; specialization; transformed patients' needs and expectations; more stress on prevention; the revolutionizing tendency of the Internet; increased development of equipment, instruments, techniques, and treatment procedures; and the creation of new medicinal products and materials used in dental care, among other enhancements, as well as demands of efficiency and effectiveness have meant that a multitude of practitioners no longer provide services in isolation (Council of European Chief Dental Officers 2013; Naylor 2006; Roemer 1977). A single practitioner cannot individually provide modern comprehensive care. A dental team, a hallmark of contemporary times, has developed in many of the EU Member States, and practitioners from diverse professions are now collaborating and, in some cases, unfortunately, competing with each other. These DCPs enhance patient safety and quality of care. They include general dentists, specialist dental practitioners, dental technicians, clinical dental technicians (also called denturists), dental chair-side assistants/dental nurses, dental hygienists, dental hygiene therapists, and orthodontic therapists. Not all these professions have developed or are active in every Member State, and sometimes different labels are assigned to the role. There is much diversity as will be seen in this discussion of these professionals.

Dentists are responsible for diagnosing oral disease; developing treatment schemes; explaining diagnostic analyses; undertaking measures to ensure the safe administration of anesthetics; watching over development of the teeth, mouth, and jaws; performing surgery on teeth, bones, and soft tissues of the oral cavity; and dealing with oral trauma and other emergencies (The dentist's role n.d.). Given that such practices can engage the abilities of diverse DCPs, the dentist is the leader of the team and assumes responsibility for patient information, diagnosis, planning, and performance of the necessary treatment.

The themes discussed in this chapter provide a general background for a study of the dental team in the framework of the European Union. In Chap. 2, the themes will be related to these DCPs and the first stage of the professionalization process, the acquisition of specialized knowledge and training, and affiliated EU activities and policies.

References

Allen, W. R. (2005). Dental education in the European Union. *British Dental Journal, 199*(5s), 33–34.

Amariei, C., & Nuca, C. (2006). Oral health and quality of life. *Oral Health and Dental Management, 5*(4), 25–29.

Anderson, K. M. (2015). *Social policy in the European Union*. London: Palgrave.

Barnard, C., & Deakin, S. (2012). Social policy and labor market regulation. In E. Jones, A. Menon, & S. Weatherhill (Eds.), *The Oxford handbook of the European Union* (pp. 542–555). Oxford: Oxford University Press.

Better Oral Health: European Platform. (2015). Best practices in oral health promotion and prevention from across Europe: An overview prepared by the Platform for Better Oral Health in Europe. http://www.oralhealthplatform.eu. Accessed 16 Oct 2016.

Better Oral Health: European Platform. (n.d.). *Oral health*. http://www.oralhealthplatform.eu. Accessed 3 Dec 2015.

Council Decision 78/688/EEC of 25 July 1978 setting up an Advisory Committee on the Training of Dental Practitioners.

Council Directive 78/686/EEC of 25 July 1978a concerning the mutual recognition of diplomas, certificates and other evidence of the formal qualifications of practitioners of dentistry, including measures to facilitate the effective exercise of the right of establishment and freedom to provide services.

Council Directive 78/687/EEC of 25 July 1978b concerning the coordination of provisions laid down by Law, Regulation or Administrative Action in respect of the activities of dental practitioners.

Council Directive 86/378/EEC of 24 July 1986 on the implementation of the principle of equal treatment for men and women in occupational social security schemes.

Council Directive 96/97 EC of 20 December 1996 amending Directive 86/378/EEC on the implementation of the principle of equal treatment for men and women in occupational social security schemes.

Council Directive 2000/78/EC of 27 November 2000 establishing a general framework for equal treatment in employment and occupation.

Council of European Chief Dental Officers. (2013). *CECDO position paper on team dentistry*. http://www.cecdo.org. Accessed 14 June 2017.

Council of European Dentists. (2015). *CED statement: Common training principles under Directive 2005/36/EC*. http://www.eudental.eu. Accessed 16 Oct 2015.

Council of European Dentists. (2017). *Proportionality and Commission proposal for a Directive on a proportionality test for adoption of new regulations for professions. (COM (2016) 822 final)*. http://www.cedentists.eu. Accessed 30 Mar 2018.

Daly, M. (2006). EU social policy after Lisbon. *Journal of Common Market Studies, 44*(3), 461–481.

Davies, R. (2008). The Bologna process: The quiet revolution in nursing higher education. *Nurse Education Today, 28*(8), 935–942.

Directive 2005/36/EC of the European Parliament and of the Council of 7 September 2005 on the recognition of professional qualifications.

Directive 2006/54/EC of the European Parliament and the Council of 5 July 2006 on the implementation of the principle of equal opportunities and equal treatment of men and women in matters of employment and occupation (recast).

Directive 2013/55/EU of the European Parliament and of the Council of 20 November 2013 amending Directive 2005/36/EC on the recognition of professional qualifications and Regulation (EU) 1024/2012 on administrative cooperation through the Internal Market Information System (the IMI Regulation).

Directive (EU) 2018/958 of the European Parliament and of the Council of 28 June 2018 on a proportionality test before adoption of new regulation of professions.

European Commission. (2017a). *Commission staff working document. Detailed report on the implementation by Member States of Directive 2003/88/EC concerning certain aspects of the organization of working time. Accompanying the document Report from the Commission to the European Parliament, the Council and the European Economic and Social Committee, Report on the implementation by Member States of Directive 2003/88/EC concerning certain aspects of the organisation of working time (COM(2017) 254 final).*

European Commission. (2017b). *Commission staff working document: Executive summary of the impact assessment accompanying the document Proposal for a Directive of the European Parliament and of the Council on a proportionality text before adoption of new regulation of professions (SWD (2016)463 final.*

European Commission Directorate-General Internal Market and Services. (2011, July 5). *Evaluation of the Professional Qualifications Directive (Directive 2005/36/EC).*

European higher education area and Bologna process. (n.d.). http://www.ehea.info. Accessed 2 Feb 2019.

Falkner, G., Treib, O., Hartlapp, M., & Leiber, S. (2009). *EU social policy over time: The role of directives*. Cambridge, UK: Cambridge University Press.

FDI (Federation Dentaire Internationale-International Dental Federation). (2016, September 6). FDI unveils new universally applicable definition of oral health. http://www.fdiworlddental.org. Accessed 1 Nov 2016.

Freidson, E. (1973). Professions and the occupational principle. In E. Freidson (Ed.), *The professions and their prospects* (pp. 19–38). Beverly Hills: Sage.

Greenwood, E. (1966). The elements of professionalization. In H. M. Vollmer & D. I. Mills (Eds.), *Professionalization* (pp. 9–19). Englewood Cliffs: Prentice-Hall, Inc..

Guimarães, L., & Freire, J.-M. (2007). Los temas de salud en la Unión Europea: Su impacto en la sanidad Española (Health policy in the European Union: Its impact on the Spanish health system). *Cadernos de Saúde Pública, 23*(suppl. 2), S143–S154.

Hollister, M. C., & Weintraub, J. A. (1993). The association of oral status with systemic health, quality of life, and economic productivity. *Journal of Dental Education, 57*(12), 901–912.

Irwin, R. (2010). EU law and health: An introduction. *Eurohealth, 16*(4), 1–2.

Jackson, J. A. (1970). Professions and professionalization: Editorial introduction. In J. A. Jackson (Ed.), *Professions and professionalization* (pp. 3–15). London: Cambridge University Press.

Johnson, T. J. (1972). *Professions and power*. London: The Macmillan Press Ltd..

Jordan, R. A., Bodechtel, C., Hertrampf, K., Hofmann, T., Kocher, T., Nitschke, I., et al. (2014). The fifth German oral health study (Fünfte Deutsche Mundgesundheitsstudie, DMS v)–rationale, design, and methods. *BMC Oral Health, 14*(161). https://doi.org/10.1186/1472-6831-14-161.

Kyrieri, K-M. (n.d.). The modernized directive on professional qualifications and its impact on national legislation. http://www.publications.eipa.eu. Accessed 27 Apr 2018.

Larson, M. S. (1977). *The rise of professionalism: A sociological analysis*. Berkeley: University of California Press.

Lisbon Treaty. (2007). http://www.eur-lex.europa.eu. Accessed 21 Jan 2018.

Martinsen, D. S., & Blomqvist, P. (2009). The European Union: Single market pressures. In J. Magnussen, K. Vrangbaek, & R. B. Saltman (Eds.), *Nordic health care systems: Recent reforms and current policy challenges* (pp. 294–315). Maidenhead: McGraw Hill, Open University Press.

Martu, S. (2008). *The impact of oral health on the quality of life for the patient with periodontal disease.* Paper delivered at the VIth International Congress of Oral Health and Dental Management in the Black Sea Countries, Constanta, Romania–Varna, Bulgaria, May 2008.

Midday Express: News from the Communication Directorate-General's midday briefing January 28, 2010. (2010, January 28). http://www.ec.europa.eu. Accessed 19 Oct 2018.

Minogiannis, P. (2003). *European integration and health policy: The artful dance of economics and history*. New Brunswick: Transaction Publishers.

Monitoring the application of Union law. (2015, May 5). *European Union Commission Newsletter.* Received from www.ec.europa.eu on 5 May 2015.

Mossialos, E., & McKee, M. (2002). *EU law and the social character of health care systems.* Brussels: Peter Lang.

Murtomaa, H. (2009). Dental education in Europe. *European Journal of Dentistry, 3*(1), 1–2.

Naylor, M. N. (2006). Dentistry. In S. Lock, J. M. Last, & G. Dunea (Eds.), *The Oxford companion to medicine* (3rd ed.). n.p.: Oxford University Press. http://www.oxfordreference.com. Accessed 20 Apr 2019.

Nugent, N. (2010). *The government and politics of the European Union* (7th ed.). Houndmills/Hampshire: Palgrave Macmillan.

Papaioannou, W., Oulis, C. J., Latsou, D., & Yfantopoulos, J. (2011). Oral health-related quality of life of Greek adults: A cross-sectional study. *International Journal of Dentistry, 2011*, 360292. https://doi.org/10.1155/2011/360292.

Patel, R. (2012). *The state of oral health in Europe: Report commissioned by the Platform for Better Oral Health in Europe.* n.p.: Commissioner.

Petersen, P. E., Bourgeois, D., Ogawa, H., Estupinan-Day, S., & Ndiaye, C. (2005). The global burden of oral disease and risks to oral health. *Bulletin of the World Health Organization, 83*(9), 661–669.

PGEU response to the consultation on proportionality in the regulation of professions. (2019). http://www.pgeu.eu. Accessed 30 Aug 2019.

Pipitone, B., & Eaton, K. (2013). Promoting oral health: A cent of prevention costs less than a euro of cure. *Eurohealth, 19*(4), 34–36.

Robinson, M. (2008). Health as a human right: Implications for the dental profession. *European Journal of Dental Education, 12*(Suppl 1), 9–10.

Roemer, M. I. (1977). *Comparative national policies on health care.* New York/Basel: Marcel Dekker.

Santiago, R., & Carvalho, T. (2015). Towards changes in professions and professionalism: Academics, doctors and nurses. In T. Carvalho & R. Santiago (Eds.), *Professionalism, managerialism and reform in higher education and the health services: The European welfare state and the rise of the knowledge society* (pp. 1–12). New York: Palgrave Macmillan. https://www.repubblica.it.

Sanz, M., Van Der Velden, U., Van Steenberghe, D., & Baehni, P. (2006). Periodontology as a recognized dental specialty in Europe. *Journal of Clinical Periodontology, 33*(6), 371–375.

Scannapieco, F. A., & Cantos, A. (2016). Oral inflammation and infection, and chronic medical diseases: Implications for the elderly. *Periodontology 2000, 72*(1), 153–175.

Scott, J. (2003). Dental education in Europe: The challenge of variety. *Journal of Dental Education, 67*(1), 69–78.

Shanks, M. (1977). *European social policy. Today and tomorrow*. Oxford: Pergamon Press.

Shanley, D. B., Dowling, P. A., Claffey, N., & Nattestad, A. (2002). European convergence towards higher standards in dental education: The DentEd thematic network project. *Medical Education, 36*(2), 186–192.

Sharma, P., Busby, M., Chapple, L., Matthews, R., & Chapple, I. (2016). The relationship between general health and lifestyle factors and oral health outcomes. *British Dental Journal, 221*(2), 65–69.

Sheiham, A. (2005). Oral health, general health and quality of life. *Bulletin of the World Health Organization, 83*(9), 644–645.

Silva, C. A. B., Grando, L. J., Fabro, S. M. L., & de Mello, A. L. S. F. (2015). Oral health related to quality of life in patients with stomatological diseases. *Stomatologija, Baltic Dental and Maxillofacial Journal, 17*(2), 48–53.

Single European Act. (1986). http://www.eur-lex.europa.eu. Accessed 21 Jan 2018.

Susskind, R., & Susskind, D. (2015). *The future of the professions: How technology will transform the work of human experts*. Oxford: Oxford University Press.

The dentist's role. (n.d.). http://www.modental.org. Accessed 10 Nov 2019.

The EU Single Market: Regulated professions database. (2018). http://www.ec.europa.eu. Accessed 3 Feb 2018.

The Maastricht Treaty. (1992). http://www.eur-lex.europa.eu. Accessed 21 Jan 2018.

Theodore, A. (1971). The professional woman: Trends and prospects. In A. Theodore (Ed.), *The professional woman* (pp. 1–35). Cambridge, MA: Schenkman Publishing Company, Inc..

Treaty Establishing the European Economic Community. (1957). http://www.eur-lex.europa.eu. Accessed 21 Jan 2018.

Treaty of Amsterdam. (1997). http://www.eur-lex.europa.eu. Accessed 21 Jan 2018.

Vural, I. E. (2011). Lisbon strategy and social policy in the enlarged European Union and in Turkey. In I. E. Vural (Ed.), *Converging Europe: Transformation of social policy in the enlarged European Union and in Turkey* (pp. 1–26). Farnham/Burlington: Ashgate Publishing Company.

Wismar, M., Busse, R., Paton, C., Silió-Villamil, F., Romo-Avilés, N., Prieto-Rodriguez, M. A., et al. (2002). Transposition of European directives into national legislation. In R. Busse, M. Wismar, & P. C. Berman (Eds.), *The European Union and health services: The impact of the single European market on member states* (pp. 49–59). Amsterdam: IOS Press.

Zabalegui, A., Macia, L., Márquez, J., Ricomá, R., Nuin, C., Mariscal, I., et al. (2006). Changes in nursing education in the European Union. *Journal of Nursing Scholarship, 38*(2), 114–118.

Chapter 2
The First Stage of Professionalization: Education

Dentist: Undergraduate Education

Why study dentistry? Over time researchers have sought an answer to this question, and many of the same responses have been given by dental students in diverse countries, regardless of the stage of their education in which they commenced their dentistry studies—postgraduate or pregraduate. The intrinsic factors for their selection of a profession include a personal interest in a fulfilling career and the desire to provide for the public and to help others, particularly, the less fortunate. Some students mentioned not only helping people, but they specifically referred to improving their appearance and to be able "to give back" to society in their future career in either the public or private sector or both. This altruistic element and, in general, intrinsic factors have been important to the motivations of dental trainees. In fact, in Sweden, 44% of future dentists indicated that these interpersonal motives related to helping people, and in a British study, 88% did the same (Belsi et al. 2013; Karibe et al. 2009). Students' desire to be able to offer a genuinely needed service to the community was important as well. The human service element offers the practitioner a sense of pride (Newton et al. 2011).

Extrinsic factors accounting for a dentistry career choice were several. These included a distinct probability of finding employment with ease and having a substantial financial remuneration with concomitant material security. Basically, dental students have believed that dentists are able to construct their desired personal lifestyles. More specifically, students have been attracted by flexible working hours and the autonomy related to self-employment, as well as their positive perception of other working conditions. They welcomed the opportunity to make creative use of manual talent and to have variations in the nature of their work that allow them to translate theory into practice. They thought they would be able to integrate scientific knowledge with practical hand skills. In short, students have been attracted to

S. Z. Koff, *The Dental Team in the European Union*,
https://doi.org/10.1007/978-3-030-72232-6_2

dentistry by features of the work (Alani 2015; Du Toit et al. 2014; Gallagher et al. 2007a, 2008; Hallissey et al. 2000; More and Kohn Jr 1960; Vigild and Schwarz 2001).

Socio-demographic factors have impacted career choice as well. These relate, in part, to gender and socioeconomic status. In terms of gender, it is noteworthy that in recent years, the feminine component of dentistry has increased substantially in many Member States. In some cases, the future student's career choice has been influenced by the occupational history of her/his family. It is believed that the higher the position of the family in terms of education, occupation, income, and status, having more resources at hand, the greater the expectation of easier access to the dentistry profession. Traditionally, few dentistry students have come from manual workers' families (Elliott 1972; Sherlock and Cohen 1972). Interpersonal factors consisting of the influence of family members and professional persons can also steer people in the direction of a specific career.

Of all these elements, the literature reports that the principal influences on the choice of a dental career have been the desire to work with people and the main features of professional work. The motives for choosing dentistry are primarily altruistic and are found among intrinsic and extrinsic factors. This holds as well for dental care professionals (DCPs) and healthcare professionals in general. Interestingly enough, having a dentist among family members or friends has not been found to be important in the choice of a dental career. Thus, research conclusions demonstrate that various types of students have selected their course of study influenced by altruism, but also pragmatic, extrinsic motives. The latter held more importance for people directly entering dentistry than for other DCPs (Belsi et al. 2013; Gallagher et al. 2007a, b; Hallissey et al. 2000; Vigild and Schwarz 2001; Wu et al. 2015).

As noted, dentistry has become an independent profession throughout the European Union (EU). However, it is noteworthy that in some institutions of higher education, it is part of the faculty of medicine for reasons of cost efficiency and integration. Of note is the fact that there are no dental training programs in Cyprus or Luxembourg, meaning students have to study abroad. Cypriots tend to study dentistry in Greece, the United Kingdom, and Hungary (Charalambous and Theodorou 2013).

In several Member States, the number of students that can be granted access to dentistry education is limited, meaning the nation has a *numerus clausus* (closed number). Member States featuring such a restriction include Austria, Belgium, Bulgaria, Croatia, France, Hungary, Italy, Latvia, Malta, Poland, Portugal, Romania, and Slovenia. Sometimes, the limitation only includes candidates for admission to dental training, and occasionally, it also specifies the number of students from other countries, as in the case of Hungary (Kivovics and Csado 2010), or, as in the case of Poland and Italy, it is applied to each faculty of dentistry. In Greece, 15 places per year are automatically allotted to Cypriots (Kravitz et al. 2015). In Malta, restrictions are set for EU students and those from outside the structure.

Belgium does not formally have a *numerus clausus*. However, federal law regulates the number of future dentists who can participate in vocational training, the period which takes place in some Member States after one finishes formal classroom dental studies and in which she/he undertakes a specified period of supervised clinical training. Spain is the Member State with the greatest increase in the number of dental practitioners over the last three decades. Due to this situation, according to its 2016 Report, the Spanish Dental Association has attempted to have a *numerus clausus* established, but its efforts have been in vain. Another nation heading toward unemployment and underemployment of dentists is Scotland which is significantly overproducing dental practitioners (Drummond 2015). In Austria, the number of foreign dental students has increased impressively. Thus, a quota system has been introduced because it was feared that many students would return to their home country to practice. And so, Austria loses. Seventy-five percent of the posts available for dentistry students have been reserved for those possessing an Austrian secondary education diploma (Hofmarcher and Quentin 2013).

Determination of the *numerus clausus* is usually the responsibility of a unit or member(s) of a nation's government. For example, in Belgium, Hungary, Latvia, and Poland, it is the Ministry of Health who takes the decision concerning quotas, whereas in Bulgaria, it is the Council of Ministers, the executive branch of government, and in Croatia, the notion is defined by the Ministry of Science, Education, and Sport. In France, it is set by the Ministry of Education and the Ministry of Health. In Romania, each university determines it autonomously. This fact means that principally it mirrors teaching capacity, not national oral healthcare needs (Albreht et al. 2016; Croatia 2015; Dimova et al. 2012; Eaton et al. 2012a; Mitenbergs et al. 2012; Vlădescu et al. 2016). The quota is frequently established on an annual basis. In fact, in Slovenia, it has to be approved each year by the National Assembly, a legislative body.

Directive 2005/36/EC provided that applicants to basic dental education be in possession of a diploma or certificate valid for entrance to a university or an institution of higher education at a similar level (Directive 2005/36/EC, Article 34 (1)). Admission procedures vary throughout the EU. Having an impact on academic achievements, all are considered important. Students, believing themselves to be specially selected, often raise the level of their desired achievement goals (Röding 2005).

Part of the admissions process in some Member States consists of completion of an entrance examination. Some Member States with such a qualifying requirement include Spain, Germany, Greece, Italy, Latvia, Romania, Slovakia, Finland, Estonia, the Czech Republic, Croatia, Bulgaria, and Belgium. In Cyprus, the entry examination is for dental study in Greece, and it is organized by the Ministry of Education of Cyprus. In Belgium, the entry examination takes place before the first year of study, as in other Member States, but in Flanders, the Flemish-speaking part of the country, and in the French-speaking universities, this examination is taken after the first year of study (Charalambous and Theodorou 2013; The Czech Republic n.d.; Džakula et al. 2014; Eaton et al. 2012b; Kravitz et al. 2015; López-Valcárcel et al. 2006). Performance on this element as well as that on a test often given in European countries when one is about to complete secondary education is taken into consideration in the dental school admissions decision.

Assuming that there is no diversity in students' scores and requirements between the two fields, some institutions adopt the same examination for medical and dentistry candidates. From their perspective, they are both equal. Over an extended period of time, researchers have compared medical and dental candidates' scores. They concluded that those starting dental studies had lower total scores on the examination than students beginning a medical program. On the cognitive section of the examination, the difference in scoring between the two fields was labeled striking. It was found that examination scores for both medical and dental students were predictors of academic grades, especially during the first 3 years of study. However, in the case of dental education, the correlation was somewhat lower. Such findings have implications for an admissions process which utilizes the same examination for two diverse programs (Buyse et al. 2010).

In Ireland, entry to dental studies has been based on one's performance on the aforementioned examination taken at the end of secondary education. Researchers found a significant relationship between performance on this exercise and the first dental examination, but it could only explain a small percentage (12%) of the variation within the achievement of students on this examination. They indicated there was no relationship between scores achieved in the secondary education leaving challenge and the final dental examination. Thus, it was concluded that a selection process based solely on one's performance on an examination of this type is of limited value (Lynch et al. 2006).

The importance of manual dexterity in the selection of dental students has also been questioned. Part of a dentistry entrance examination in Croatia is based on the results of a manual skills examination (Croatia 2015). In an Italian study, differences concerning this capacity were found among applicants. Diverse types of high schools and prior educational experience produced differences within the group. Those having a university degree and those from a scientific high school were more capable. Moreover, it was found that students' manual ability improved significantly with attendance in a dental training program. Thus, the variable of manual dexterity was deemed not essential in the selection of a dental class (Giuliani et al. 2007).

A full spectrum of variables affiliated with the backgrounds of applicants to dental school are used as predictors of course performance. More specifically, questions have been raised about the validity of the variables of students with prior dental assisting experience and having a parent who is a dentist. Can these be used as predictors of a student's performance in a dental program? It seems that these two variables have minimum merits as predictors and concern should lie instead with an applicant's motivation and interest in the dental sector (Park et al. 2010).

In some Member States, admission to dental training programs requires completion of mandatory courses prior to application. For example, in the United Kingdom, an applicant must have successfully completed three "A-level" (advanced-level) science courses in high school, and in the Netherlands, specific courses are designated: physics, biology, and chemistry. In Malta, application requisites include a minimum grade of C in examinations in advanced chemistry and biology and three subjects at an intermediate level of which physics is compulsory (Kravitz et al. 2015).

Often applicants to dental training are already in possession of a university degree. The appropriateness of a standard admissions process based on information contained on the application form, and in a personal statement, as well as academic performance for the first degree has provided a subject for research in Scotland. The outcome suggests that instead of admissions decisions being based on the standard documents required for graduate-entry dental schools, they should be founded on multiple mini-interviews that can predict academic performance in this type of situation. These confrontations, it is affirmed, should be used to discuss previous relevant work experience and to reveal team-working capacity, communication skills, and manual dexterity. These elements were found to have greater predictive value of subsequent academic and clinical success in graduate-entry dental programs. It is noteworthy that in Malta, applicants for basic dental training with the highest grades are admitted following an interview (Foley and Hijazi 2013).

Research has indicated that applicants to dental faculties increasingly reflect the upper social classes (Gallagher et al. 2009; Vigild and Schwarz 2001). A British study noted that if you are a male from a lower social class and a minority ethnic group and have attended an institution of higher education, the chances for acceptance to dental training are low. In fact, successful applicants for such programs are most likely to be from higher social classes and a minority ethnic background than those who apply to higher education, in general. Gender, ethnicity, and school type, comprehensive or private, are identified with the probability of acceptance to medical and dental faculties. Also, it has been demonstrated that dentistry does not seem to be attracting black applicants. Obviously, these circumstances raise issues of widening access to entrance and social justice. Moreover, healthcare providers should reflect somehow the population that they serve.

Financial support in various forms is available to students throughout the EU and in all academic programs. This support is found in various forms: grants, both need-based and merit-based, loans, tax benefits for parents of students, and family allowances. There is great variation in the number of students who pay fees in public institutions and how much they are charged. For example, in Slovenia, only part-time students pay fees. In the Czech Republic, the amount charged is less than 50 euro ($54.33) annually, and it is viewed as a contribution to administrative expenses.

The United Kingdom has the highest cost established by the universities, and it has been capped at 11,377 euro per year ($12,361.91). Other countries with relatively high fees include Ireland, Italy, Latvia, Lithuania, Hungary, the Netherlands, and Slovenia. In Lithuania and Hungary, students can benefit from state-funded places, and thus, they study at no cost. Such funding is awarded on the basis of academic performance. It has been criticized for not confronting social inequity and demonstrating little effort to enlarge participation in higher education.

In terms of grants, nearly all Member States have support systems that combine those that are need-based and merit-based. The former tend to be prevalent. Greece is the only Member State where need-based criteria have no role. Iceland, as part of the EEA, is the only nation without grants. In 12 support systems, either all or a majority of students receive grants of one type or another. In addition, there are family allowances and tax benefits for parents of students who are dependent on household income based on the number of dependents. In these instances, the student is viewed as a family member and not as an individual. This type of support is to be found in approximately one-half of the European higher education systems (European Commission/EACEA/Eurydice 2015).

A variety of support mechanisms for higher education students exists within the confines of the EU. However, it is to be stressed that not all are available in every Member State. Furthermore, the requirements of the programs differ from one nation to another along with the operation of their structures. Still, it is evident that there is a multitude of programs of a diverse nature. Not every area of the globe is as fortunate.

Directive 2013/55/EU provides standards for dental training. Incorporating a feature of the aforementioned Bologna Declaration, it proclaims that programs may be expressed in terms of ECTS credits and shall consist of at least 5000 hours of full-time theoretical and practical study at a university or institution at a similar level or at one supervised by a university. Furthermore, such programs are to have a duration of at least 5 years (Directive 2013/55/EU, Recital 26). Several Member States have dental training programs with a duration of 5 years. In the remainder, dental majors require at least 6 years of study. These nations include Austria, Bulgaria, Croatia, France, Italy, the Netherlands, Romania, Slovakia, and Slovenia. It must be remembered, as aforementioned, that Cyprus and Luxembourg do not offer this training (Amariei and Eaton 2009; Charalambous and Theodorou 2013; Croatia 2015; The Czech Republic n.d.; Eaton et al. 2012a; ERO-FDI 2012; Federal Ministry of Health, Division II 2016; Friedman 2011; Kravitz et al. 2015; Matrix Insight 2012; Olejaz et al. 2012). In the United Kingdom, the General Dental Council is of the opinion that students already in possession of a university degree are able to complete a degree in dentistry in less time, meaning 3 or 4 years, depending on the type of their first degree. Given the length of dentistry education and the cycles provided for in the aforementioned Bologna Declaration, some Member States, such as Estonia and Bulgaria, use an integrated curriculum of bachelor's and master's studies. At the end of the dental program, a participant is awarded a master's degree.

Dentistry is both an art and a science and also a practice-based and academic discipline. Such is evident in EU legislation, given the mandates of what the student is supposed to receive from dentistry education. Directive 2005/36/EC stipulates that basic dental training is to provide the student specific knowledge and skills. These include knowledge of the sciences that stand at the base of dentistry, an understanding of scientific methods, and multi-faceted erudition of healthy and ill persons and of the structure and function of healthy and diseased teeth, mouth, jaws, and associated tissues. In addition, it is to furnish the dental trainee adequate knowledge of clinical disciplines and methods related to preventive, diagnostic, and therapeutic dentistry, as well as appropriate supervised clinical experience (Directive 2005/36/EC, Article 34 (3a-3f)).

In addition to these provisions, the directive also includes subjects to be part of a study program for future dental practitioners. Mention is made of basic courses, such as chemistry, physics, and biology. Medico-biological subjects and general medical ones provide a classification for another group of courses that involve, among others, anatomy; pharmacology; hygiene; radiology; general surgery; general pathology; general medicine, including pediatrics; and anesthetics. A third group of courses is composed of subjects specifically related to dentistry, such as conservative dentistry, preventive dentistry, anesthetics and sedation, special surgery, dental materials and equipment, clinical practice, orthodontics, dental radiology, professional organization, ethics and legislation, social aspects of dental practice, prosthodontics, special pathology, pedodontics, periodontics, dental occlusion, and functioning of the jaw (Directive 2005/36/EC, Annex V.1, point 5.3.1). In the amending directive (Directive 2013/55/EU, Recital 26), the Commission is assigned authority, with respect for the Member States' responsibility for education, to update this list in order to keep it congruent with technical and scientific changes.

In December 2016, the Council of European Dentists passed a resolution expressing its dissatisfaction with the dentistry curriculum as stated in Annex V.3/5.3.1 of Directive 2005/36/EC. The purpose of its document was to be certain that accurate terminology is utilized in the professional qualifications law and that dental practitioners are in possession of appropriate skills and competences. It suggested three types of changes to the professional qualifications statement in order to foster congruence with present-day curricula. The resolution noted the need to change some of the names of listed subjects. For example, biology should not stand alone, but should be listed as biology and genetics. The list to be changed cited in the resolution was quite long. Also suggested were modifications of titles linked with groups of courses.

In addition, the Council stated that certain subjects should be deleted from the study program as they were outdated and no longer listed in any contemporary dental curricula. Finally, the resolution suggested courses to be added to the professional qualifications document. These included forensic dentistry, biostatistics (evidence-based approach), gerodontology, and emergency medical care, especially cardiopulmonary resuscitation, among others. It was noted that the suggested modifications have already been integrated into most curricula and approved by prominent cross-national professional and dental student associations.

In 2013 and 2014, the Council of European Dentists and the Executive Committee of the Association for Dental Education in Europe, respectively, approved a resolution for the modernization of the professional qualifications directive. The document set forth five competence domains which should be integrated into dentistry education. They were professionalism, ethics, and communication; knowledge base and information literacy; clinical examination, diagnosis, and treatment planning; therapy and maintaining oral health; and prevention and oral health promotion.

Some Member States offer basic dental training programs in a language or languages other than that or those of the country involved. For example, those who follow dentistry courses in Romania have to choose between Romanian, English, or French as their language of choice for their studies. In Hungary, dentistry studies are available in three languages: Hungarian, English, and German. Also, English is used in Lithuania, Poland, and Bulgaria, along with the native language (Eaton et al. 2012a; Janulyte et al. 2014; Kavadella 2014).

At the end of their academic road, future dentists in some Member States, such as Belgium, Bulgaria, Croatia, Germany, Poland, Slovenia, and the United Kingdom, must undertake vocational training which is "the organized education of the newly qualified dentist in supervised practice" (Scott 2003, p.76). It takes place in a period of transition between academia and the world of work. During this period, the professional works in a dental office, clinic, or healthcare facility usually under the supervision of mentors, professors, and/or authorized professionals for a specific period of time which can range from 6 months to a year or more.

In Germany, vocational training is compulsory, if one desires to eventually provide care within the sick fund system. To do so, an individual with a German diploma must complete 2 years of approved supervised practice in a dental office in vocational training. A person holding an EEA diploma does not require this experience. The United Kingdom has a similar requisite. To eventually practice in the National Health Service, one must participate in vocational training and Dental Foundation Training. The latter program entails clinical practice 4 days a week plus 1 day devoted to academia. Vocational training candidates in the United Kingdom compete with each other. They are ranked nationally and assigned training placements according to their standing. The system has been labeled mechanistic (Alani 2015; Eaton et al. 2012a; Germany's dental health care system 2015; Kravitz et al. 2015).

Several Member States no longer feature vocational training because it has been incorporated into the last year of dental education. This is the case in France, where students in their sixth year are supervised in a practice by a referenced dentist for at least 200 h. In Finland and Lithuania, a similar arrangement exists (Eaton et al. 2012a; Profile of dental education in France 2010). Then, in a few Member States, such as Ireland and Malta, vocational training programs exist, but participation is not compulsory.

With an adviser always close at hand, this post-qualification experience is considered most valuable to the new practitioner as an aid to increasing self-confidence, improving competence, allying theoretical knowledge with practice, and providing managerial and decision-making experience. The amended professional qualifications directive (Directive 2013/55/EU) notes that such systems are useful for guaranteeing employment for the younger set and for providing a transition from academia into the world of work without difficulty (Directive 2013/55/EU, Recital 10). In 2014, the Council of European Dentists in a resolution issued a call for national governments to acknowledge the significance of these programs.

In Poland, vocational training was scheduled to be ended in 2017. Academicians and dental students opposed such action. It was quite obvious that the decision was based solely on financial reasons and the value of the experience was not given consideration. Eventually, a law confirmed a supervised 12-month internship prior to obtaining the right to independent practice. Frequently, participants in vocational training, as in the Polish case, are paid a salary. Sometimes it has limits. In Romania, the Collegiums of Dental Physicians oppose the introduction of vocational training based on issues of patient safety and quality of care. On the other hand, the Spanish Dental Association has undertaken efforts without success to introduce mandatory vocational training. The organization even proposed it to the Council of European Dentists in the hope of having it formally incorporated into Directive 2013/55/EU (ERO-FDI 2012; Kravitz et al. 2015; Regional European Organisation of the FDI 2012). At the EU level, there have been other attempts to make vocational training obligatory. However, the concept has not met with a favorable response because costs have been believed to be excessive. Moreover, realization of such an EU program would present an obstacle to freedom of movement. European legal measures prohibit any Member State from imposing such a scheme save on its own citizens graduating from educational institutions in its own territory. Directive 2013/55/EU (Recital 27) provided that if one undertakes a traineeship in another Member State, it should be given recognition in the home Member State.

Reasons for the choice of dentistry as a career have been set forth. These are subject to change as one progresses throughout the educational program and its vocational training. A study of participants in England and Wales reveals such modification. The choice of a dentistry career originally followed the aforementioned reasons. However, these were transformed due to changes in educational and healthcare arrangements, and thus, career paths became related to personal student indebtedness, national workforce modifications, clinical practice limitations, and expenses for additional training (Gallagher et al. 2007a, b).

At the end of the educational path, dental students often confront the challenge of a State examination or another type of course termination exercise by a university or dental body, in order to be eligible for registration. This occurs in several Member States, including France, Ireland, Germany, Croatia, Poland, and Bulgaria. For future French practitioners, the challenge is not over. In order to practice, they have to complete a thesis project which has to be presented within 18 months after their sixth year of study.

In 2015, there were 13,500 new dentistry graduates in the Member States. Germany led the way with the highest number, 2300. Romania, Spain, the United Kingdom, and France recorded more than 1000 each. Relative to the total population, Romania had the highest number of dentists who graduated in 2017. There were 10.6 graduates per 100,000 inhabitants. Portugal and Lithuania, that same year, scored relatively high ratios with both 6.2 graduates per 100,000 inhabitants, respectively. These three Member States featured an increase in dentistry graduates per 100,000 population over a decade. The majority of Member States for which data have been reported had between 1.7 and 4.1 dentistry graduates per 100,000 inhabitants. The Netherlands, Malta, and Italy scored lower (Healthcare personnel statistics n.d.).

Hopefully, the described training will "produce a dental practitioner who is ethically competent to practice general dentistry at a level commensurate with the reasonable expectations of the society he or she is destined to serve and committed to career-long education and professional improvement" (Scott 2003, p. 69). In addition, the new graduate should have acquired communication, leadership, organizational, problem-solving, and management skills, the capacity to work within the principles of equity and diversity, the ability to accept responsibility for the care provided, meaning diagnosis, treatment planning, and the quality control of oral health care. Also, of importance is the ability to delegate and collaborate with the dental squad, regardless of its nature. The value of characteristics, such as detail orientation, dexterity, patience, and stamina, also should have been acquired (Dentists-Latvia n.d.). Moreover, it is during the training process that future practitioners begin socialization to the profession. They become attuned to its values and culture.

Dentists: Specialization

Just as professionalization has various stages, the same holds true for specialization. In the first place, as a result of scientific and technological advances, persons in a specific field develop a new skill or skills. These are transmitted through educational institutions, and an association is usually established for purposes of exchanging ideas and featuring the new capacities. Associational membership comes to symbolize a certain status within the specific field, and certification of excellence or specialization takes place in an effort to externally make known such recognition. Eventually, certification as proof of competence is accepted by units responsible for healthcare quality and practice within that sector, and it is restricted to those duly authorized (Strasberg 1980). They are labeled specialists, experts in a specialty, in this case, a dental specialty, which is defined as "a nationally or internationally recognized branch of dental specialisation for which a structured postgraduate training programme exists" (Widström and Eaton 2006, p. 718).

According to Directive 2013/55/EU (Recital 22), dental specialties are to be covered by the original professional qualifications directive (Directive 2005/36/EC), if the specialization is common to at least two-fifths of the Member States. Entry to specialist dental programs is contingent on having completed basic dental training or being in possession of named valid documents. Full-time duration of study is 3 years minimum, according to the law. Moreover, during this period, the person following the route to a specialty is to participate in the activities and the responsibilities of the training institution. Also, the Commission was granted authority to maintain the congruity of the minimum time period for training with scientific and technical change. In addition, it was empowered to include new dental specialties in the directive, if they are common to two-fifths of the Member States.

The number of recognized specialties varies from Member State to Member State. The aforementioned sectoral directives recognized only two dental specialties: orthodontics and oral surgery. At this time, there are three Member States, Austria, Luxembourg, and Spain, that do not recognize any specialties. However, this does not mean that specialist practices are non-existent. Some nations have many practicing specialists who are not formally recognized. Since 2007, the Spanish Dental Association has undertaken efforts to formally introduce specialization based on a medical residency model. Opposition has arisen from some academics and scientific associations who seem to see threats and competition related to the teaching of graduate courses. However, the effort might be on the road to success. Some institutions have favorably evaluated the project, and detailed plans are eventually to be developed (Regional European Organisation of the FDI 2014).

The number of specialties can be explained by the nature of a national oral healthcare system, rather than general socioeconomic factors. It seems that nations with publicly provided oral health care have more specialty services as in the case of the United Kingdom (Widström and Eaton 2006). Also, several of the newer Member States, such as Bulgaria, Croatia, Latvia, Lithuania, Poland, and Slovenia, claim more recognized dental specialties than the older members.

Many of the same specializations exist in several Member States and are most common. Some of these are orthodontics (relates to the correction and prevention of irregularities of the teeth, bite, and jaw), oral surgery, endodontics (relates to the diagnosis, treatment, and prevention of diseases and injuries of the tooth root, dental pulp, and encircling tissue), pediatric dentistry, oral and maxillofacial surgery, periodontics (focuses on supporting structures of the teeth, jawbone, and gums and periodontal ligament), and prosthodontics (relates to substitutes for missing teeth). It is noteworthy that a specialty unique to Croatia is that of family dentistry which focuses on oral health of all family members throughout the life cycle (Sanz 2010; Widström and Eaton 2006).

Consideration might be given to the expansion of the latter and other specialties as well. One of these is dental public health. Given the alliance of general and oral health care, plus the dental squad's stress on prevention of oral maladies and difficulties with resources planning in many Member States, this particular specialization's focus on the epidemiological, demographic, clinical, social, and economic facets of health and oral health care would be of extreme value to many communities (Eaton et al. 2009).

Another expertise to be further developed lies in the area of legal dentistry and/or forensic dentistry. Dentists are involved in cases related to fitness to practice, car and other accidents, missing person investigations, and work-related or non-accidental injuries. Such situations frequently require reliance on combined multifaceted knowledge: biological, technical, medico-legal, and forensic knowledge. Forensic and legal knowledge is of importance to dental practitioners in that many societies have become more litigious than in the past. Nuzzolese (2013) makes a forceful call for special consideration to be given to the role of forensic odontologists in these situations. Failure to do so, it is argued, can cause delays in positive identification of a person, a longer grieving period, and, furthermore, a violation of human rights (Nuzzolese et al. 2013; A revolution in disaster victim identification 2012).

Special care dentistry is another specialty that, if further developed, would serve a need throughout the EU. It would not only meet the needs and demands of an important population, but it would also offer significant support for primary care dental practitioners. This specialty achieved recognition by the General Dental Council in the United Kingdom after more than 20 years of lobbying by the British Society for Disability and Oral Health and the British Society of Gerodontology (Special care dentistry recognized by GDC 2008).

Factors impacting dental students' decision to specialize and their choice of specialty have differed from those influencing their decision to study dentistry. The most important factor is gratification in providing the service. Other elements are the influence of faculty members and mentors as well as being in debt (Dhima et al. 2012; Shin et al. 2015). At the postgraduate level, in some Member States, enrollment in dental specialty studies is limited. The *numerus clausus* exists at this level as well. For example, in Romania, only 30 students per year may enter specialist training programs. A restriction also exists in Finland, Poland, Bulgaria, Slovenia, and Sweden. It is noteworthy that specialist training is not available in Cyprus, Luxembourg, Malta, and Spain (Amariei et al. 2009; Dimova et al. 2012; Kravitz et al. 2015). Such programs usually take place in universities and their clinics, hospitals, or other recognized training facilities, public or private.

Also, at this level as well, courses are sometimes offered in languages other than the national one, as in Sweden, where several specialist training programs are offered in English. In some Member States, specialist trainees are remunerated, and in others, they are not. Postgraduate dental students seeking the title of specialist are paid in Ireland, Germany, Latvia, Belgium, Denmark, Poland, Romania, Finland, the Czech Republic, the Netherlands, and Bulgaria. There is no remuneration for postgraduate trainees in Italy and Portugal. In some nations, such as Sweden, the systems for remuneration vary. In Austria, there are no official guidelines pertaining to this subject. It is purely a matter to be taken up by the trainee and the university (Dimova et al. 2012; Germany's dental health care system 2015; Kravitz et al. 2014, 2015).

Frequently, entry requirements for specialist training include a specific amount of time spent in post-qualification work experience prior to application. This is the case in Sweden, the Czech Republic, Denmark, Greece, Germany, the United Kingdom, Ireland, Slovakia, Slovenia, and Finland. The timeline for this post-qualification experience ranges from 1 to 3 years in these Member States. A 2-year period is the most common. As noted, according to EU law, full-time specialist dental training must last a minimum of 3 years. Most programs of this nature throughout the EU are between 3 and 4 years with the exception of oral and maxillofacial surgery which has a longer duration. Specialty training in this field usually lasts 5 years and, in a few cases, 6. In some Member States, it is considered a specialty of medicine. The Hellenic Dental Association is concerned that it is not considered a part of dentistry as well. In fact, in Hungary, such training programs are open to physicians only. In the Netherlands, Belgium, and Greece, eligibility for this training requires both medical and dentistry qualifications. In Lithuania, after 6 years of studying general medicine, the trainee in this specialty needs to spend another 5 years as a student (Damaskinos and Economou 2012; Eaton et al. 2012b; Janulyte et al. 2014; Kivovics and Csado 2010; Swedish Dental Association 2003).

Postgraduates finish specialty training in diverse ways. Practices vary from one Member State to another and also between specialties in the same nation. For example, in Portugal, the orthodontics and oral surgery specializations end with a presentation of clinical cases to a committee appointed by the national dental association, the Ordem dos Médicos Dentistas. Another practice involves an end of training university final examination as in Finland, Estonia, and Poland. This requirement is accompanied by a mandatory thesis in Croatia. In the Czech Republic, the examination is organized by a committee appointed by the Minister of Health. A formal State examination is to be taken in Bulgaria and an examination under the auspices of the regional dental chamber in Germany (The Czech Republic n.d.; Dimova et al. 2012; Germany's dental health care system 2015; Kravitz et al. 2015; Tallinn Tervishoiu Kõrgkool n.d.).

Neither Directive 2013/55/EU nor the one which it amended speak to the content of specialist training. Reference to a study program as in the case of undergraduate curricula for dentistry or to a set of knowledge, skills, and competences does not take place. This is the responsibility of national competent authorities or entities. The Council of European Dentists is fully supportive of this practice. However, the Council of European Chief Dental Officers is not so complacent. It is of the opinion that in order to enhance standardization and harmonization, a Pan-European list of competences should be groomed for each specialty (Council of European Chief Dental Officers 2012). As specialty training developed throughout the EU, much diversity has been identified in the Member States' curricula for specific specialties. To confront this situation, several European specialist societies came to an agreement related to the curricula and criteria to be utilized for specialist training programs (Council of European Dentists 2016; Widström and Eaton 2006).

Dental practitioners have increasingly been placed under pressure. Their workload has changed in nature, and oral healthcare challenges have mounted. Patients' needs and demands have transformed. The population has aged throughout the EU, and as a group, the elderly have more of their own teeth. Cosmetic embellishment has become fashionable along with modified societal priorities across the Member States. Aesthetics have assumed an importance. Such changes have the potential to increase the need for complex restorative dentistry. In addition, patient expectations have grown. Scientific knowledge has advanced, and skills have become more sophisticated. The techniques and instruments used by practitioners in providing services have multiplied. Such changes have cast doubts on the capacity of undergraduate dentistry programs to appropriately educate future practitioners to meet the new needs and demands placed on the profession. Evidently, many sophisticated skills are not included in the undergraduate dentistry curriculum. Thus, it has been argued that competences and proficiencies at the EU level should be developed for dental specialties. Several Member States, including Romania, Poland, Sweden, the United Kingdom, Spain, and France, want or have wanted more specialists and/or specialties. On the other hand, a majority of German dentists are not in favor of additional dental specialties. In spite of this opposition, it appears that both specialties and specialists will continue to increase in order to meet the needs and demands of the new era (Amariei et al. 2009; ERO-FDI 2012; Sanz et al. 2008).

Dental Hygienists and Dually Qualified Dental Hygienists-Therapists

A significant participant in some dental teams is the dental hygienist who provides various oral prophylaxis services and oral health education. However, across the Member States, the rules vary as to what services these figures are allowed to offer. Moreover, the profession is not recognized throughout the EU. Several Member States do not regulate the profession in terms of required professional qualifications for access to it and practice of it. These countries include Austria, Bulgaria, Cyprus, Estonia, France, Germany, Luxembourg, and Romania. In fact, not every Member State, such as Luxembourg, has a training program for this DCP (Damaskinos and Economou 2012; Eaton et al. 2012b; European Commission 2016; Goldie 2013). The movement to develop dental hygiene practice was spurred by the American emphasis on preventive care and in Eastern Europe by the same care in Switzerland. In nations where this profession has been recognized, there has been a focus on preventive and prophylactic oral care instead of corrective dental care (European Commission 2016; Luciak-Donsberger 2003b).

For dental hygienists, there is currently no European standard for professional training. The aforementioned professional qualifications directives do not cover this subject. However, the European Regional Organisation of the World Dental Federation has passed a resolution that contained a dental hygienist healthcare profile (ERO 2015). In addition to acquiring the skills and knowledge of dental chair assistants and dental preventive assistants, the dental hygienist is to better capacities and knowledge related to specific technical and professional skills and oral health prevention. Admission to a training program, according to the resolution, should require having completed the requirements of a dental chair assistant and dental preventive assistant. In addition, the applicant should have practiced as the latter DCP for a year. With this preparation, further education is to consist of at least 300 additional hours. The end of training and qualification is to be achieved via completion of a final examination in front of a committee consisting of competent authorities and representatives from the national dental association.

In terms of present-day education, dental hygienists have travelled a long path from short periods of diploma or certificate training to longer ones culminating in a bachelor's degree. Training for this particular DCP throughout the EU requires 2 to 4 years of post-secondary education. Two-year training in either general or vocational programs is found in Spain, Ireland, Latvia, and Slovenia. In the United Kingdom, the course, lasting 24 to 27 months takes place alongside dental trainees in special units of dental schools. Hungary offers a short training course of 360 hours outside of the formal school system. Entrance is open to those who have completed a 2-year education as a dental assistant. Secondary courses awarding a certificate on completion are available in the Czech Republic, Liechtenstein, and Norway. The latter two nations, as noted, are part of the EEA.

Other courses are found at the university level with diverse duration. Such programs in Poland, Sweden, and the United Kingdom last for 2 years. Those in the

Czech Republic, Denmark, Italy, Malta, Portugal, Slovakia, and Romania require 3 years' study. Another year is needed to complete the 4-year course in Finland, Hungary, Lithuania, the Netherlands, and Poland. Lithuania awards a professional bachelor's degree after 3 years as does a course in the United Kingdom. After finishing these programs successfully, the participant receives a degree or diploma, depending on the type of completed program. In any case, professional qualification has been achieved (Bachelor of Dental Hygiene: College of Education and Therapy in Poznan 2016; The Czech Republic 2008, 2018, n.d.; Eaton et al. 2012b; European Commission 2016; The EU Single Market: Regulated professions database 2018; Jongbloed-Zoet et al. 2012; Kivovics and Csado 2010; Slot 2013). It is noteworthy that in Italy there is a postgraduate specialization in dental hygiene that requires 2 years' participation. Also, in Portugal, it is possible to obtain a master's degree and a doctorate in the field. In addition, both Swedish and Dutch institutions offer doctoral programs in dental hygiene (Araújo 2013; Kravitz et al. 2015).

Sometimes, there are admission requirements affiliated with such programs as aforementioned in the case of Hungary with required completion of training as a dental assistant. In the United Kingdom, the 24- to 27-month courses require that applicants be qualified as a dental nurse and sometimes have an "A level." Then, as in the case of other healthcare professionals, there are programs that require an entrance examination, as in Italy and Latvia. Unfortunately, there are indications that equal access to dental hygiene education has been affected by gender bias (Luciak-Donsberger 2003a). Hopefully, this negativity has been tempered.

Very often, training courses involve a mandatory traineeship. Some dental hygienists have to participate in these, as do some dentistry trainees in vocational training. Such participation is mandatory for dental hygienists studying in the Czech Republic, Denmark, Finland, Ireland, Latvia, Lithuania, Slovenia, and Spain. A last step to achieve professional qualification for many dental hygienists is successful completion of a State examination. This does not take place in every Member State. Included in those that require it are Denmark, Latvia, Lithuania, Poland, and Slovenia. In other instances, often, there is an end-of-course university examination, such as in Romania (The EU Single Market: Regulated professions database 2018). Those dental hygiene students who follow university training and receive a bachelor's degree, frequently, are required to write a thesis, as in Poland (Bachelor of Dental Hygiene: College of Education and Therapy in Poznan 2016).

Programs that have moved to the university, such as those in the Netherlands, have devised courses for practitioners who hold a 2- or 3-year post-secondary diploma so that they too may have the higher qualification. The time needed for this "catch-up" depends on one's knowledge and competences (Slot 2013). Also, many students work in dental practices part-time while studying dental hygiene. This was found to hold true for 75% of Dutch students. Working on the average of 8 h per week in dental practices, they assumed many tasks usually performed by the dentist (Poorterman et al. 2010). Also, the International Federation of Dental Hygienists makes research grants available to trainees. Its purpose in doing so is to stimulate interest and experience in the research arena with the dissemination of research results in order to enlarge dental hygiene's body of knowledge and evidence-based practice.

It is evident that there is much diversity in the programs that educate dental hygienists. There has been no harmonization of their education or even basic agreement as to skills and competences to be acquired. This creates difficulty in terms of free movement of services. A recent situation in Italy illustrates the circumstance. The Unione Nazionale di Igienisti Dentali (National Union of Dental Hygienists) announced that chair-side assistants who have completed hygienist training in Austria may not undertake any dental hygiene activities in Italy (Unione Nazionale Igienisti Dentali 2016). The development of legislation governing dental hygiene education across the Member States would contribute to truly needed equitable standards and opportunities in education as well as in employment. Unity can be achieved with diversity.

Given the close relationship between dental hygienists and periodontology and based on consultation with a variety of professional groups, the European Federation of Periodontology (n.d.) has developed guidelines for dental hygienist education. These are intended to reap high standards on the continent and to stimulate countries in which dental hygienist practice is not recognized to establish training schools. These guidelines refer to the permitted work of these professionals and related entry requirements, principles of education and training, and preparation for employment and assessments. This document features defined learning outcomes and professional competences. If only it was to be considered valid by all stakeholders.

A relatively new member of the dental team is the dually qualified dental hygienist-therapist. This combined professional model, utilized in the Netherlands, was first developed in New Zealand with dental nurses. The profession was born in a period of crisis. During World War I, many recruits were rejected for military service due to an epidemic of serious dental disease. It was realized that the country did not have enough dental practitioners to deal with the particular situation as well as others of a similar nature and that a new professional figure was needed.

In 1920, dental nurses were trained and deployed in schools to provide basic dental care to children. These oral care providers performed a range of dental functions, including diagnoses of oral diseases, as well as drilling and filling of carious teeth (Roemer 1977). At a later date, these practitioners came to be called therapists. Eventually, in some areas, the training was integrated with that of dental hygienists. It prepares students to carry out the majority of routine dental activities for both adults and children. In other words, they are limited practitioners who provide basic dental care just like a dentist (Friedman 2011; Nash et al. 2008, 2012).

In the United Kingdom, there is more than one way to become dually qualified in dental hygiene and therapy. One can follow an integrated program which combines the two fields, or one can obtain two separate qualifications. The integrated course has a duration of 3 years, and completion reaps a Bachelor of Science Degree in Dental Hygiene and Dental Therapy or in Oral Health Sciences. Entry requirements relate to a certain number of "A levels" and, in some cases, a dental nurse qualification. Another option resulting in a Bachelor of Science degree with honors is a course with a 4-year duration.

The majority of diploma courses last for 27 months, and the award is a Diploma in Dental Hygiene and Dental Therapy. There are also diploma programs of lesser duration. These focus on only one of the two fields and last from 36 weeks to 2 years. Entry qualifications depend, it seems, on the focus of the course. Those having a central theme of dental therapy require the applicant to be a qualified dental hygienist. Those with a concentration on dental hygiene mandate the applicant be qualified in dental nursing. In addition, one has to have completed a certain number of "A-level" courses and, often, specific sciences.

In the Netherlands, the combined profession still carries the name of dental hygienist. Training was lengthened from 3 to 4 years resulting in a bachelor's degree. People have become more aware of these professionals, due to the Internet, and the fact that they meet many needs and demands, especially those of the elderly (Friedman 2011; Rowbotham et al. 2009).

Dental Technicians

The dental technician is recognized as a member of the dental team throughout the EU. This DCP, who constructs various oral appliances following the written prescription of a dentist, is also known as a dental craftsman or a dental mechanic in Ireland and, sometimes, elsewhere as well. Training takes place in various sites, including vocational institutions, both secondary and post-secondary, dental laboratories, medical colleges, and programs within dental schools and universities. It is noteworthy that Cyprus has no structures for training in this profession. Cypriots must study the subject matter in another nation.

Length of training differs across the Member States. It ranges from 2 to 5 years. At the low end of the continuum, 2-year post-secondary programs are to be found in Denmark, France, the Netherlands, Spain, and the United Kingdom. Part-time participation is available in the Dutch course, and thus, in this case, completion requires 4 years. Two-and-a-half-year programs are found in Latvia and Poland (Eaton et al. 2012a; The EU Single Market: Regulated professions database 2018).

A common type of training for the profession is one that lasts for 3 years. Such programs take place in Belgium, the Czech Republic, Germany, Greece, Lithuania, Luxembourg, Portugal, Romania, Slovakia, and Sweden. These programs tend to be at the post-secondary level, and a diploma is awarded to a successful participant. Usually theoretical and dental laboratory training are combined. In the Portuguese case, one more year of study reaps a degree instead of a diploma (The Czech Republic n.d.; Eaton et al. 2012b; The EU Single Market: Regulated professions database 2018; Germany's dental health care system 2015).

A half-year more is required to complete a training program in a Finnish polytechnic institute. The same amount of time is needed for a diploma of professional higher education in Estonia. It is noteworthy that in 1945 Tallinn Medical School featured dental technician training and the curriculum included an offering on the

Soviet Communist Party and the Russian language. In addition, military training was offered as well (Kravitz et al. 2015; Tallinn Health Care College 2016; Tallinn Tervishoiu Kõrgkool n.d.). These courses, obviously, were a sign of the political times, not the field of dental technology.

Four-year programs, both secondary and post-secondary, are to be found in Austria, Croatia, the Czech Republic, Hungary, Ireland, Malta, the Netherlands, Slovenia, and the United Kingdom. Secondary education courses of this length for dental technicians are available in Croatia, the Czech Republic, Slovenia, and the United Kingdom (Eaton et al. 2012a; The EU Single Market: Regulated professions database 2018; Kravitz et al. 2014). Also, in Ireland, an apprenticeship program exists. Usually secondary training terminates with a certificate.

University programs for dental technicians have become much more common. Currently, they exist in 12 of the Member States: Bulgaria, the Czech Republic, Estonia, Greece, Ireland, Malta, Poland, Portugal, Slovakia, Slovenia, Sweden, and the United Kingdom. A bachelor's degree is awarded upon completion. Degree programs last usually between 3 and 4 years. Also, of note is that Estonia and Sweden feature master's studies in the field, and in Sweden, it is possible to complete a Ph.D. The program in Estonia is offered in the national language and in English (An Comhairle Fiaclóireachta 2010; Cini 2008; The Czech Republic 2008, n.d.; Katrova 2009; Ministry of Interior of the Slovak Republic 2016; Tallinn Health Care College 2016; Zagoričnik 2011).

The longest period of training is found in Italy and Slovakia. In the former Member State, after 3 years of training and successful completion of an examination, employment is permitted. However, self-employment requires two more years of study and success on another examination. In Slovakia, vocational secondary education to become a dental technician requires 5 years as well (The EU Single Market: Regulated professions database 2018; Kravitz et al. 2015). An entrance examination is an admission requirement in only a few programs. In Latvia, one is required for training as a dental technician at Riga Medical College. Also, the same is a requisite for the noted 3.5-year program in Finland.

As mentioned, educational programs for diverse oral health professions terminate in diverse ways across the Member States. The same holds true for dental technicians. Some Member States require a mandatory traineeship. Such occurs in Bulgaria, Croatia, the Czech Republic, Denmark, Finland, Germany, Greece, Lithuania, the Netherlands, Slovakia, and Slovenia. There is no standard duration. Some are a year in length. It is interesting that in Bulgaria, the university bachelor's degree in dental technology includes 600 h in pregraduate practice, and then the traineeship is mandatory in order to exercise the profession of dental technician.

In terms of examinations to be completed at the end of training, the 3.5-year program in Estonia requires a final examination or a thesis with a positive grade. This was the only case that mentioned an exercise of this type. Other Member States require successful completion of a State examination. Such is mandatory in Bulgaria; Croatia; Denmark; France; Germany, where it is prepared by the Chamber of Handicraft; Italy; Poland (for the 2.5-year program only); and Slovenia (The EU Single Market: Regulated professions database 2018; Germany's dental health care system 2015).

This presentation reveals that in the EU different ways are followed to educate dental technicians. In fact, several Member States follow more than one path to accomplish the same goal. This happens in the Czech Republic, Greece, Ireland, Italy, Malta, Poland, Portugal, Slovakia, Slovenia, Sweden, and the United Kingdom. A survey of the programs available in these individual nations reveals that they are usually found at different educational levels. A study of European dental technicians' training was undertaken not too long ago (Zagoričnik 2011). It found that in the Member States, 5% of these DCPs had a master's degree and 5% had a doctorate. The low percentages are understandable in that graduate studies in the field were made available relatively recently and are not offered everywhere. It was also revealed that 21% of the dental technicians were in possession of a Bachelor of Science degree. This is a program that has grown at a rapid pace. On the other hand, 49% of the profession was educated in secondary programs which, at one time, represented the standard. Also, it was found that 19% of these DCPs achieved professional status via another system.

Clinical Dental Technicians

A relatively recent addition to some dental squads is the clinical dental technician. These DCPs provide complete removable prosthetic appliances directly to the public without the involvement of a dentist. They work independently. This is a major difference between this profession and that of the dental technician. These figures are known by various names throughout the Member States. Dental-prosthetist-denturist is used in Belgium, dental prosthetician in the Netherlands, clinical dental technician or special dental technician/technologist in Denmark and the United Kingdom, and denturologist in France (European Parliament 2000).

The profession is not recognized in all Member States. Currently, the Malta Dental Technology Association is involved in a legal battle for its recognition. Also, noteworthy is the fact that as of 2016, a 41-year battle was won when denturism was finally recognized as an autonomous profession in Belgium (IFD 2016, 2017). Even though the profession is not recognized in all Member States, the aforementioned latest Professional Qualifications Directive and Council Directives 90/385/EEC, 93/42/EEC, and 98/79/EC, pertaining to medical devices, support the provision of goods and services by these professionals throughout the EU. They also have the privilege of workers' freedom of movement as mentioned in the Treaty of Rome (Engelbrecht 2016). The Medical Devices Regulations (Regulation (EU) 2017/745 and Regulation (EU) 2017/746) will amend the cited directives pertaining to the subject after transition periods of 3 and 5 years, respectively.

Denturism is a subset of dentistry. Whereas dental students study a wide scope of disciplines, future clinical technicians concentrate on only one of these subjects—removable prosthetics. Once again, professional training for this figure is not uniform across the Member States. Belgium, Denmark, Finland, Ireland, the Netherlands, and the United Kingdom provide education for denturists. With the exception of Denmark, admission requires one to be a qualified dental technician.

The United Kingdom mandates that an applicant have post-technician training in science, clinical and interpersonal skills, as well as customer care. Professional experience as a dental technician in a laboratory is required in Finland, Ireland, the Netherlands, and the United Kingdom. This mandate ranges from at least 5 years in Finland and the Netherlands to 3 years in Ireland. In Finland, applicants are required to take an entry examination, and in the Netherlands, dentists may apply for admission after a practical examination.

Program length also varies. In the Netherlands, it consists of 4 years at a university or 3 years part-time in a program offered by the Dutch Denturist Federation. The Danish and Finnish programs require 4 years to complete; in Belgium, 3 years (580 h); in the United Kingdom, 2 years; and in Ireland, 18 months (European Commission 2016; The EU Single Market: Regulated professions database 2018). Once again, a program is offered in a language other than the national one. In Finland, a university course is available in both Finnish and English.

Dental Assistants/Dental Nurses

Another member of some dental teams is the dental assistant, also commonly referred to as the dental nurse or chair-side assistant. This is the person who helps the dentist prepare for and carry out oral health care and who also has some organizational and administrative responsibilities. In Bulgaria, this DCP is not found (Katrova 2009).

Once again, diverse training exists across the Member States. In several Member States (Cyprus, Italy, Luxembourg, Portugal, Slovenia, and Spain), training is normally undertaken by the employer. In the Netherlands, in spite of the availability of many courses, the dentist is the major trainer, and in Sweden, there is no uniform formatted training program. The shortest training courses are found in Belgium (Flanders) and in Poland. These are diploma post-secondary programs and duration is 1 year. Qualification level, in the United Kingdom, is certificate post-secondary, and program length is 18 months. The same time is allotted to complete the 590 h mandated in a French dental practice (Focus on Belgium, the Netherlands, and Luxembourg 2007; Kravitz et al. 2015; Swedish Dental Association 2003).

Two-year post-secondary courses exist in the Czech Republic, Greece, Ireland, and Malta. In Greece, after completing course work, the future DCP is expected to spend at least 6 months gaining experience in a dental practice. In Hungary, one is also allowed to train for 1400 h outside academia, and in the Czech Republic, dentists are allowed to provide formal training for general nurses. Two and a half years are required to obtain professional qualifications in Denmark and Finland. University training is offered in the former Member State, and in the latter, training takes place with a dentist with institutional support. Diplomas are the reward for completion of the program (The Czech Republic n.d.; The EU Single Market: Regulated professions database 2018; Olejaz et al. 2012).

Six months longer or 3 years are needed to qualify in Austria, Germany, Latvia, Lithuania, and Romania. In Romania and Austria, nurses are trained at the secondary level. A minimum of 600 h is to be devoted to theoretical instruction and at least 3000 h to practical training. Formation takes place in post-secondary education in Latvia and Lithuania. In Germany, training is provided in a dental practice and a vocational school. Then, specialization is available. This education is offered in a Dental Chamber. A specialized chair-side assistant requires 700 h of further training. A dental prophylaxis assistant needs a minimum of 400 more hours of preparation, and the dental administrative assistant must complete 350 additional hours of instruction (The EU Single Market: Regulated professions database 2018; Federal Ministry of Health, Division II 2016; Germany's dental health care system 2015; Health systems in transition (HiT) profile of Germany 2016; Kravitz et al. 2014).

In Estonia, training involves basic nurse preparation for 3.5 years followed by a special short course on dental care. Tallinn Health Care College was supposed to begin a program for the training of dental assistants in Estonia. The longest educational path for this profession is found in Croatia and Slovakia where 4 years is required for completion of requirements. In both cases, certificate training is at the secondary level (Croatia 2015; The EU Single Market: Regulated professions database 2018; Tallinn Tervishoiu Kõrgkool n.d.). As is the case with other DCPs, training for many EU dental assistants terminates differently. For example, in Latvia, professional qualification ends with a mandatory traineeship, similar to the previously mentioned vocational training. Latvia and Poland require successful performance on a State examination in order to access the profession. In Germany, a similar examination organized by a regional Dental Chamber is mandated, and in Austria, an examination takes place before an examination commission. Romania and Slovakia also have a course-ending final examination (The EU Single Market: Regulated professions database 2018; Germany's dental health care system 2015; Kravitz et al. 2015).

Orthodontic Therapists

The orthodontic therapist, also called an orthodontic auxiliary, is a member of the dental squad in only a few Member States. This figure performs some orthodontic care. The qualification level is post-secondary. With the exception of Ireland, training lasts for a year. In Ireland, the duration is 3 years, and there is a mandatory traineeship. In the United Kingdom, candidates for admission to the training program must be a qualified dental nurse, dental hygienist, dental therapist, or dental technician with clinical experience, and in Ireland, to pursue this qualification, one must be a qualified dental hygienist or dental nurse (The EU Single Market: Regulated professions database 2018; Swedish Dental Association 2003).

Treatment Coordinators

It is possible for this figure to be a member of the clinical or non-clinical squad. The position, according to the literature, appears to be unique to the United Kingdom. Application of this role throughout the EU appears very limited. This person facilitates the new patient process and closes the gap between the new patient, the practice, and the staff. Training for the position can be personalized and delivered by a Treatment Coordinator Trainer, or there are courses offered that last for a day or so. The aim of the course is for the participant to be able to carry out the role effectively and efficiently and to deal with patients in a sensitive and effective manner.

Student Attitudes and Behavior

Given the multiple professions represented in the dental team across the EU, it is quite obvious that a multitude of persons is educated annually to fulfill the various roles involved. These trainees' oral health attitudes and behaviors toward their own health reflect their understanding of the significance of prevention of oral health problems. Moreover, their own oral health behavior holds consequences for patients' oral well-being as well. As future DCPs, the oral health habits, attitudes, and lifestyles of these students have been studied. It was found that dental students had superior oral health behavior and knowledge in comparison to others and this superiority was expected to increase. Students involved with clinical dental training reported improved dental behavior due to their studies (Pacauskiene et al. 2014).

Other research projects have found that a majority of oral healthcare trainees adopted inappropriate oral health attitudes and behaviors. However, the year of study had the most impact on comportment. As students progressed throughout their program, oral health attitudes and behaviors improved. Thus, it has been asserted that the teaching of self-care techniques should be assigned more importance and stressed early in all programs (Dias et al. 2016). In addition, for dental students, especially Croatians, it was affirmed that oral hygiene should be a compulsory course taken at the beginning of training. It has been an elective and, as such, it has exerted little influence on students' oral health behaviors (Badovinac et al. 2013). Cross-culturally, differences have also been found in dental school students' oral health attitudes and behavior. The impact of culture was recognized, but the conclusion was similar to that aforementioned. The year of study was important as was a course focusing on preventive dentistry techniques (Kawamura et al. 2000; Polychronopoulou and Kawamura 2005). Positive attitudes toward the preventive approach should always be cultivated.

The Learning Environment

Student perceptions of the learning environment are important. Not only does it influence their overall academic performance, but it also may contribute to the development of psychosocial difficulties and impact their resolution. In Greece, dental care students have positively evaluated their educational environment. There was concern related to students' stress, tiredness, and lack of appropriate feedback from teachers. These criticisms were generated during clinical experiences. On the other hand, trainees were content with their colleagues and felt socially comfortable in the classroom (Kossioni et al. 2012).

Bullying and intimidation are not restricted to pre-secondary and secondary education. According to a cross-national study, they exist in oral healthcare training institutions on the part of instructors and fellow students. Negative training experiences involving these activities could eventually exert a significant impact on the future of a profession in that its members are its best recruiters (Rowland et al. 2010).

In oral healthcare training, students and faculty are affected by gender discrimination and inequality. Furthermore, a full-strength workforce faces a serious barrier due to this phenomenon. It has been observed that the gender role of dental hygienists with the profession being composed of a large majority of females has contributed to disparities in educational attainment within Europe. In order to meet the mandates of the EU, immediate effort should be undertaken to promote equal access to educational attainment. Remedy of this situation is of major importance because it bears consequences that go beyond education. All efforts should be viewed as integral parts of institutional and instructional reform (Newman et al. 2016).

The appropriate penalty for specific academic offenses has been a subject for debate between oral healthcare students and faculty. It seems that Greek dental school faculty members would assign more severe sanctions for various academic offenses than students. This was especially true in the case of academic dishonesty. Even though extenuating circumstances could sometimes significantly change the recommended sanctions, it appears that faculty members are generally more severe than students in recommending penalties for the same misbehaviors (Koletsi-Kounari et al. 2011).

A malady that many oral healthcare students, unfortunately, encounter is stress and its various consequences. According to research results, in Greece, most stress is caused by the encountered workload, performance pressure, and self-efficacy beliefs. The most perceived stressors reflect gender differences, whereas stress intensity varies a great deal according to the year of study, as in Sweden (Schéle et al. 2012). More specifically, fourth-year students showed more stress in reference to their professional future, whereas those in their first year were stressed over the lack of time for relaxation (Polychronopoulou and Divaris 2005). Other reported sources of stress concern examinations, clinical requirements, and oral healthcare supervisors (Alzahem et al. 2011).

In Germany, research identified the same sources of stress and found that marked gender differences on stress appraisal persisted overtime. In another Greek study, however, the significance of workload and clinical training factors decreased overtime, whereas faculty and administrative factors increased (Pohlmann et al. 2005; Polychronopoulou and Divaris 2010). These stressors take their toll on future professionals. They have adverse effects on students' health and well-being. More specifically, they put trainees at risk for problems, such as anxiety, depression, and burnout (Elani et al. 2014).

In an earlier cross-national survey of dentistry trainees in five Member States (the Netherlands, Ireland, Germany, Finland, and the United Kingdom) (Humphris et al. 2002), 36% reported significant psychological distress or morbidity, and 22% revealed high scores on emotional exhaustion. These figures represent a definite large part of the participants. Another research effort (Gortner et al. 2008) on the same topic identified high burnout rates in the fifth year of the dental program. A direct effect of stress on both burnout and physical symptoms was found. Also illustrated was an indirect effect of stress on mental health via burnout. Stress and burnout are also alive and well in postgraduate dental education, but without gender differences. Perceived stress in this case also correlated with burnout (Divaris et al. 2012).

Students develop diverse strategies to cope with these maladies. Some utilize reflection and appraisal skills. Others select social and interpersonal capacities, while still others invoke organization and time-management talents. Unfortunately, there are those who engage in health-damaging behaviors, such as risk taking, smoking, substance abuse, and depersonalization and social isolation from family, friends, and society, in general. It is imperative that the psychosocial environment of the institutions where oral healthcare training takes place be upgraded so that psychological problems are not as prevalent. The environment should be such that students are able to construct a work-life balance that allows for the maintenance of their endurance, capacity to perform, and commitment (Aulak et al. 2016). These traits they can take with them as they enter the world of work. They will be most useful.

Faculty

As far as dental school faculty members are concerned, recruitment is cited as a problem in several Member States (Continued decline in dental academics 2016). As is the international trend, in Ireland, the oral healthcare faculty has been dominated by males who hold senior academic positions, have considerable clinical experience, and are over a certain age, meaning retirement is just around the corner. There is support from part-time clinical staff, which represents general practitioners, but it has much less teaching experience (O'Sullivan 2009).

These part-timers have an important role to play in clinical teaching. Many perceive it as long-term, even though opportunities to progress in the system are limited. Not all hold this perspective. In the United Kingdom, 27% expect higher rewards related to recognition and status. Many are dissatisfied with their position. In that dental training institutions are extremely dependent on these people, and recognizing the amount of dissatisfaction, it has been suggested that formal training in teaching skills be offered, so that all can adequately meet their mandated responsibilities and that a career pathway be developed as well (Davies et al. 2013). Trainers and practitioners have common professional knowledge. However, in spite of this, the emphasis they place on its theoretical and practical sectors is diverse (Becher 1990).

Curricula

Oral healthcare curricula face many challenges. The Association for Dental Education in Europe claims that they should reflect the history, culture, and political system of the specific nation (Murtomaa 2009). This is especially important, but nowadays more difficult than ever. Europeanization and globalization carry implications for DCPs. It cannot be assumed that what is practiced in one culture is directly applicable in another. Cultural sensitivity is a significant part of a DCP's education, especially given the development of the single market and migration trends. Furthermore, it is well-established that people from different cultures react diversely to treatments, practices, and maladies. To be culturally competent, members of the dental team should develop generic cultural competence, the knowledge and skills usable with all ethnic groupings, as well as culture-specific competence, the knowledge and skills concerned with a specific ethnic cluster (Gerrish 2004). DCPs must accommodate the needs generated by cross-national mobility and, at the same time, those in their own Member State.

The European Dental Students' Association has as one of its goals, the promotion of exchange programs and student participation in them. The organization participates in a project involving volunteers in Ladakh, India, known as the Amçhi Programme. The Amçhi are Buddhist nuns who provide some health care to the community. Volunteers, who include European physicians, dentists, and trainees, educate the Amçhi on how to prevent and contain the spread of oral maladies and provide service to those who need it (www.adee.org). In another project, the organization, in collaboration with the Tanzanian Dental Students' Association, located at Muhimbili University of Health and Allied Sciences, sponsors a program to educate school children about oral health. These children are examined for oral diseases and treated, if necessary (King 2014).

One way to develop cultural sensitivity and respect is to have an international learning experience. Health care in general and specifically oral health care can no longer be taught within the context of a single nation. Not only is specific knowledge gained via study abroad, but horizons, in general, are expanded. Programs for foreign study have been developed and funded by the EU. Moreover, many oral healthcare schools in the Member States have an exchange program or programs providing trainees and faculty with opportunities to spend time in another site. Also joint degree programs have been established between academic institutions in different nations (Joint degree agreement signed 2009). Such initiatives weaken or remove obstacles to mobility which was the rationale for establishing the aforementioned joint European Higher Education Area. Unfortunately, there have been barriers to intercultural education endeavors. These include overcrowded curricula, lack of faculty and administrative support, and financial constraints (Rafter et al. 2006).

Interprofessional Education

Diagnosis and care have become more complex and thus, frequently, require that practitioners from more than one field be involved. When this situation initially arose, training in some Member States was difficult because many professionals were in private individual practice. Teaching trainees to work with other professionals was not easy because the setting needed for this type of teaching was rare or non-existent (Mustard 1978). However, Sweden, for more than 30 years, has featured interprofessional education. Caregiving services in the hospital and ambulatory sector are integrated. Healthcare practitioners with university degrees are awarded extended competences and rights, including restricted prescription and first-line consultation. Education prepares personnel for these responsibilities and functions. Common learning of the various tracks and training on real patients are the principal pillars of interprofessional teaching which initially started as an experiment and became national in scope. The established goals and educational and caregiving outcomes are duly considered by the accreditation and quality assurance authority when making decisions. However, it has been noted that such an approach would be deemed a restriction on academic freedom outside Sweden (Sottas et al. 2016).

Sweden has also devised an interprofessional program between dentists and dental hygienists in view of a foreseen decrease in the former practitioners and an increase in the latter and the need for well-developed collaboration between the two professions. The program includes dental trainees for dental hygiene students, as well as planning and treatment for shared patients. These two features rank high with both sets of trainees. Teamwork is encouraged, knowledge of the other profession is enhanced, and a holistic perspective on patients and oral care is developed and reinforced. Both groups of students due to interprofessional education are better prepared for the world of work (Leisnert et al. 2012).

The importance of introducing oral care trainees to implementation science and evidenced-based elements has been made known (Laurence 2015). Implementation science encompasses the use of strategies to adapt and use of evidence-based interventions in targeted settings to realize improvements in people's health. Trainees are exposed to interpretation and systematic reviews of materials. They also become aware of newer methodologies utilized by other healthcare practitioners, such as physicians and nurses, with whom they often work. Furthermore, interprofessional collaboration is enhanced. Trainees also learn the significance of stakeholder engagement. After all, services provided are to fulfill the needs of the population served. Familiarity with implementation science, multiple methodologies, and evidence-based interventions, plus use of stakeholder engagement, definitely make decision-making much easier and more appropriate.

Interprofessional education in various healthcare sectors and at both pre- and post-qualification levels has received positive evaluations. It has augmented professionals' capacities to work as a team and to communicate more effectively among themselves and with patients as well as with other practitioners in diverse fields. Moreover, practitioners have a greater understanding of each other's work and responsibilities. In spite of the positive evaluations, in an Irish study of dental and DCP interprofessional education, obstacles to the approach arose. Dental hygiene trainees thought that they had a shared role in many tasks assigned solely to the dentist by dental and dental nurse trainees. Dental hygiene students perceived their role as a partner in care and not basically as offering support to the dentist. These divisive attitudes indicate that professional identity and role development must be given attention by oral healthcare educators (Morison et al. 2008).

Also, in Austria, many physicians view the field of public health as one fully identified with medicine. Thus, other professionals involved in multidisciplinary efforts are viewed with suspicion (Ladurner et al. 2011). This attitude has been confirmed in a most recent British study. Interprofessional education was viewed as beneficial in terms of teamwork and as deficient in reference to professional identity and roles (Salazar et al. 2017).

It is noteworthy that the Association for Dental Education in Europe has been collaborating with the Association for Medical Education in Europe, especially on interprofessional education. The goal is to provide medical education for dentistry trainees and dental education for medical students. Such is deemed critical for the interprofessional delivery of healthcare services, given the close relationship between general health and oral health (ADEE & Council of European Dentists (CED) collaboration 2015; European update: ADEE-CED taskforce 2016; Van Dyke 2016). Most recently, Germany has recognized the need to insert new elements in the dentistry curriculum to create closer links with medicine in the early years of undergraduate dental education (German Dental Association 2016).

Interprofessional education focuses on an understanding of the roles, scope of practice, and education of all team members, their basic language, and mind-sets. In order to encourage cooperation, efforts are also undertaken to develop appropriate attitudes and comportment (World Health Organization 2013). There are several subjects that lend themselves to more than one profession and, thus, could be offered in an interprofessional manner. These include ethics, communication and motivational interviewing, evidence-based practice, and informatics (Rafter et al. 2006). Another feasible topic would be smoking which has been added to a Hungarian curriculum. Healthcare professionals serve as role models for patients and students concerning smoking. The patient-practitioner relationship affords a chance for guidance and a personalized consultancy (Johansson et al. 2014).

Claiming that clinical training and work are not presently defined in European legislation and are not optimal in some institutions, the European Dental Students' Association had suggestions for curriculum revision. These related to clinical training and called for a revision of the Annex of Directive 2005/36/EC in relation to harmonized clinical training. Some trainees, it was asserted, are lacking in the needed experience to become fully competent practitioners. Thus, the organization issued a call for the establishment of minimal clinical training requirements throughout the Member States so that qualified dentists would have a proper education, would offer patients equally safe treatment, and would be fully mobile (EDSA press release 2015; EDSA update 2015).

Another area cited for development in curricula is that of special care dentistry. Those needing such a service are people with "a disability or activity restriction that directly or indirectly affects their oral health, within the personal and environmental context of the individual" (Yeaton et al. 2016, p. 10). The literature implies that qualified practitioners often lack the necessary knowledge, skills, and experience needed to provide services to these patients. Irish dental schools have recognized this deficiency and integrated the subject matter into interprofessional education. Unfortunately, all members of the dental team still felt a low level of confidence in dealing with patients requiring special care dentistry, due to insufficient clinical exposure (Yeaton et al. 2016). Efforts should be made to correct such a situation throughout the Member States. There have been other calls for this type of training and some to make it mandatory. Other suggestions, as noted, include the creation of another specialty of Special Care Dentistry. Such would require enhanced faculty training in gerontology, geriatrics, and special patient care. It could certainly meet the needs of many EU citizens (Damning inquiry report 2008; Dolan 2013).

Outreach

A not too recent teaching tool that has been adopted in several Member States, including the United Kingdom, Finland, Germany, and Sweden, is known as Outreach. It concerns "teaching which although, coordinated by a traditional provider of dental education, such as a dental school, takes place at a site, distant to the traditional centre" (Eaton et al. 2006, p. 186), or in other words, it is "clinical teaching away from the home dental school" (Smith et al. 2011, p. 85). In that oral health care is, for the most part, based on primary care, it was considered appropriate to train students in community dental clinics as well as in university facilities. Furthermore, such a training method helped relieve pressures from a shortage of suitable patients and oral care faculty members. In these clinics, students perform a full range of restorative dentistry procedures, preventive treatment and advice, extractions, and emergency treatment, among other services. They also work with a complete dental team. Thus, they have an opportunity for interdisciplinary learning. Part-time general practitioners deliver this educational experience. Firm, ongoing support for them is of major importance as is aid to facilitate their transition from an experienced practitioner to a clinical instructor (Eaton et al. 2006; Elkind et al. 2005; Radford et al. 2014).

Outreach participation was found to be of value to both teachers and trainees. Teachers are exposed to a new environment, and they do not have to worry about a shortage of patients for students. For students, it has contributed to personal development, sense of professional responsibility, knowledge of the practice environment, and further development of clinical skills. The Outreach environment in terms of training has been judged as more demanding than that of a university facility. For the DCP trainees, the volume and diversity of treatment procedures carried out have been highly appreciated and considered an important contribution to their enhanced clinical maturity. The experience has been of significance for students because of the increase in their confidence in performing clinical tasks. It has been said that augmented confidence relates to increased competence. In addition, trainees are exposed to organizational issues, such as patient history-taking, record keeping, and the like (Eaton et al. 2006; Lynch et al. 2010). Moreover, participants see more patients with diverse needs in a period of time than they do in a dental school clinic. Not only is the clinical experience different in the community setting, but the social one is as well. The patients are from the "real world" and are socially diverse. This is important in terms of experiencing a wide range of cultural norms, using communication skills, and developing management talents. Patients reap benefits as well in terms of access to care and the costs involved (Craddock 2008; Eaton et al. 2006; Elkind et al. 2007; Eriksen et al. 2011; Lynch et al. 2010; Radford et al. 2014; Smith et al. 2006).

In addition, in England, DCP trainees have participated in community-based oral health education for the homeless community. The rewards have been the same as those cited above, but a socialization tool is also involved. In this environment, a sense of social responsibility can be nurtured and, hopefully, carried forward to be utilized in one's career (Pritchett et al. 2014). In Germany, trainees have worked in the area of oral health promotion in day care centers and schools. In addition to the aforementioned rewards from a community program, these trainees became more comfortable in handling children which can often pose a problem in the oral healthcare world (Schüler and Heinrich-Weltzien 2010).

The Outreach program seems to be a win-win situation for all: trainees, patients, and clinical teachers. It provides access to additional resources and, as noted, reaps benefits for all participants. Most important, students are also furnished a notion of their future professional demands and the tenor of their work schedule (Smith et al. 2011).

Teaching Methods

Teaching techniques have also furnished a subject for debate. The lecture method and learning facts have been deemed inappropriate. It has been asserted that these should be substituted with the problem-solving approach and the appropriate use of information technology in all oral care training institutions, so as to remove obstacles to mobility (Murtomaa 2009). Invented in the 1960s, and adopted by many medical and dental schools, problem-based learning uses problem-solving as a way to increase knowledge and understanding. It is a pedagogy in which students learn about a subject via solving an open-ended problem. They do independent self-directed study and then in a group, an essential part of the process, discuss and perfect their newly acquired knowledge. Problem-based learning portrays a student-centered approach, and the teacher acts as a facilitator, rather than a disseminator (Problem-based learning 2001).

A survey of two groups of students, one taught via lecture-based learning and one by problem-based learning, revealed that students who were taught by the latter method outperformed the group who learned via the former approach. Such results indicate that problem-based learning might be better for curriculum integration of clinical cases likely to be encountered in the world of work (Iigüy et al. 2014).

In Scotland, problem-based learning was implemented in a dental nurse program. Participants termed the experience enjoyable. They were of the opinion that the methodology could be useful for learning in depth and improved care of patients. However, they had doubts as to their own ability to acquire knowledge via this methodology. They signaled the necessity for improved feedback (Anderson and Reid 2012).

Online discussion boards are a relatively new arrival to oral healthcare education. Reference has been made to a shortage of patients for clinical purposes. Online case-based discussions represent a solution to the problem and the synchronization of clinical and theoretical education. There appears to be no difference in faculty and student use of the tool. Students mainly post messages for discussion purposes, and faculty mostly reply to them and answer questions. This tool provides for group interaction. Users can share experiences, knowledge, and ideas. These boards have been evaluated as valuable and most successful (Koole et al. 2012; Linjawi et al. 2012).

Peer-assisted learning is another method used to teach dental skills in which students participate in the teaching of their colleagues. In a Scottish case, fifth-year dental trainees, peer tutors, teach entry-level students. These sessions are useful to those who enter dental school with a lack of confidence in their preparation. The peer tutors received high grades from their students on their teaching skills and level of feedback. Also, they were considered less intimidating and more approachable than faculty members. Tutors were pleased with the experience as well, claiming that they also learned from the encounters. In addition, they had an opportunity to enhance graduate attributes (Luk et al. 2016). Examination performance revealed no significant difference between the performance of peer-led groups and those led by faculty (Cameron et al. 2015).

Conclusion

As is evident in this presentation of DCPs' education in the Member States, there is much diversity. This holds true within individual Member States and professions. For example, such has been revealed in Spanish schools of dentistry, both public and private, in relation to the teaching of removable partial dentures used in the treatment of partly dentate patients (de Oyagüe and Lynch 2011). First of all, there was a difference in the duration of the preclinical course between the two types of institutions. In public schools, the course lasted 38 h and in private structures, 60.5 h. Each public school trainee made more removable partial dentures prior to graduation than those in private institutions. Moreover, each student, unlike private school colleagues, was obliged to make a minimum number using specific materials. Not only does such a situation, which is not unique, carry implications for education but also for the mobility of students among dental schools, of graduates across the Member States, and professional recognition, in general.

Health professional education programs and the structures in which their graduates work are under constant pressure resulting, especially from society, internationalization, scientific and technological advances, professional interactions, and government policies. Professional training must be fashioned in such a manner that it meets the needs of tomorrow's healthcare system. The EU Directorate-General for Education and Culture of the Commission has held a stakeholder consultation on skills and qualifications. Noteworthy is the fact that there was overwhelming majority support for implementation of an approach focusing on learning outcomes related to training at all levels of education (Walmsley and Kavadella 2012). The aforementioned requisites for dental training as mandated in the professional qualifications directives are based on input measures, such as workload and time required for a course or programs.

In fact, the Association for Dental Education in Europe in conjunction with the Council of European Dentists jointly affirmed that competences of dental practitioners should be included in the directive concerned with recognition of professional qualifications. They identified five competence domains: professionalism, ethics, and communication; knowledge base and information literacy; clinical examination, diagnosis, and treatment planning; therapy and maintenance of oral health; and prevention and oral health promotion (Association for Dental Education in Europe and Council of European Dentists 2013). Also, they assigned learning outcomes to each domain. Implementation of the learning outcomes approach requires much effort from many sources. However, it would definitely be worthwhile and should be applied to all DCPs, not only dentists. It represents a giant step forward in the right direction.

References

A revolution in disaster victim identification. (2012). *British Dental Journal, 213*, 10.

ADEE (Association for Dental Education in Europe) & Council of European Dentists (CED) collaboration. (2015, August). *ADEE newsletter special edition European activities update, 2*. http://www.adee.org. Accessed 19 June 2018.

Alani, A. (2015, April). *Graduation: A minefield for the younger generation of dentists*. Dental Tribune United Kingdom Edition, pp. 10–12.

Albreht, T., Brinovec, R. P., Jošar, D., Poldrugovac, M., Kostnapfel, T., Zaletel, M., et al. (2016). Slovenia: Health system review. *Health Systems in Transition, 18*(3), 1–207.

Alzahem, A. M., van der Molen, H. T., Alaujan, A. H., Schmidt, H. G., & Zamakhshary, M. H. (2011). Stress amongst dental students: A systematic review. *European Journal of Dental Education, 15*(1), 8–18.

Amariei, C., & Eaton, K. A. (2009). Systems for the provision of oral care in the Black Sea countries: Part 1: Romania. *Oral Health and Dental Management, 8*(1), 3–6.

Amariei, C., Eaton, K., Zaharia, A., & Bartok, F. (2009). *The need for dental specialties in Romania*. Paper prepared for delivery at the European Association for Dental Public Health 2009 Conference, Tromso, Norway. September 3–5, 2009.

An Comhairle Fiaclóireachta (Irish Dental Council). (2010, March). *Dental technicians information dental council newsletter*. http://www.dentalcouncil.ie. Accessed 28 Nov 2016.

Anderson, V., & Reid, K. (2012). Students' perception of a problem-based learning scenario in dental nurse education. *European Journal of Dental Education, 16*(4), 218–223.

Araújo, M. R. (2013). *Dental hygiene around the world*. http://www.dentalcare.com. Accessed 4 Dec 2015.

Association for Dental Education in Europe & Council of European Dentists. (2013). *Modernisation of the recognition of professional qualification directive: Directive 2005/36/EC*. http://www.eudental.eu. Accessed 6 Oct 2015.

Aulak, D. S., Quinn, B., & Wilson, N. (2016). Student burnout. *British Dental Journal, 220*(5), 219–220.

Bachelor of Dental Hygiene: College of Education and Therapy in Poznan. (2016). http://www.healthcarestudies.com. Accessed 2 Nov 2016.

Badovinac, A., Božić, D., Vučinac, I., Vešligaj, J., Vražić, D., & Plančak, D. (2013). Oral health attitudes and behavior of dental students at the University of Zagreb, Croatia. *Journal of Dental Education, 77*(9), 1171–1178.

Becher, T. (1990). Professional education in a comparative context. In R. Torstendahl & M. Burrage (Eds.), *The formation of professions: Knowledge, state and strategy* (pp. 134–150). London: SAGE.

Belsi, A., Asimakopoulou, K., Donaldson, N., & Gallagher, J. (2013). Motivation to study dental professions in one London Dental Institute. *European Journal of Dental Education, 18*(1), 24–30.

Buyse, T., Lierens, F., & Martens, L. (2010). Admission systems to dental school in Europe: A closer look at Flanders. *European Journal of Dental Education, 14*(4), 215–220.

Cameron, D. A., Binnie, V. I., Sherriff, A., & Bissell, V. (2015). Peer assisted learning: Teaching dental skills and enhancing graduate attributes. *British Dental Journal, 219*(6), 267–272.

Charalambous, C., & Theodorou, M. (2013). Systems for the provision of oral health care in the Black Sea countries: Part 13: Cyprus. *Oral Health and Dental Management, 12*(1), 3–8.

Cini, R. (2008, August 15). Standards of health care. *Times of Malta*. http://www.timesofmalta.com. Accessed 8 Mar 2017.

Continued decline in dental academics. (2016). *British Dental Journal, 221*(5). https://doi.org/10.1038/sj.bdj.2016.477.

Council Directive 90/385/EEC of 20 June 1990 on the approximation of the laws of the Member States relating to active implantable medical devices.

Council Directive 93/42/EEC of 14 June 1993 concerning medical devices.

Council Directive 98/79/EC of the European Parliament and of the Council of 27 October 1998 on in vitro diagnostic medical devices.

Council of European Chief Dental Officers. (2012). *CECDO position paper on specialization in dentistry*. http://www.cecdo.org. Accessed 14 June 2017.

Council of European Dentists. (2016). *CED Statement: Specialist dentists*. http://www.cedentists.eu. Accessed 12 June 2016.

Craddock, H. L. (2008). Outreach teaching – The Leeds experience: Reflections after one year. *British Dental Journal, 204*(6), 319–324.

Croatia. (2015). *The Health Systems and Policy Monitor (with modifications since publication of printed version 2015)*. http://www.hspm.org. Accessed 18 Sept 2015.

Damaskinos, P., & Economou, C. (2012). Systems for the provision of oral health care in the Black Sea.countries – Part 10: Greece. *Oral Health and Dental Management, 11*(1), 3–10.

Damning inquiry report calls for training in learning disabilities to be made mandatory. (2008). *British Dental Journal, 205*(4), 170.

Davies, B. R., Leung, A. N., & Dunne, S. M. (2013). Why do general dental practitioners become involved in clinical teaching? A pilot study exploring the views of part-time practitioner teachers, Kings College London. *British Dental Journal, 214*(9), 461–465.

de Oyagüe, R. C., & Lynch, C. (2011). Variations in teaching of removable partial dentures in Spanish dental schools. *Medicina Oral, Patologia Oral y Cirugia Bucal, 16*(7), e1005–e1013.

Dentists-Latvia. (n.d.). http://www.latviaeducation.info. Accessed 26 Aug 2016.

Dhima, M., Petropoulos, V. C., Han, R. K., Kinnunen, T., & Wright, R. F. (2012). Dental students' perceptions of dental specialties and factors influencing specialty and career choices. *Journal of Dental Education, 76*(5), 562–573.

Dias, A. M., Dias, A. R., Veiga, N., Saraiva, R. C., & Dias, I. M. (2016). Oral health attitudes and behaviours among Portuguese dental students. *Atención Primaria, 48*(Espec Cong 1), 218–222.

Dimova, A., Rohova, M., Moutafova, E., Atanasova, E., Koeva, S., Panteli, D., et al. (2012). Bulgaria: Health system review. *Health Systems in Transition, 14*(3), 1–186.

Directive 2005/36/EC of the European Parliament and of the Council of 7 September 2005 on the recognition of professional qualifications.

Directive 2013/55/EU of the European Parliament and of the Council of 20 November 2013 amending Directive 2005/36/EC on the recognition of professional qualifications and Regulation (EU) 1024/2012 on administrative cooperation through the Internal Market Information System (the IMI Regulation).

Divaris, K., Polychronopoulou, A., Taoufik, K., Katsaros, C., & Eliades, T. (2012). Stress and burnout in postgraduate dental education. *European Journal of Dental Education, 16*(1), 35–42.

Dolan, T. A. (2013). Professional education to meet the oral health needs of older adults and persons with disabilities. *Special Care in Dentistry, 33*(4), 190–197.

Drummond, J. R. (2015). Overproducing dentists. *British Dental Journal, 218*(4), 211.

Du Toit, J., Jain, S., Montalli, V., & Govender, U. (2014). Dental students' motivations for their career choice: An international investigative report. *Journal of Dental Education, 78*(4), 605–613.

Džakula, A., Sagan, A., Pavić, N., Lončarek, K., & Sekelj-Kauzlarić, K. (2014). Croatia: Health system review. *Health Systems in Transition, 16*(3), 1–162.

Eaton, K. A., De Vries, J., Widström, E., Gait, T. C., Bedi, R., Meyers, I., et al. (2006). 'Schools without walls?' Developments and challenges in dental outreach teaching – Report of a recent symposium. *European Dental Journal, 10*(4), 186–191.

Eaton, K. A., Widström, E., & Katrova, L. (2009). Education in and the practice of dental public health in Bulgaria, Finland and the United Kingdom. *Oral Health and Dental Management, 8*(2), 30–37.

Eaton, K., Garcia, A., Patel, R., & Rincon, V. (2012a). *A practical resource to help in the support of non-UK, EEA qualified dental practitioners practicing in the UK*. http://www.oxforddeanery.nhs.uk. Accessed 17 Jan 2017.

Eaton, K. A., Harris, M., Ross, M. K., & Arevalo, C. (2012b). A survey of dental hygienists in the United Kingdom in 2011. Part 1—Demographics and working patterns as dental hygienists. *British Dental Journal, 213*(10), E18. https://doi.org/10.1038/sj.bdj.2012.1041.

EDSA (European Dental Students' Association) press release. (2015, August 1). *A need to revise the annex of the 2005/36 Directive for harmonized clinical training*. http://www.edsaweb.org. Accessed 20 May 2016.

EDSA (European Dental Students' Association) update. (2015, December). *ADEE (Association for Dental Education in Europe) Newsletter, 11*(3), 10.

Elani, H. W., Allison, P. J., Kumar, R. A., Mancini, L., Lambrou, A., & Bedos, C. (2014). A systematic review of stress in dental students. *Journal of Dental Education, 78*(2), 226–242.

Elkind, A., Potter, C., Watts, C., Blinkhorn, E., Duxbury, J., Hull, P., et al. (2005). Patients treated by dental students in outreach: The first year of a pilot project. *European Journal of Dental Education, 9*(2), 49–52.

Elkind, A., Watts, C., Quahbough, A., Blinkhorn, A. S., Potter, C., Duxbury, J., et al. (2007). The use of outreach clinics for teaching undergraduate restorative dentistry. *British Dental Journal, 203*(3), 127–132.

Elliott, P. (1972). *The sociology of the professions*. London: The Macmillan Press Ltd..
Engelbrecht, E. W. (2016, February). European Committee news. *IFD Newsletter*, Edition 2, 8. http://www.international-denturists.org. Accessed 5 Feb 2017.
Eriksen, H. M., Bergdahl, M., Byrkjeflot, L.-I., Crossner, C.-G., Widström, E., & Tilberg, A. (2011). Evaluation of a dental outreach teaching programme. *European Journal of Dental Education, 15*(1), 3–7.
ERO (Europäische Regionale Organisation) (European Regional Organisation-FDI (Fédération Dentaire Internationale) (International Dental Federation). (2012). *Summary of national reports--Prague 2012*. http://www.erodental.org. Accessed 12 Mar 2017.
ERO (The European Regional Organisation of the FDI (International Dental Federation). (2015). *Resolution: Dental hygienist profile 25/04/2015*. http://www.ec.europa.eu. Accessed 3 Feb 2018.
European Commission. (2016). *Mutual evaluation of regulated professions. Overview of the regulatory framework in the health services sector – Dental hygienists and related professions*. Report based on information transmitted by Member States and discussion in the meeting of 20 April 2015. GROW/ES- 29 April 2.
European Commission/EACEA (Education, Audiovisual and Culture Executive Agency)/Eurydice. (2015). *National student fee and support systems in European higher education 2015/16: Facts and figures: Education and training*. Luxembourg: Publications Office of the European Union.
European Federation of Periodontology. (n.d.). *Curricular guidelines in dental hygienist education*. http://www.efp.org. Accessed 11 June 2016.
European Parliament. (2000, January 11). *Parliamentary questions*. http://www.europarl.europa.eu. Accessed 14 Nov 2016.
European update: ADEE (Association for Dental Education in Europe)-CED (Council of European Dentists) taskforce. (2016, April). *ADEE Newsletter, 12*(1), 3.
Federal Ministry of Health, Division II. (2016). *Healthcare professions in Austria*. Vienna: Author.
Focus on Belgium, the Netherlands, and Luxembourg. (2007). *Infodent International*, n. 4. http://www.gnydm.com. Accessed 16 Oct 2016.
Foley, J. I., & Hijazi, K. (2013). The admissions process in a graduate-entry dental school: Can we predict academic performance? *British Dental Journal, 214*(2), E4. https://doi.org/10.1038/sj.bdj.2013.56.
Friedman, J. W. (2011). The international dental therapist: History and current status. *Journal of the California Dental Association, 39*(1), 23–29.
Gallagher, J. E., Clarke, W., Eaton, K. A., & Wilson, N. H. F. (2007a). Dentistry – A professional contained career in healthcare: A qualitative study of vocational dental practitioners' professional expectations. *BMC Oral Health, 7*, 16. https://doi.org/10.1186/1472-6831-7-16.
Gallagher, J. E., Patel, R., Donaldson, N., & Wilson, N. H. F. (2007b). The emerging dental workforce: Why dentistry? A quantitative study of final year dental students' views on their professional career. *BMC Oral Health, 7*, 7. https://doi.org/10.1186/1472-6831-7-7.
Gallagher, J., Clarke, W., & Wilson, N. (2008). Understanding the motivation: A qualitative study of dental students' choice of professional career. *European Journal of Dental Education, 12*(2), 89–98.
Gallagher, J. E., Niven, V., Donaldson, N., & Wilson, N. H. F. (2009). Widening access? Characteristics of applicants to medical and dental schools, compared with UCAS (University and College Admissions Services). *British Dental Journal, 207*(9), 433–445.
German Dental Association. (2016). *ERO (European Regional Organisation) country report: Plenary session on 29 and 30 April 2016 in Baku*. http://www.erodental.org. Accessed 16 Sept 2017.
Germany's dental health care system. (2015). *Dental Abstracts, 60*(5), 248–250.
Gerrish, K. (2004). The globalization of the nursing workforce: Implications for education. *International Nursing Review, 51*, 65–66.
Giuliani, M., Lajolo, C., Clemente, L., Querqui, A., Viotti, R., Boari, A., et al. (2007). Is manual dexterity essential in the selection of dental students? *British Dental Journal, 203*(3), 149–155.

Goldie, M. P. (2013). *Dental hygienists in Belgium: Fact or myth?* http://www.dentistryiq.com. Accessed 16 Oct 2016.

Gortner, R., Freeman, R., Hammen, S., Murtomaa, H., Blinkhorn, A., & Humphris, G. (2008). Psychological stress and health in undergraduate dental students: Fifth year outcomes compared with first year baseline results from five European dental schools. *European Journal of Dental Education, 12*(2), 61–68.

Hallissey, J., Hannigan, A., & Ray, N. (2000). Reasons for choosing dentistry as a career – A survey of dental students attending a dental school in Ireland during 1998-99. *European Journal of Dental Education, 4*(2), 77–81.

Health Systems in Transition (HiT) profile of Germany. (updated April 24, 2016). *The health systems and policy monitor*. http://www.hspm.org. Accessed 5 May 2016.

Hofmarcher, M., & Quentin, W. (2013). Austria: Health system review. *Health Systems in Transition, 15*(7), 1–291.

Humphris, G., Blinkhorn, A., Freeman, R., Gorter, R., Hoad-Reddick, G., Murtomaa, H., et al. (2002). Psychological stress in undergraduate dental students: Baseline results from seven European dental schools. *European Journal of Dental Education, 6*(1), 22–29.

IFD (International Federation of Denturists). (2016, February). Breaking news: Belgium. *IFD Newsletter*, Edition 2, 8.

IFD (International Federation of Denturists). (2017).Working for denturists worldwide: News from around the world. *IFD Newsletter*, Edition 3, 6–9.

Iigüy, M., Iigüy, D., Fişekçioğlu, E., & Oktay, I. (2014). Comparison of case-based and lecture-based learning in dental education using the SOLO taxonomy. *Journal of Dental Education, 78*(11), 1521–1527.

Janulyte, V., Aleksejuniene, J., Puriene, A., Peciuliene, V., & Benzian, H. (2014). Current employment characteristics and career intentions of Lithuanian dentists. *Human Resources for Health, 12*, 74. https://doi.org/10.1186/1478a.-4491-12-74.

Johansson, A.-C., Johannsen, G., Uhlin, L., & Johannssen, A. (2014). Dental hygienist students' learning about motivational interviewing. *Dentistry Journal, 2*(2), 65–77.

Joint degree agreement signed. (2009). *British Dental Journal, 207*(6), 259.

Jongbloed-Zoet, C., Bol-van den Hil, E. M., La Rivière-Ilsen, J., & van der Sanden Stoelinga, M. S. E. (2012). Dental hygienists in the Netherlands: The past, present and future. *International Journal of Dental Hygiene, 10*(3), 148–154.

Karibe, H., Kawakami, T., Suzuki, A., Warita, S., Ogata, K., Aoyagi, K., et al. (2009). Career choice and attitudes towards dental education amongst dental students in Japan and Sweden. *European Journal of Dental Education, 13*(2), 80–86.

Katrova, L. (2009). Systems for the provision of oral health care in the Black Sea countries, Part 2: Bulgaria (2009). *Oral Health and Dental Management in the Black Sea Countries, 8*(2), 3–6.

Kavadella, A. (2014, April). Secretary general's report. *ADEE (Association for Dental Education in Europe) Newsletter, 10*(1), 2–3.

Kawamura, M., Honkala, E., Widström, E., & Komabayashi, T. (2000). Cross-cultural differences of self-reported oral health behaviour in Japanese and Finnish dental students. *International Dental Journal, 50*(1), 46–50.

King, O. J. (2014, August). EDSA (European Dental Students Association)-Tanzania volunteer work programme. *ADEE (Association for Dental Education in Europe) Newsletter, 10*(2), 3.

Kivovics, P., & Csado, K. (2010). Systems for the provision of oral health care in the Black Sea countries. Part 7. Hungary. *Oral Health and Dental Management, 9*(4), 193–198.

Koletsi-Kounari, H., Polychronopoulou, A., Reppa, C., & Teplitsky, P. E. (2011). Penalties for academic dishonesty in a Greek dental school environment. *Journal of Dental Education, 75*(10), 1383–1389.

Koole, S., De Wever, B., Aper, L., Veivaeke, S., Derese, A., & De Bruyn, H. (2012). Using online periodontal case-based discussions to synchronize theoretical and clinical undergraduate dental education. *European Journal of Dental Education, 16*(1), 52–58.

Kossioni, A. E., Varela, R., Ekonomu, I., Lyrakos, G., & Dimoliatis, I. D. K. (2012). Students' perceptions of the educational environment in a Greek dental school, as measured by DREEM. *European Journal of Dental Education, 16*(1), e73–e78.

Kravitz, A. S., Bullock, A., & Cowpe, J., with Barnes, E. (2014). *Council of Dentists manual of dental practice 2014* (5th ed.). n.p.: Council of European Dentists.

Kravitz, A. S., Bullock, A., & Cowpe, J. with Barnes, E. (2015). *Council of European Dentists: EU manual of dental practice 2015*. (5.1 ed.). Brussels, Belgium: Council of European Dentists.

Ladurner, J., Gerger, M., Holland, W. W., Mossialos, E., Merkur, S., Stewart, S., et al. (2011). *Public health in Austria: An analysis of the status of public health*. Copenhagen: World Health Organization on behalf of the European Observatory on Health Systems and Policies.

Laurence, B. (2015). Dental education: Why introducing implementation science and stakeholder engagement belong in evidence-based dental education. *British Dental Journal, 219*(6), 246.

Leisnert, L., Karlsson, M., Franklin, I., Lindh, L., & Wretlind, K. (2012). Improving teamwork between students from two professional programmes in dental education. *European Journal of Dental Education, 16*(1), 17–26.

Linjawi, A. I., Walmsley, A. D., & Hill, K. B. (2012). Online discussion boards in dental education: Potential and challenges. *European Journal of Dental Education, 16*(1), e3–e9.

López-Valcárcel, B. G., Quintana, C. D. D., & Socorro, E. R. (2006). Spain. In G. Rechel, C.-A. Dubois, & M. McKee (Eds.), *The health care workforce in Europe: Learning from experience* (pp. 115–127). World Health Organization on behalf of the European Observatory on Health Systems and Policies: Copenhagen.

Luciak-Donsberger, C. (2003a). The effects of gender disparities on dental hygiene education and practice in Europe. *International Journal of Dental Hygiene, 1*(4), 195–212.

Luciak-Donsberger, C. (2003b). Origins and benefits of dental hygiene practice in Europe. *International Journal of Dental Hygiene, 1*(1), 29–42.

Luk, G. D., Glasheen, M. H., & Quock, R. L. (2016). Near-peer facilitated learning in a dental school: A student reflection. *International Dental Journal of Students' Research, 4*(2), 66–70.

Lynch, C. D., McConnell, R. J., & Hannigan, A. (2006). Dental school admissions in Ireland: Can current selection criteria predict success? *European Journal of Dental Education, 10*(2), 73–79.

Lynch, C. D., Ash, P. J., Chadwick, B. L., & Hannigan, A. (2010). Effect of community-based clinical teaching programs on student confidence: A view from the United Kingdom. *Journal of Dental Education, 74*(5), 510–516.

Matrix Insight. (2012). *EU level collaboration on forecasting health workforce needs, workforce planning and health workforce trends--A feasibility study*. http://www.ec.europa.eu. Accessed 18 Feb 2015.

Ministry of Interior of the Slovak Republic. (2016). *Dental technics*. http://www.minv.sk. Accessed 3 Nov 2016.

Mitenbergs, U., Taube, M., Misins, J., Mikitis, E., Martinsons, A., Rurane, A., et al. (2012). Latvia: Health system review. *Health Systems in Transition, 14*(8), 1–191.

More, D. M., & Kohn, N., Jr. (1960). Some motives for entering dentistry. *The American Journal of Sociology, 66*(1), 48–53.

Morison, S., Marley, J., Stevenson, M., & Milner, S. (2008). Preparing for the dental team: Investigating the views of dental and dental care professional students. *European Journal of Dental Education, 12*(1), 23–28.

Murtomaa, H. (2009). Dental education in Europe. *European Journal of Dentistry, 3*(1), 1–2.

Mustard, J. F. (1978). Health professional education. In P. Slayton & M. J. Trebilcock (Eds.), *The professions and public policy* (pp. 142–155). Toronto: University of Toronto Press.

Nash, D. A., Friedman, J. W., Kardos, R. I., Schwarz, E., & Satur, J. (2008). Dental therapists: A global perspective. *International Dental Journal, 58*(2), 61–70.

Nash, D. A., Friedman, J. W., & Mathu-Muju, K. R. (2012). *A review of the global literature on dental therapists in the context of the movement to add dental therapists to the oral health workforce in the United States*. http://www.depts.washington.edu. Accessed 11 Sept 2016.

Newman, C., Ng, C., Pacqué-Margolis, S., & Frymus, D. (2016). Integration of gender-transformative interventions into health professional education reform for the 21st century: Implications of an expert review. *Human Resources for Health, 14*, 14. https://doi.org/10.1186/s12960-016-0109-8.

Newton, P., Cabot, L., Wilson, N. H. F., & Gallagher, J. E. (2011). The graduate entry generation: A qualitative study exploring the factors influencing the career expectations and aspirations of a graduating cohort of graduate entry dental students in one London institution. *BMC Oral Health, 11*, 25. https://doi.org/10.1186/1472-6831-11-25.

Nuzzolese, E. (2013). Missing and unidentified persons: Implications for human rights and forensic odontology. *Journal of Forensic Odonto-Stomatology, 31*(Supplement 1), 31–32.

Nuzzolese, E., Manica, S., Cuković-Bagić, I., Rosie, J., Alqahtani, S. J., & Untoro, E. (2013). Under the lens: Dental expert witnesses in Brazil, Croatia, UK, Saudi Arabia, Indonesia and Italy. *The Journal of Forensic Odonto-Stomatology, 31*(Suppl 1), 160.

O'Sullivan, E. M. (2009). The demographic and academic profile of Irish dental school faculty members. *Journal of the Irish Dental Association, 55*(6), 296–301.

Olejaz, M., Nielsen, A. J., Rudkjøbing, A., Birk, H. O., Krasnik, A., & Hernández-Quevedo, C. (2012). Denmark: Health system review. *Health Systems in Transition, 14*(2), 1–192.

Pacauskiene, I. M., Smailiene, D., Siudikiene, J., Savanevskyte, J., & Nedzelskiene, I. (2014). Self-reported oral health behavior and attitudes of dental and technology students in Lithuania. *Stomatologija, Baltic Dental and Maxillofacial Journal, 16*(2), 65–71.

Park, S. E., Da Silva, J. D., Barnes, J. L., Susarla, S. M., & Howell, T. H. (2010). Predicting dental school performance based on prior dental experience and exposure. *European Journal of Dental Education, 14*(1), 1–6.

Pohlmann, K., Jonas, I., Ruf, S., & Harzer, W. (2005). Stress, burnout and health in the clinical period of dental education. *European Journal of Dental Education, 9*(2), 78–84.

Polychronopoulou, A., & Divaris, K. (2005). Perceived sources of stress among Greek dental students. *Journal of Dental Education, 69*(6), 687–692.

Polychronopoulou, A., & Divaris, K. (2010). A longitudinal study of Greek dental students' perceived sources of stress. *Journal of Dental Education, 74*(5), 524–530.

Polychronopoulou, A., & Kawamura, M. (2005). Oral self-care behaviours: Comparing Greek and Japanese dental students. *European Journal of Dental Education, 9*(4), 164–170.

Poorterman, J. H. G., Dikkes, B. T., & Brand, H. S. (2010). Dental hygiene students' part-time job in dental practices in the Netherlands. *International Journal of Dental Hygiene, 8*(2), 143–146.

Pritchett, R. M., Hine, C. E., Franks, M. A., & Fisher-Brown, L. (2014). Student-led oral health education for the homeless community of East London. *British Dental Journal, 217*(2), 85–88.

Problem-based learning. (Winter 2001). *Speaking of Teaching, 11*(1), 1–7.

Profile of dental education in France. (2010, June). ADEE (Association for Dental Education in Europe) Newsletter, pp. 6–7.

Radford, D. R., Hellyer, P., Jones, K. A., & Meakin, N. (2014). Experienced general practitioners as clinical teachers: A qualitative study of their experience over the first three years as novice clinical teachers in an outreach setting. *JBR Journal of Interdisciplinary Medicine and Dental Science, 2*(6), 147–154.

Rafter, M. E., Dent, B., Pesun, I. J., Herren, M., Linfante, J. C., Mina, M., et al. (2006). A preliminary survey of interprofessional education. *Journal of Dental Education, 70*(4), 417–427.

Regional European Organisation of the FDI (International Dental Federation). (2014). *National report—Spanish Dental Association 2014*. http://www.erodental.org. Accessed 3 Nov 2016.

Regulation (EU) 2017a/745 of the European Parliament and of the Council of 5 April 2017 on medical devices, amending Directive 2001/83/EC, Regulation (EC) No. 178/2002 and Regulation (EC) No. 1223/2009 and repealing Council Directives 90/385/EEC and 93/42/EEC.

Regulation (EU) 2017b/746 of the European Parliament and of the Council of 5 April 2017 on in vitro diagnostic medical devices and repealing Directive 98/79/EC and Commission Decision 2010/227/EU.

Röding, K. (2005). Perceptions of admission committee members: Some aspects on individual admission to dental education at Karolinska Institutet. *European Journal of Dental Education, 9*(3), 115–122.

Roemer, M. I. (1977). *Comparative national policies on health care*. New York/Basel: Marcel Dekker, Inc..

Rowbotham, J. S., Godson, J. H., Williams, S. A., Csikar, J. I., & Bradley, S. (2009). Dental therapy in the United Kingdom: Part 1. Developments in therapists' training and role. *British Dental Journal, 207*(8), 355–359.

Rowland, M. L., Naldoo, S., Abdulkadir, R., Moraru, R., Huang, B., & Pau, A. (2010). Perceptions of intimidation and bullying in dental schools: A multi-national study. *International Dental Journal, 60*(2), 106–112.

Salazar, F. B. C., Andiappan, M., Radford, D. R., & Gallagher, J. E. (2017). Attitudes of the first cohort of student groups trained together at the University of Portsmouth Dental Academy towards dental interprofessional education. *European Journal of Dental Education, 21*(2), 91–100.

Sanz, M. (2010). *EFP (European Federation of Periodontology) guidelines for seeking the specialty in periodontology*. http://www.efp.org. Accessed 11 June 2016.

Sanz, M., Widström, E., & Eaton, K. A. (2008). Is there a need for a common framework of dental specialties in Europe? *European Journal of Dental Education, 12*(3), 138–143.

Schéle, I. A., Hedman, L. R., & Hammarström, A. (2012). A model of psychosocial work environment, stress, and satisfaction among dental students in Sweden. *Journal of Dental Education, 76*(9), 1206–1217.

Schüler, I. M., & Heinrich-Weltzien, R. (2010). *Oral health promotion in day-care centres provided by dental students*. Poster session at the European Association of Dental Public Health Meeting, September 10–11, 2010, Constanta, Romania.

Scott, J. (2003). Dental education in Europe: The challenge of variety. *Journal of Dental Education, 67*(1), 69–78.

Sherlock, B., & Cohen, A. (1972). The strategy of occupational choice: Recruitment to dentistry. In R. M. Pavalko (Ed.), *Sociological perspectives on occupations* (pp. 79–95). Itasca, IL: F. E. Peacock Publishers, Inc..

Shin, J. H., Kinnunen, T. H., Zarchy, M., Da Silva, J. D., Chang, B. M., & Wright, R. F. (2015). Factors influencing dental students' specialty choice: A survey of ten graduating classes at one institution. *Journal of Dental Education, 79*(4), 369–377.

Slot, D. E. (2013). *Dental hygiene in the Netherlands*. http://www.dentistryiq.com. Accessed 30 Jan 2017.

Smith, M., Lennon, M. A., Brook, A. H., & Robinson, P. G. (2006). A randomized controlled trial of outreach placements' effect on dental students' clinical confidence. *Journal of Dental Education, 70*(5), 566–570.

Smith, M., Ash, P., Gilmour, A. S. M., Austin, T., & Robinson, P. G. (2011). Outreach training: The special interest group's report. *European Journal of Dental Education, 15*(2), 85–89.

Sottas, B., Mentrup, C., & Meyer, P. C. (2016). Interprofessional education and practice in Sweden. *International Journal of Health Professions, 3*(1), 3–13.

Special care dentistry recognised by GDC. (2008). *British Dental Journal, 205*(6), 300.

Strasberg, M. A. (1980). Graduate medical education, specialists and specialization – The tangled web. *Journal of Health Politics, Policy and Law, 4*(4), 559–569.

Swedish Dental Association. (2003). *Dentistry in Sweden*. http://www.mah.se. Accessed 9 Oct 2016.

Tallinn Health Care College. (2016). *Curriculum: Dental technician*. http://www.ttk.ee. Accessed 11 Feb 2017.

Tallinn Tervishoiu Kõrgkool. (n.d.). *Estonia: Oral and dental care*. http://www.ttk.ee. Accessed 11 Oct 2016.

The Czech Republic. (2008). http://www.dent.cz. Accessed 17 Oct 2016.

The Czech Republic. (2018, February). *International Federation of Dental Hygienists eNEWS*. http://www.ifdh.org. Accessed 3 Aug 2018.

The Czech Republic. (n.d.). http://www.dent.cz. Accessed 1 Sept 2016.

The EU Single Market: Regulated professions database. (2018). http://www.ec.europa.eu. Accessed 3 Feb 2018.

Unione Nazionale Igienisti Dentali (National Union of Dental Hygienists). (2016, August 4). *Titolo acquisito in Austria.* (Qualification acquired in Austria). http://www.unid.it. Accessed 8 Dec 2016.

Van Dyke, T. E. (2016, giugno (June)). La formazione odontoiatrica deve avere come base quella medica e viceversa (Dentistry training should have a medical base and viceversa). *Dental Tribune Italian Edition*, pp. 9–10. http://www.dental-tribune.com. Accessed 11 June 2016.

Vigild, M., & Schwarz, E. (2001). Characteristics and study motivation of Danish dental students in a longitudinal perspective. *European Journal of Dental Education, 5*(3), 127–133.

Vlădescu, C., Scîntee, S. G., Olsavszky, V., Hernández-Quevedo, C., & Sagan, A. (2016). Romania: Health system review. *Health Systems in Transition, 18*(45), 1–170.

Walmsley, D., & Kavadella, A. (2012, December). Are we taking enough care of our teeth? The case for a European oral health policy. *ADEE (Association for Dental Education in Europe) Newsletter, 8*(3), 4–5.

Widström, E., & Eaton, K. A. (2006). Factors guiding the number of dental specialists in the European Union and Economic Area. *Norwegian Dental Journal, 116*, 718–721.

World Health Organization. (2013). *Transforming and sealing up health professionals' education and training: World Health Organization guidelines 2013*. Geneva: Author.

Wu, L. T., Low, M. M. J., Tan, K. K., Lopez, V., & Liaw, S. Y. (2015). Why not nursing? A systematic review of factors influencing career choice among healthcare students. *International Nursing Review, 62*(4), 547–562.

Yeaton, S., Moorthy, A., Rice, J., Coghlan, D., O'Dwyer, L., Green, E., et al. (2016). Special care dentistry: How prepared are we? *European Journal of Dental Education, 20*(1), 9–13.

Zagoričnik, M. (2011). *Education and training for dental technicians in Europe: Research and results*. http://www.online.scuola.zanichelli.it. Accessed 3 Mar 2017.

Chapter 3
Dental Care Professionals: Regulation

Dentists

Professions are deemed to be regulated when entry and practice are dictated by possession of a particular preparation or qualification. Regulation came about because it was thought that the public did not possess appropriate knowledge to judge the competence of professionals (Shinberg 2000). A regulatory mechanism is that of licensure or that of a registration or recognition requirement. Licensing is "an arrangement under which one must obtain a license from a recognized authority in order to engage in the occupation" (Wright 1978, p. 125). The basis for professional licensure, which is founded on the government's power to protect the health, safety, and welfare of the citizenry, to a large extent, depends on educational preparation. This requirement and others related to entry, such as fees, experience, etc., function as a constraint on admission to a profession because entry is only granted after verification of requisites.

Member States utilize diverse types of regulatory processes. Some of them regulate the professions of dental care professionals (DCPs) using the reserves of activities method. In other words, the profession cannot be practiced without meeting the requisites of the professional qualification. Other nations regulate these professions protecting the use of the professional title without any reserves of activities. Still others combine methods and protect use of the professional title with a reservation of professional activities to individuals in possession of obligatory professional qualifications. For example, when the profession of dental assistant/nurse was recognized in France in January 2016, the combined approach was utilized.

Moreover, licensure also has a publicity function as well. Being included in a professional register allows for individual publicity. The citizenry has a chance to review a professional's background (European Economic and Social Committee 2013). Many professional registers nowadays are viewable via the Internet. This opportunity grants professional authority to an individual and affords the consumer confidence that the named professional can meet her/his needs. Those listed in the professional document possess a protected title, in that only registered professionals

S. Z. Koff, *The Dental Team in the European Union*,
https://doi.org/10.1007/978-3-030-72232-6_3

can utilize the title affiliated with the profession. In addition, their activities are termed reserved in that only they, who have been given official permission via licensure, may carry out designated procedures. A multitude of healthcare professionals and DCPs are subject to registration and recognition. The process relates to many facets of their careers, including training, career paths, nomenclature rights, the right to practice, ethical behavior, disciplinary procedures, and continuing education, to cite a few (Greenwood 1972).

Diverse structures have responsibility for recognition and other processes. One model assigns this task to a governmental unit. For dentists, this occurs in Belgium (Federal Ministry of Health), the Czech Republic (Ministry of Health), Denmark (Danish Patient Safety Authority), Estonia (Ministry of Health and Labour, Health Board), Finland (Valvira, National Supervisory Authority for Welfare and Health), Germany (subnational Länder ministries responsible for health), Hungary (Ministry of Health, Office of Health Authorization and Administrative Procedures), Latvia (Ministry of Health, Health Inspectorate), Luxembourg (Ministry of Health), the Netherlands (Ministry of Public Health, Welfare, and Sport), and Sweden (National Board of Health and Welfare). It should be noted that in the case of the Czech Republic, Czech citizens do not register with the Ministry of Health, but with the Czech Dental Chamber which maintains the dental register. The Ministry of Health only recognizes foreigners' qualifications. In Denmark, in order to be a principal in private practice and to receive payments from the government, one must also register with the Danish Dental Association (Alexa et al. 2015; Anell et al. 2012; Azzopardi-Muscat et al. 2017; Eaton et al. 2012a; Gaál et al. 2011; Government and healthcare in the Czech Republic 2008; Health systems in transition (HiT) profile of Germany 2016; Kravitz et al. 2015; Lai et al. 2013; Olejaz et al. 2012).

A second regulatory structure is known as the chamber model. In this case, chambers are autonomous institutions assigned responsibility for the registration and supervision of a profession. Basically, they are self-regulatory boards composed of members of the profession involved. Thus, the profession acquires control over admission into the group. Such a system is relied on in Austria (Austrian Dental Chamber), Croatia (Croatian Dental Chamber), the Czech Republic (Czech Dental Chamber—Czech citizens only), France (Ordre National des Chirurgiens-Dentistes—National Order of Dental Surgeons), Greece (Hellenic Dental Association on behalf of the Ministry of Health), Italy (Federazione Nazionale degli Ordini dei Medici Chirurghi e degli Odontoiatri—National Federation of Doctors' and Dental Practitioners' Orders), Lithuania (Dental Chamber of Lithuania), Poland (Chamber of Physicians and Dentists), Portugal (Ordem dos Médicos Dentistas—Order of Dental Physicians), Slovakia (Slovak Chamber of Dentists), Slovenia (Medical Chamber of Slovenia), and Spain (Consejo General de Colegios Oficiales de Odontólogos y Estomatólogos de España—General Council of the Official Colleges of Spanish Odontologists and Stomatologists) (Albreht et al. 2016; Analysis of the relationship between national dental associations (NDAs) and dental faculties within the ERO zone: A NDA perspective n.d.; Džakula et al. 2014; Eaton et al. 2012a; ERO-FDI 2012b; Government and healthcare in the Czech

Republic 2008; Hofmarcher and Quentin 2013; Kravitz et al. 2015; Murauskiene et al. 2013; Regional European Organisation of the FDI 2012; Sagan et al. 2011; Smatana et al. 2016).

These self-regulatory units came into being because it was deemed that public authorities did not possess the necessary capacity to make appropriate decisions on dental subjects. Thus, regulatory authority became the responsibility of self-regulatory boards or chambers, rather than being based on governmental action. These units consist of practitioners in the regulated profession who are judged to have the appropriate knowledge and experience to make professional decisions. Primarily, due to their composition, self-regulatory boards became subject to a great deal of criticism. They were charged with being benefactors of the regulated profession because such boards or chambers consisted, for the most part, of members from the regulated profession. For critics, a conflict of interest existed (Shinberg 2000). Obviously, the board's or chamber's responsibility is to be committed to the public, not the professional group. Very often, such groups include in their membership representatives of the public, known as public members. After all, the chambers' objective is to protect the public and to ensure that consumers receive services of superior quality. It seems only natural that these people have some input into decision-making.

Many nations around the globe rely on self-regulation as a tool to achieve public policy objectives. It is believed that self-regulation generates compliance because it is based on the know-how of the profession. Also, it is assumed that with adoption of this tool, acceptance of the profession's regulations by those who should obey them is easier to achieve. Furthermore, self-regulation is evaluated as a responsive and flexible regulatory mechanism that allows for more responsive and faster reactions to rapidly changing technologies. It is also thought that innovative developments are easier to stimulate under this system (Vrielink and van Bockel 2013).

The third basic regulatory model is identified with councils. Utilization of this model takes place in Cyprus (Cyprus Dental Council), Ireland (Dental Council of Ireland), Malta (Medical Council of Malta), and the United Kingdom (General Dental Council) (Boyle 2011; Eaton et al. 2012a; European Economic and Social Committee 2013). These structures somewhat resemble the chambers. Both are responsible for regulatory tasks and both function as monitors. However, there are some variations in organization. For example, in Cyprus, the Council's regulatory decision-makers are appointed by the Council of Ministers, an executive governmental structure. In the United Kingdom, some members of the body are elected by registered dental practitioners, and others, lay or public members, are appointed by a governmental advisory organ, the Privy Council, and in Malta, these decision-makers are elected by registered dental practitioners. Lay members are of significance because in deliberations they allow for another perspective, a nondental one. Moreover, they create an important link for the organization with consumers and the general public.

It has been observed that the Romanian Collegium of Dental Physicians, the body responsible for registration tasks, requires further research as to its legal status. It is debatable whether it is a chamber or a private law structure (European Economic and Social Committee 2013). The latter units also carry out dentists' registration and supervisory duties in some Member States. Such occurs in Bulgaria.

Very often the same institution registers specialist dental practitioners as well. This appears to be the prevalent practice. However, there are some Member States, where specialists are dealt with by a different structure, as in the Netherlands, where the Specialisten-Registratie Commissie (Specialist Registration Board) is involved. In Malta, dentists are obligated to have their specialty recognized by the Specialist Accreditation Committee. In Poland, specialists are accredited by the Medical Centre for Postgraduate Training and Voivodeship Centres for Postgraduate Training (European Economic and Social Committee 2013). Also, it is noteworthy that sometimes specialist dentists are named in a specific register, as in the United Kingdom and Ireland. As noted, the number of featured dental specializations differs throughout the European Union (EU). Several Member States, including France, Belgium, Germany, Malta, the Netherlands, and Slovakia, feature only two or three, whereas Poland features eight and the United Kingdom, thirteen (European Economic and Social Committee 2013).

Renewal of registration is often linked to participation in continuing professional development (CPD). If so, usually, candidates for renewal must document a certain number of credits, points, or hours of continuing education completed in a specific time period. If the requirement is not met, usually, one must pay a price. For example, in Slovenia, if a dentist fails to meet the established standard, she/he must take a re-certification examination (Albreht et al. 2016). Also, retention fees are involved in most nations. There is much variation in the amount.

Very often when professional registration is processed by a public or private law association, compulsory membership in the organization is targeted. This practice takes place in several Member States, including Croatia, Cyprus, the Czech Republic, Germany, Greece, Hungary, Lithuania, Poland, Portugal, Romania, Slovenia, and Spain (Albreht et al. 2016; Alexa et al. 2015; Czech Dental Chamber 2016; Džakula et al. 2014; Eaton et al. 2012a; Hlawacek and Orsulova 2003; Kovács et al. 2013; Kravitz et al. 2015; Sagan et al. 2011; Traxlor and Adam n.d.; Vlădescu et al. 2016).

Not only are the structures that have responsibility for registration and supervision of the dentistry profession diverse, but the same holds true for the validity of the professional's registration. For example, Slovakia and Denmark have no recertification system. Other Member States, such as the United Kingdom and Italy, require annual renewal. Times are longer in other nations. Seven years are noted in the case of Slovenia, where after age 70, one has possession of a lifetime license. In the Netherlands and Latvia, re-registration takes place every 5 years and every 3 in Spain. Based on this information, it is evident that registration validity time varies throughout the EU (Albreht et al. 2016; Azzopardi-Muscat et al. 2017; García-Armesto et al. 2010; Mitenbergs et al. 2012; Olejaz et al. 2012; Smatana et al. 2016; Traxlor and Adam n.d.).

Auxiliaries

Some members of the dental team, other than dentists, are subject to regulatory mechanisms. However, not all DCPs are registered or regulated in every Member State. For example, only three (Ireland, Sweden, and the United Kingdom) have practicing orthodontic therapists. In Sweden, this profession is not regulated (personal communication 16 November 2017). Luxembourg, apart from dental technicians, does not recognize other auxiliaries. France only recognizes dental chair-side assistants, receptionists, and dental technicians and Austria only dental chair-side assistants and dental technicians (Kravitz et al. 2015). The only auxiliaries practicing in Greece are dental technicians and chair-side assistants. Like Greece, Austria, Belgium, Bulgaria, Cyprus, Estonia, France, and Germany do not regulate dental hygienists in terms of professional qualifications. If this is the case, dental hygiene tasks are performed by general or specialized dental practitioners, chair-side assistants, etc. (Eaton et al. 2012b; European Commission 2016; Koletsi-Kounari et al. 2011). However, in January 2016, a reconstruction of the oral healthcare system in Belgium was announced. After a long struggle, regulations were to be developed to allow dental hygienists to work in the oral cavity (IFD 2016). Thus, throughout the Member States, there is much diversity in the composition of the formal dental squad. In spite of this situation, the structures that accredit professional qualifications where required are of the same type as those for dentists.

Dental Hygienists

For dental hygienists, the regulatory model based on governmental units is prevalent. For these DCPs, this framework is utilized in the Czech Republic (Ministry of Labour and Social Affairs), Denmark (Danish Patient Safety Authority), Finland (Valvira—National Supervisory Authority for Welfare and Health), the Netherlands (Ministry of Health, Welfare and Sport—CIBG, an executive organization of the Ministry), Portugal (Ministry of Health—Central Administration of Health Systems), and Sweden (National Board of Health and Welfare) (International Federation of Dental Hygienists 2015).

In relation to dental hygienists, the chamber model applies in Lithuania (Lithuanian Dental Chamber), Slovakia (Slovak Chamber of Medical and Technical Staff), and Romania (Romanian Order of Medical Assistants and Midwives). Perhaps the same observation may be made in reference to the latter organization as was made regarding the aforementioned Romanian Collegium of Dental Physicians. Also, in Italy, the Parliament, in December 2017, passed a law after many years of conflict, establishing orders for the various health professions. Thus, dental hygienists will eventually have a national register for themselves after the decision as to how the law should be implemented.

Dental hygienists have adopted the council model in Ireland (Dental Council of Ireland), Malta (Council for Professions Complimentary to Medicine), and the United Kingdom (General Dental Council). In the latter Member State, the named body also is responsible for regulating dental therapists as is the aforementioned unit in the Netherlands (Amariei and Eaton 2009; Boyle 2011; Cylus 2015; Nash et al. 2012). From the length of this list, it is evident that not all Member States regulate dental hygienists. Included in the group of non-regulators are Austria, Bulgaria, Cyprus, Estonia, France, Germany, and Luxembourg. Hungary is included in this list, but future registration and regulation of dental hygienists have been acknowledged. Furthermore, in some Member States, such as Germany and Greece, the profession does not even exist (Eaton et al. 2012b; European Commission 2016; Koletsi-Kounari et al. 2011).

Dental Assistants/Dental Nurses/Chair-Side Assistants

Member States which regulate dental assistants, known in some countries as dental nurses, and chair-side assistants, tend to be about equal in number to those that regulate dental hygienists. Once again, some of these professions are not regulated in individual Member States. For example, there is no register for dental nurses in Bulgaria and Sweden (Eaton et al. 2012b). Also, some professional registration is not recorded in the Czech Republic, Denmark, France, Ireland, Italy, and Portugal, among other Member States.

On the other hand, governmental entities accredit these DCPs in Estonia (Health Care Board), Finland (Valvira—National Supervisory Authority for Welfare and Health), and Greece (Ministry of Health and Welfare). In Poland, the Ministry of Science regulates dental nurses, and it is intended that future legislation will govern all DCPs (Eaton et al. 2012b; Kravitz et al. 2014, 2015).

Chambers are used, primarily in Eastern Europe, to regulate auxiliary dental personnel in addition to other professionals. This model is adopted in Croatia (Croatian Dental Chamber), Hungary (Chamber for Non-medical Health Professionals), Lithuania (Lithuanian Dental Chamber), Romania (Romanian Order of Medical Assistants), and Slovakia (Slovak Chamber of Medical and Technical Staff). Again, the aforementioned observation about Romanian orders comes to mind (Eaton et al. 2012b; ERO-FDI 2012a, b; Gaál et al. 2011). Latvia assigns regulatory responsibility to an association, the Latvian Nurses Association. In Ireland and the United Kingdom, the Dental Council of Ireland and the General Dental Council, respectively, assume the task of regulating these professionals (Amariei and Eaton 2009; Cylus et al. 2015; The EU Single Market: Regulated professions database 2018).

Dental Technicians

The same type of structures used to regulate dental auxiliaries in general is found in the case of dental technicians. These professionals are not required to register in every Member State. Governmental authorities regulate the profession in Belgium (Federal Ministry of Health), Bulgaria (Ministry of Health), Denmark (Danish Patient Safety Authority—clinical dental technicians), Estonia (Healthcare Board), Finland (Valvira—National Supervisory Authority for Welfare and Health), Greece (Ministry of Health and Welfare), Italy (Ministry of Health), Portugal (Ministry of Health), and Sweden (National Board of Health and Welfare) (Eaton et al. 2012a; Enterprise Finland: Ministry of Economic Affairs and Employment n.d.; Kravitz et al. 2015; Olejaz et al. 2012).

Self-regulation in the form of a chamber is used in the following countries: Croatia (Croatian Dental Chamber), Germany (German Dental Technicians Guild), Hungary (Chamber of Non-medical Health Professionals), Lithuania (Lithuanian Dental Chamber), Slovakia (Slovak Chamber of Dental Technicians), and Slovenia (Economy Chamber) (Croatia 2015; Džakula et al. 2014; ERO-FDI 2012b; Gaál et al. 2011). Perhaps debatable as a chamber, based on aforementioned comments, is the Order of Romanian Dental Technicians.

The council model is adopted in Cyprus (Cyprus Council for the Registration of Dental Technicians and Laboratories), Malta (Council for Professions Complementary to Medicine), and the United Kingdom (General Dental Council) (Charalambous and Theodorou 2013; Council for the Professions Complementary to Medicine-Malta 2015). Clinical dental technicians or denturists are registered by the Danish Patient Safety Authority, the Dental Council of Ireland (but not dental technicians), Valvira, and the National Supervisory Authority for Welfare and Health, in Finland, and by the General Dental Council in the United Kingdom (Boyle 2011; Cylus et al. 2015; Kravitz et al. 2015). An association regulates dental technicians in Latvia (Latvian Confederation of Professional Organizations of Health Care Personnel) (Eaton et al. 2012a; Mitenbergs et al. 2012).

As in the case of dentists, there is variation in the validity of these DCPs' registration. Also, it is possible that relicensing is not required. Several Member States have a recognition validity of 5 or 6 years, and relicensure is not necessary in Denmark or Cyprus (Mitenbergs et al. 2012; Olejaz et al. 2012).

Compulsory registration for some DCPs has been relatively recent, and it has not served as a subject for a great deal of scholarly research in terms of its impact on the profession concerned. Such an affirmation is applicable to dental nurses in the United Kingdom. One research team (Turner et al. 2012a, b) studied the views of these professionals concerning mandatory CPD which is linked to registration. Over a majority of the participants in the researchers' survey (67%) approved of the practice, and 51% approved of its compulsory nature. However, the registration fee was viewed in a most unfavorable manner. It was sanctioned by only 6% of the participants, most of whom did not think that compulsory registration had affected their beliefs related to their career, their role, or their status within the dental team. Some positive comments focused on enhanced professionalism, more respect or status, greater responsibility, a larger quantity of knowledge, or job interest. Those who felt their opinions had been influenced believed the impact, for the most part, was positive.

The same research team undertook a similar study of dental technicians who acquired registration requirements at the same time as dental nurses. Although the percentages differed, the outcomes of the projects were somewhat analogous. Registration and its compulsory nature were endorsed, respectively, by 52% and 54% of the participants. The registration fee was viewed in a negative light, receiving the approval of only 13%. Most of those surveyed were of the opinion that compulsory registration had either no impact or a negative impact on their opinions concerning their career (80%), role (78%), or status within the dental squad (85%). The attitudes toward the registration fees in both studies demonstrated that they require attention. Also, the negative effects of compulsory registration merit the same.

Registration affords a profession the exclusive right to utilize or evaluate a particular group of skills and knowledge. This exclusive right, a profession, acquires possessing power and privilege and becomes linked with formal political processes. These attributes, having a legal foundation, result from governmental decisions, and thus, they have a political base (Freidson 1973). Changes in constraints related to professional entry and the tasks licensed practitioners can carry out can impact stipends and employment in a particular profession as well as the quality of delivered services (White 1979).

Continuing Professional Development

Professions, including those of DCPs, are not static. Facing pressures from internal and external transformations, their structure and requirements change. DCPs have been confronted with more health issues and increasingly complex oral health needs. At the same time, their patients manifest higher expectations for their performance. Also, there have been modifications in the patterns of oral health. In the new environment, DCPs require a wider knowledge base than that which they received in their initial training. Moreover, it is practitioners' obligation to offer services that reflect improved and current criteria, experience, and knowledge. The significance of competence has changed as well. Originally, purely, a condition for admission to a regulated profession, it has become a continuing and enlarged concept. It has stressed requirements that society be protected from all types of incompetence (Bullock et al. 2013; Sheppard 1978). The grip of regulatory mechanisms has augmented. These factors, among others, enhanced a debate focused on CPD.

Continuing education is a defining characteristic of professional work. In health care, it has become an accepted practice. It has been defined "as a continuing structured learning process of dental practitioners, aimed to maintain, update or enhance knowledge, technical skills or professional clinical or behavioural standards, all of which can improve the provision of oral healthcare to the public" (Council of European Dentists 2013). It is deemed essential for practitioners to enhance patient safety in general and at the EU level within the context of cross-border mobility. Furthermore, CPD is related to safety at work, the maintenance of skills, the acquisition of new ones and their integration into practice, and the satisfaction of patients' expectations that the dental squad will keep its skills and knowledge up-to-date. The latter factor instills confidence in the practitioner. Other purposes of CPD are to inform participants of developments in dental research, to guarantee activity levels and competency, and to satisfy public expectations. It is a learning process that complements initial training and a method to hold practitioners accountable, to guarantee and regulate their competence, to improve clinical practice and outcomes, and to motivate professionals' participation in lifelong learning (Bullock et al. 2013; Directive 2013/55/EU; Eaton et al. 2011; Executive Agency for Health and Consumers 2014; Irish Dental Association n.d.; Merkur et al. 2008).

According to a Council of European Dentists' resolution (2013) for these practitioners, CPD should fill the voids in their dental knowledge, skills, and competences and, at the same time, take into consideration the maturity of the dental profession and epidemiology of oral health exigencies. These elements help to ensure evidence-based oral health care of high quality.

The structures related to DCPs' continuing education programs throughout the Member States are far from harmonized. Basically, there are three types of systems: compulsory, voluntary, and mixed. Compulsory programs require no explanation. Most Member States feature CPD of this type. This system is the most common. In fact, 81% of the participants in the DentCPD Project were of the opinion that dental continuing education should be obligatory. The project, entitled Harmonization and Standardisation of European Dental School Programs of Continuing Professional Development for Graduate Dentists, sought to develop guidelines for the administration, delivery, and harmonization of CPD by dental faculties. It was initiated in 2010 by the Association for Dental Education in Europe and was funded by the EU. It lasted for 2 years (DentCPD 2010).

In order to provide better patient management and to aid promotion of practitioner mobility, it was thought, given throughout the EU the variable quality of CPD courses and their lack of regulation, activities in this sector should be harmonized. An inventory of existing CPD programs, their sponsors and core components, guidelines for the organization and management of such programs, and an example of a competence-based activity, in addition to a CPD reference manual, resulted from the project.

One would think that a voluntary CPD system is completely diverse from obligatory arrangements. Obviously, from its name, it should lack mandatory requirements, but often, it includes cases where CPD is mandatory for a part of the profession, such as providers in a statutory health system. Voluntary CPD systems are found in Austria, Cyprus, Denmark, Estonia, Finland, Malta, and Sweden (Eaton et al. 2012a; Executive Agency for Health and Consumers 2014).

As noted, a voluntary system may exist side-by-side with a compulsory one, as in Denmark, Portugal, and Finland. In the first-named Member State, CPD is not obligatory for dental practitioners. However, the Danish Dental Association organized a CPD program which obliges members, but not those employed in the public dental service, to annually complete 25 h of continuing education. In Portugal, there is mandatory CPD and in addition, a voluntary continuing education framework founded on the regulations of the Ordem dos Médicos Dentistas (Order of Dental Physicians). The program is monitored by the same association. In Finland, the voluntary facet is subsidized by the Finnish Dental Association, and it is based on law, governmental regulations, and practitioners' ethical obligations. The last-mentioned basis of the system is especially important in terms of responsibility to participate in the voluntary facet of CPD.

In the new code of ethics for dentists in the EU, one of the guiding principles of the profession is that practitioners are "to apply current standards of practice and update professional knowledge and skills throughout their professional life" (Council of European Dentists 2017, 1.1). Consequently, CPD becomes an ethical obligation. A large-scale study of CPD in the EU concluded that neither the voluntary or obligatory structure is superior. Each one serves diverse purposes and must be viewed in its national context (Executive Agency for Health and Consumers 2014).

Requirements in terms of the amount of CPD also vary among the Member States. For example, in Ireland, which had a voluntary CPD system for dental practitioners and where a statutory CPD scheme was implemented in 2010, dentists were advised to complete at least 50 h per year or 250 h over 5 years as part of their ethical obligations. In the statutory arrangement, this was the requirement as well. Broken down, the obligation is to complete 50 h of CPD a year, 20 of which should be verifiable or documented. A minimum of 100 h over the 5-year cycle must be verifiable and the rest undertaken personally and in activities approved in advance by the Dental Council (Dental Council of Ireland 2015). Practitioners are required to undertake CPD in core topics designated as infection prevention and control (10 h), radiology information and radiation protection (5 h), professional communication (10 h), medical emergencies (5 h), audit (7 h), record keeping (5 h), and governance (8 h). The indicated hours represent a minimum time period. In addition to the required core subjects, one is obliged to undertake work in Basic Life Support and to maintain accreditation. In other Member States, options are diverse. For example, Bulgaria, which has a mandatory CPD system, merely adopted a credit arrangement in which a minimum of 30 credits must be acquired over 3 years (Katrova 2009).

Other Member States have core topics as well. These include Belgium, the Czech Republic, Poland, and the United Kingdom. The DentCPD Project in its survey found great support for medical emergencies, infection control, and the medically compromised patient as core topics. It was concluded that these topics plus radiation protection should be compulsory core CPD subject matter and that recommended core topics to be undertaken should include health and safety, pain management, and safeguarding children and vulnerable adults (Bailey et al. 2013).

All the designated core topics are significant. However, medical emergencies and basic life support are particular. Studies have demonstrated that medical emergencies are not sparse in dental offices. They do occur. In a project focused on dentistry in Great Britain and Germany, researchers uncovered 793 emergency incidents in a year in the former nation, and in the same time period in Germany, 57% of respondents to a survey had the challenge of facing up to 3 emergencies and 36% had to deal with up to 10 (Jevon 2012; Malamed 2015).

In Denmark, as noted, the CPD requirement for members of the Danish Dental Association is completion of a minimum of 25 h annually. However, for the first 3 years after one's graduation, this minimum is reduced to 10 h. There are no direct consequences for noncompliance, even though one could be dismissed from membership. Also, in voluntary CPD systems, noncompliance could become a factor in fitness to practice decisions (Dental Council of Ireland 2015; Executive Agency for Health and Consumers 2014). In Luxembourg's mandatory CPD arrangement, each dental practitioner determines the amount needed to provide appropriate service (Kravitz et al. 2015). The requirement in Germany for the mandatory CPD component is different again. A credit system has been adopted with a minimum requirement over a 5-year period of 125 credits which represents 125 h of CPD (Germany's dental health care system 2015).

Failure to meet established requisites or recommendations related to continuing education is handled in diverse ways throughout the Member States. Consequences vary significantly from loss of the right to practice to no automatic consequence. In Slovakia, such failure might be reported to an employer whose responsibility becomes rectification of the situation or to the Office for Supervision of Health Care. Other options are retesting, as in Romania and Slovenia, temporary license suspension, or complete license withdrawal, as in Hungary (Albreht et al. 2016; Kivovics n.d.; Vlădescu et al. 2016). Obviously, the latter sanction is the most severe. In the United Kingdom, the same sanction may result. To be restored to the register, CPD requirements must be met (General Dental Council n.d.). For noncompliance occurring in voluntary continuing education frameworks, penalties are much less harsh (Executive Agency for Health and Consumers 2014).

The Danish Dental Association issues a diploma that certifies compliance with CPD requisites, and in the Czech Republic, a Certificate of Proficiency is issued by the Czech Dental Chamber to the practitioner who has met continuing education requirements. The person designated on the document receives approximately 10% more in health insurance payments for some services (Czech Dental Chamber 2016; Czech Republic 2018; Executive Agency for Health and Consumers 2014). Such practices are aimed at generating enhanced participation.

Due, in part, to the diversity displayed in the oral healthcare arrangements of the Member States, the core CPD topics are diverse as well. Many subjects are noted on individual rosters. As aforementioned, a survey of dental educators (Bullock et al. 2013) revealed majority support for medical emergencies, infection control, and the medically compromised patient as mandatory CPD subjects. Directive 2013/55/EU mentions CPD (Recital 15) and notes its importance. It also states that continuing education should include technical, scientific, regulatory, and ethical elements and that programs should motivate participation.

A relatively recent statement of the European Regional Organisation of the Federation Dentaire Internationale (International Dental Federation) (2015b) recommended that related medical topics be included in dental continuing education. It was underscored that dentistry's congresses and other scientific activities should feature these topics as well and that dental and medical associations should collaborate on the development of CPD programs and other scientific events. Such would recognize the aforementioned relationship of oral and general health. Moreover, given social transformations, as noted, practitioners will have to treat more elderly persons. Frequently, these people have multiple diagnoses that require specific action prior to commencing oral health care. In addition, the dental practitioner will become knowledgeable about contemporary medical treatment procedures so as to be able to appropriately address dental problems with medical specialists (Jaquiery 2012).

In 2011, in France, a new and separate framework for continuing education was introduced. Entitled Developpement Professionnel Continu (Continuing Professional Development), it differs from traditional CPD in the EU. Annually, it lasts for a day and a half and is organized by different dental associations and is coordinated by the Ministry of Health (Kravitz et al. 2015). Also noteworthy is that the General Dental Council in the United Kingdom announced an enhanced CPD scheme that started for dentists on 1 January 2018 and for auxiliaries on 1 August 2018. Principal modifications in the arrangement include the requisite that all DCPs must have a personal development plan. Also, the number of verifiable hours of CPD has been augmented and should be spread more evenly across the 5-year period. DCPs no longer have to report non-verifiable hours to the General Dental Council. In addition, CPD activities must be congruent with specific development outcomes. Lastly, professionals' CPD programs must be planned according to their fields of practice (Education & CPD n.d.).

Methods for acquiring CPD are multiple. They include participation in national and international congresses, symposia, seminars, courses, research and its dissemination, lecturing, peer review, clinical audit, self-directed readings, study clubs, task forces, private study, workshops, staff or governance board training, distance learning, multimedia learning, etc. The most popular forms of CPD delivery have been conferences, symposia, traditional lectures, and seminars. It has been stated that the most effective methods relate to sustained, repeated, or longer-term CPD activities that include interactive arrangements utilizing multimedia. Interactive methods have been found to be most efficacious (Dental Council of Ireland 2015; Eaton et al. 2011; Executive Agency for Health and Consumers 2014; Katrova 2009; Stewart and Kinirons 2015).

CPD providers are multiple as well. They include universities, professional dental associations, scientific dental societies, regulatory authorities, and commercial enterprises. Of these structures, the most common providers have been university dental faculties and professional dental associations (Bullock et al. 2013).

Revalidation or relicensure is practiced to ensure healthcare professionals remain fit to provide services. Linking relicensure with CPD creates a regulatory control mechanism for competence, quality, and accountability of services. This linkage creates pressure on the professional who is noncompliant in terms of fulfilling required or recommended CPD. Such a practice should decrease noncompliance. This arrangement exists in some Member States which include Belgium, Croatia, Hungary, Latvia, Lithuania, Romania, Slovenia, and the United Kingdom (Executive Agency for Health and Consumers 2014).

As noted, all types of dental auxiliaries are not recognized in all Member States. In some nations, continuing education is required of all DCPs. This group includes Latvia, Lithuania, the Netherlands, Romania, Slovakia, and the United Kingdom. It is noteworthy that requisites vary from Member State to Member State. In the United Kingdom, each DCP must complete in a 5-year period 150 h of CPD of which 50 h must be verifiable. However, as noted, a modified program was scheduled to be introduced in August 2018. For automatic recertification in Latvia, DCPs must collect at least 250 points of CPD over 5 years. In Lithuania, the requirement is based on the type of DCP. Requisites are related to the particular dental auxiliary. Dental technicians require at least 60 h as do dental hygienists, and dental assistants/nurses must complete 50 h of CPD. Compulsory topics are medical emergencies, disinfection/decontamination, medical ethics, and prophylaxis of oral diseases. A minimum number of hours must be devoted to these subjects. For dental nurses, required subject matter consists of infection control and emergency care. In the Netherlands, all DCPs must complete 240 h of CPD every 5 years, and in Slovakia, dental hygienists must earn 100 CPD credits in the same period. Fifty credits are awarded for full practice, and 3 days of participation in an international hygiene symposium garners 19 credits (Amariei and Eaton 2009; Eaton et al. 2012b; Gough and Bagnall 2012; Lithuanian Dental Chamber A. Šeikus n.d.; Mitenbergs et al. 2012; Newsome 2011; Ross et al. 2012; Turner et al. 2012b).

In some nations, the amount of CPD is related to confirmation of the license to practice a profession, as noted above. This relates to the case of dental technicians in Croatia, the Czech Republic, the Netherlands, and Slovakia. In Croatia, this DCP needs to complete 10 points or one course annually to confirm certification (personal communication 13 December 13 2017). In the Czech Republic, 40 credit points must be acquired over 6 years and in Slovakia, 50 credit points in a 5-year period (Zagoričnik 2011). Certain subjects are recommended. They include radiography and radiation protection with materials and equipment because radiography application is not part of formal training (Newsome 2011). In Estonia, dental nurses are required to attend at least one supplementary course a year (Tallinn Tervishoiu Kõrgkool n.d.).

In Romania, it is obligatory for dental hygienists, dental technicians, and dental nurses or chair-side assistants to undertake CPD (Amariei and Eaton 2009). Also, it is noteworthy that the European Regional Organisation of the Federation Dentaire Internationale (International Dental Federation) in 2015 in its Plenary Assembly passed a resolution that detailed the dental hygienist profile. One provision reads: "A DH is expected to attend continuing education courses in line with the specific requirements of the country concerned" (European Regional Organisation of the Federation Dentaire Internationale (International Dental Federation 2015a). Among the Member States that require dental hygienists to complete CPD are Hungary, Italy, Lithuania, Latvia, the Netherlands, Slovakia, Slovenia, Spain, and the United Kingdom. In Denmark, the situation is somewhat different. Consensus on the matter is to be achieved between employees and employers, although these professionals usually participate in CPD. A voluntary scheme prevails for dental hygienists in Ireland. Thus, CPD is not compulsory (European Commission 2016; personal communication 13 November 13 2017).

Studies have been undertaken of the impact of CPD on dental chair-side assistants/nurses and dental technicians in the United Kingdom. Compulsory CPD for these professionals was introduced in 2008. Interestingly enough, most dental nurses (76%) were of the opinion that CPD did not enhance their capacity to do their job. Criticism related to the costs and relevance of continuing education. In fact, the cost was viewed as impacting their career in negative fashion. For 41% of the survey participants, funding of CPD posed a problem, and some claimed they could only attend free courses. Moreover, CPD failed to contribute to their job satisfaction (Turner et al. 2012a, b). As mentioned, results of the dental technicians' survey were similar, although the percentages were diverse. A majority (66%) thought that CPD did not contribute to an improvement in the way they carried out their work tasks. Furthermore, they held negative opinions concerning the costs, accessibility, and relevance of CPD. It is noteworthy that a majority of the dental nurse and dental technician participants, 56% and 51%, respectively, claimed job satisfaction was lacking (Gough and Bagnall 2012; Ross et al. 2012). In terms of implementing changes in procedures followed at the workplace, research has identified significant barriers. These include lack of materials, resources, and collegial support (Barnes et al. 2013).

In the United Kingdom, if DCPs do not meet the minimum of CPD hours, the penalty is severe. The professional's name could be dropped from the register. Thus, she/he would be unable to practice. To be relicensed, it is mandatory that the CPD requirement be completed. Furthermore, a restoration fee plus the annual fee has to be paid. In addition, a character reference and health certificate have to be submitted to the General Dental Council. If a professional is taking a break from practice and thus, from the register, CPD must be kept up-to-date so that she/he can return to practice without discussion (Gough 2012). It is obvious that CPD for auxiliaries is taken seriously in the United Kingdom. At the same time, the results of these studies undertaken 4 years after obligatory CPD was introduced for these two professions are quite surprising, especially in terms of CPD's contribution to one's work abilities and job satisfaction.

The dental team's participation in CPD is affected by several factors. These include age, the time that has elapsed since training, postgraduate qualification(s), work and private life commitments, employment status, the work environment, convenience of access to continuing education, interest in it, and cost (Barnes et al. 2013; Bullock et al. 2010; Eaton et al. 2011).

From this brief presentation of CPD as it applies to DCPs across the EU, it is quite evident that there is much diversity. Variance relates to the nature of the system (voluntary, obligatory, or mixed), the relationship of the system to the various dental care professions, the amount of continuing education required and how it is measured, the time period involved, the relationship of CPD to other regulatory mechanisms, the providers, etc. It is quite clear that diversity is "the name of the game." Harmonization of professional qualifications was achieved for several professions, as noted earlier in this work, via the aforementioned professional qualifications directives and the Bologna Declaration that contributed to different facets of the harmonization concept. However, harmonization of CPD should not be limited to graduate dentists. The dental team should be included in and participate in any such efforts. CPD and the total dental squad are of significant value to patient safety, up-to-date high-quality oral health care, and provider mobility. CPD for each dental care profession should be harmonized. The present diversity of continuing education systems throughout the EU serves as a formidable restraining device for the needed harmonization. Mutual agreement and recognition of the significance of CPD, uniformity of accreditation standards, accessible providers, and mutual performance assessment are necessary for the realization of harmonization (Horsley et al. 2010).

Formal and informal support for the development of lifelong skills and competences has been forthcoming from the European Commission. The organ is also known as a promoter of the role of modern technology in education (Bjegovic-Mikanovic et al. 2014). The most recent professional qualifications directive (Directive 2013/55/EU) refers to the importance of CPD and assigns the Member States the task of encouraging it. Moreover, they are to communicate to the Commission the methods they adopt to do so. In addition, they are to exchange best practices (Directive 2013/55/EU, Recital15). All of these efforts are of utility to the achievement of CPD harmonization.

Codes of Ethics

It is generally acknowledged that one of the phases in the professionalization process involves elaboration of a formal code of ethics (Elliott 1972; Greenwood 1972). Each profession which compels ethical behavior on the part of its members is bound by a common set of values detailed in these documents that relate to the normative dimension of a profession and its members' service orientation and their distinctive ethics (Larson 1977; Susskind and Susskind 2015). All professional groups develop criteria of behavior concerning relations with group members as well as with individuals external to the unit. A code serves as a thermometer of professionalization, and it usually speaks to relations between practitioners and patients or clients, colleagues, and the general public. Ostensibly, its purpose is to protect all concerned (Vollmer and Mills 1966).

Much behavioral self-control exercised by codes of ethics are internalized in the work socialization process and via voluntary organizations founded and administered by professionals themselves (Johnson 1972). It is believed that professionals' activities should be congruent with clearly stated standards of conduct and ethical codes. Although an ethical professional code specifies a required social standard, it may not be of major importance for a professional practicing in an institutional setting. In this case, the organizational code might claim more authority. This code has been imposed on an individual, whereas the professional document is accepted by the person (Jenkins 1970).

Part of the code is informal in nature, while the rest is purely formal. The former portion commands the same authority as the formal prescriptions (Greenwood 1966). Across the Member States and their professions, the subject matter of formal codes of ethics reflects again diversity. However, the essential topics tend to be uniform. Included in this category are patient-professional and colleague-colleague relations. In terms of the former relationships, the practitioner usually must furnish services to all who request them. Such a provision prohibits discrimination of any kind. However, it is noteworthy that the Latvian ethical code provides that a practitioner may refuse treatment when a patient's life is not in danger. As for colleague-colleague relationships, one is supposed to be egalitarian. Furthermore, intraprofessional recognition is to be based solely on the theoretical or practical aspects of professional performance (Greenwood 1966; Kravitz et al. 2015).

Many diverse topics are mentioned in codes. These include the practitioner's rights and duties, professional competences, scope of practice, relationship with and position within society, patient referral, professional confidentiality, payment for services, contracts with patients, patient consent, electronic commerce, continuing education, promotion of services and advertising, participation and promotion of social well-being, relationships with patients, client responsibilities, treatment quality, emergency care, practice organization, research and experimentation, international relationships, partnership agreements, and code infringement and penalties. The topics are numerous (Kovács et al. 2013; Kravitz et al. 2015; Mayol et al. 2013). Non-governmental organizations have promoted education related to codes, dental law, and ethics. One such association is the Dental Law and Ethics Forum in the United Kingdom that schedules bi-monthly discussions for dental practitioners, attorneys, and any other interested professionals.

In general, dentists in each Member State have an ethical code. It is noteworthy that Austrian practitioners lack such a document and, in Estonia, the code does not command obligatory compliance. It only serves as a recommendation. Usually, a dental code of ethics is administered by a professional body of one type or another, as in the Czech Republic or France (Cini 2008; Kravitz et al. 2014). Very often, ethical guidelines are established by these national organs, as in Sweden, where the Swedish Dental Association penned a code for its members. The Swedish Association of Private Dental Practitioners has done the same (Swedish Dental Association 2003). Cross-national units have been active as well in the same sector. Also, the Federation of European Competent Authorities and Regulators penned a European Code of Conduct for Dentists. The Council of European Dentists followed suit and developed a Code of Ethics for Dentists of the European Union that served as a model for some Member States' guidelines, such as Estonia's (Council of European Dentists 2017).

Dentists have not been the only members of the dental team to be subjected to a code of ethics. The General Dental Council in the United Kingdom released

Standards for the Dental Team (2013) that contain guidance for the conduct, performance, and ethics of the entire dental squad. Also, the Unione Nazionale Igienisti Dentali (National Dental Hygienists Union) in Italy issued a deontological code (2012) as did its Maltese counterpart, the Maltese Association of Dental Hygienists. In Malta, the Council for the Professions Complementary to Medicine did the same for dental technicians. In Ireland, dental assistants/nurses are governed by a Code of Ethics and Conduct for Dental Nurses held by the Dental Council.

The teaching of ethical decision-making in dental education has stimulated debate. It has been acknowledged that dental practitioners need more than the theoretical and practical knowledge to provide oral health care of high quality. Equally important is the manifestation of integrity in the provision of service. In fact, the American Dental Education Association has claimed that a dental graduate should have competence to apply ethical and legal standards in her/his practice (Greenwood 1966; Iigüy et al. 2015; Nash 2007).

A research project (Iigüy et al. 2015) compared dental students' capacity for ethical decision-making before and after a course on ethics. The researchers found no statistically significant difference between the mean scores related to judgment of ethical decisions. Also, scores after the course was taken were significantly higher. Thus, they concluded that in order to enhance student awareness and interest, more materials on ethical issues should be included in dental education. Unfortunately, dental students, at least in the Netherlands, are pessimistic about the role of ethics in their future profession (Brands et al. 2011). Professionalism and integrity should not be stressed only in dental education, but they have a role in the training of the entire dental squad. Ethical behavior is important to the various facets of high-quality oral health care.

Patient Complaints and Fitness to Practice

It was mentioned that competence has become a continuing concept. It is no longer evaluated solely in terms of intellectual knowledge, practical experience, and adoption of modern techniques. In this day and age, it can also involve physical or mental fitness (Sheppard 1978). Another concept that has become fashionable and is growing is patient empowerment. It relates to situations in which individuals are urged to assume an active role in the management of their own health status.

Previously, relations between healthcare providers and patients were hierarchical and paternalistic in nature. As a profession matures, it acquires professional privilege. In this situation, the privilege involved immunity from public judgment on technical matters. Society was assumed to lack the capacity to understand professional standards and to invoke them to identify poor practice. Thus, a professional's performance, it was believed, could only be judged by peers (Greenwood 1966). Times and beliefs have changed.

Patients have become involved in decision-making with providers of service. Such has been found to improve the outcomes of care. Also, it has stimulated patient compliance with treatment measures and positively impacted healthcare cost efficiency. Moreover, patient satisfaction has been enhanced, and more responsibility has been assumed by an individual for her/his own health (Winblad and Ringard 2009). Patient empowerment has put pressure on practitioners, and most Member States have taken steps to enlarge and strengthen patients' roles. For example, in 2011, in Denmark, the National Agency for Patients' Rights and Complaints was created. It has the task of looking after patients' complaints and undertaking activities that prevent the reoccurrence of errors. In addition, it administers a system for reporting inadvertent healthcare incidents, and it advises other nations on patients' rights. Responsibility for monitoring developments concerned with patients' rights in Greece is assigned to the Independent Service for the Protection of Patients' Rights, under the jurisdiction of the Secretary General of Health (Economou 2010; Olejaz et al. 2012).

Social development and global consciousness assigned specific rights to society and, at the same time, defined obligations to professionals. In spite of an increase of conflicts between professionals and those whom they serve, the importance of dialogue has been underscored. A new bilateral and professional relationship has developed (Minervino and Souza 2004). Member States have structured systems for dealing with complaints resulting from oral health care. However, once again, the overall picture is characterized by diversity.

In many Member States, there are several stages to the complaints process. In several, they commence with a discussion between the oral healthcare provider and the complainant. In fact, in Estonia, most complaints are settled in this confrontation. If, however, damage to the patient's health is suspected, or there are serious problems of quality in the care delivered, official complaints appear before the Health Care Quality Expert Commission linked to the Minister of Social Affairs. The organ's principal task is to act as an independent advisor to patients. If the practitioner is deemed guilty of malpractice, the patient has an automatic right to be heard in court. The Health Board then possesses the authority to fine the practitioner or cancel her/his license to practice (Lai et al. 2013).

In the Netherlands, as well, complaints are first directly made known to the oral healthcare provider, each one of whom, according to the Healthcare Quality, Complaints and Disputes Act (WKKGZ) which went into effect on 1 January 2016, must have in their practice a complaints officer. If the problem is not resolved, the complainant can turn to an independent complaints commission composed of legally qualified members and health professionals which is easier than initiating court proceedings. The commission's outcome is binding on both parties, and the unit has the authority to award damages. Another option is to involve the Health Care Inspectorate, an institution within the Ministry of Health, which can initiate disciplinary proceedings and issue enforceable sanctions. It is also possible to contact the Health Care Information and Complaints Service which was established to provide patients with information and support concerning their complaints. In addition, patients can bring their complaints to professional associations. Professional councils, chambers, and other organizations have established complaint systems and arbitration boards for the extrajudicial resolution of malpractice claims. In the

Netherlands, pursuit of an oral healthcare complaint affords many options. It is noteworthy that 75% of the patients filing injustices were satisfied with the outcomes (Kroneman et al. 2016).

The same is true of other Member States as well. For example, in Lithuania, patient complaints can be dealt with at the provider level, at the Health Ministry's Commission on Evaluation of the Damage Caused to Health of Patients, or, as a last resort, in court (Murauskiene et al. 2013). Hungary also offers multiple routes for patient complaint procedures. As in other cases, complaints must first be perused by the practitioner who has a fixed time period in which to do so. If the problem is not resolved, the patient can contact the appropriate professional council or chamber which can apply its own disciplinary measures. One can also contact the State Secretariat for Healthcare or the Parliamentary Commissioner for Civil Rights. Once again, the initiation of judicial proceedings is also possible (Gaál et al. 2011).

Maltese practice concerning patient complaints is somewhat different. The route followed is determined by the sector in which the incident occurred—the private or public sector. Dental care is offered in both sectors. Complaints concerning incidents that happened in the public sector are brought to the attention of Customer Care of the Health Department. Those taking place in the private sector are communicated to the Medical Council of Malta (Kravitz et al. 2015). The sectoral divide is also essential to Swedish patient complaints. If the dentist is unable to resolve the conflict, two paths can lead to a solution. One consists of the Local Boards for Private Practice composed of dental practitioners or the Local Boards for Public Dental Services which may be staffed with people outside the dental profession. The second option consists of the Medical Responsibility Board on behalf of the National Board of Health and Welfare. In Poland, the route to be taken depends on whether the provider has a contract with the National Health Fund or not. If so, it has a complaint department that can impose sanctions on a DCP. If not, the complainant can make contact with a Civil Rights Ombudsman or utilize the judicial system (Eaton et al. 2012a; Sagan et al. 2011).

In Slovakia, after communication with the practitioner and no satisfactory response, complaint routes are determined by the subject of the allegation. Complaints concerning user fees, ethics, and the organization of care are to be lodged with a relevant body, such as the Ministry of Health, self-governing regions, professional chambers, etc. Issues related to the adequacy of care are handled by the Health Care Surveillance Authority, a structure responsible for the supervision of public health and healthcare provision (Smatana et al. 2016). These few illustrations demonstrate the variety of practices involved. All of these formal complaint routes afford patients a voice in incidents of discontent. Furthermore, all stress citizens' rights.

The subjects of patient complaints are multitudinous. A popular topic relates to staff. There is concern about the attitudes and personal behavior of staff involving written and oral communications, adverse reactions, alcohol and/or drug use, sexual improprieties, offensive racial comments, rudeness in general, and deficient personal treatment. Complaints have also concerned wrong clinical treatment, no or a deficient result after treatment, lack of or insufficient follow-up care, disagreement with care practices, dissatisfaction with treatment delegated to a dental hygienist, complications after treatment, incorrect diagnosis, scams, mutilations, over-treatment, working outside scope of practice, prescribing issues, radiation use, patient consent, failure to appropriately store hazardous waste, practice of illegal tooth whitening, use of misleading publicity, fraud, fees, poor record keeping, the appointment process, and waiting times. The list is long. In the United Kingdom, the most common treatments with which patients have expressed dissatisfaction have been fitting of crowns, fillings, ill-fitting or broken dentures, root canal work, and orthodontic treatments in that order (Bruers et al. 2015, 2016; García-Armesto et al. 2010; General Dental Council 2015; Steel and Cylus 2012; Why do dental patients complain? 2013).

A Finnish research project (Hiivala et al. 2015) focused on the ability of patients to detect hazardous dental practice. The researchers concluded that they were quite capable of identifying hazards as well as substandard practices and serious safety risks. Thus, it was affirmed that patient complaints must be taken seriously and that DCPs and patients might collaborate in the future to develop methods to prevent errors in practice.

The number of cases filed annually throughout the EU has increased. In the United Kingdom, in 2014, the General Dental Council received 3099 complaints, an increase of 4.4% in a year. In the same year, hearings were held involving 322 dentists, 56 dental nurses, 35 dental technicians, 7 dental hygienists, 3 clinical dental technicians, and 1 dental therapist. All DCPs were involved (General Dental Council 2015). In Estonia, the number of complaints in a few years almost doubled (Lai et al. 2013). The increase in filed cases has resulted from the enhancement of patient awareness, empowerment, and expectations. Also, as in the United States, society in the Member States has become more litigious. Another factor accounting for the increased number of patient complaints is the annual augment in the number of DCPs, especially dentists (Singh et al. 2009). Due to the increase in cases, it has been suggested that training programs spend more time on methods to prevent lawsuits and charges. Although this matter is an important part of oral health care, it tends to be neglected in curricula (Patients tend to go to court more often nowadays 2015). It would be an appropriate topic for CPD.

More hearings are taking place than previously. Frequently, a legal dental expert witness is called upon to deliver a professional opinion. There have not been any specific qualifications developed for such participants. Thus, in Germany, most recently, special training for legal dental expert witnesses was established. The program, part of CPD, trains dentists to prepare written expert opinions and to perform as expert witnesses in legal matters. So far, it has realized success (Brauer et al. 2012).

There are several disciplinary measures that are issued to DCPs found guilty of misconduct. The most severe is cancellation of one's license to practice her/his profession. Also, restrictions may be placed on the right to practice professional activities for a fixed period or until further notice. Such a sanction amounts to limited disqualification. The practitioner is not allowed to undertake certain procedures.

Other penalties include monetary fines, admonition, caution, reprimand, assignment to additional training, and expulsion from a professional society's compulsory membership (CIBG n.d.; Health Care Professionals Act No. 559/1994). Most of the Member States make use of the same penalties. Also, usually, both patients and DCPs can take advantage of the right of appeal, customarily to a superior disciplinary unit or a tribunal.

A case heard by a French court not too long ago received a great deal of press. It involved the so-called horror dentist, a Dutch practitioner practicing in France, who had about 100 complaints filed against him. He was accused of illegal practice, mutilating and disabling patients over a 3-year period, overcharging them, and billing for imaginary treatment. He was found guilty of assault and fraud as well as 85 counts of deliberate violence and other crimes. He was sentenced to 8 years in prison, fined, and barred from practice permanently. The case was considered extraordinary (Sotto and Gaschka 2016).

Directive 2005/36/EC stated that Member States should communicate with one another with all due respect for personal data protection about disciplinary or criminal penalties issued to professionals. The amending directive (Directive 2013/55/EU) addressed the subject with specificity. Such information as well as any other likely to impinge on a practitioner's performance is to be communicated via the aforementioned Internal Market Information System. Moreover, a time limit was established for this task. It is to be accomplished within 3 days of the announcement of a sanction. Thus, penalized professionals cannot immediately attempt to register in another Member State. In the same vein, authorities are to be informed when restrictions have been lifted.

Some Member States, such as the Netherlands, Denmark, and the United Kingdom, make public the outcomes of patient complaints. The website of the General Dental Council in the United Kingdom (www.gdc-uk.org) contains information on all hearings. The listing reveals the date of the hearing, name of the DCP involved, registration number, profession, and the outcome. On the site, there is also information on forthcoming hearings and where they are being held. This specific listing contains the aforementioned information, obviously, without an outcome. The public can attend all or part of the hearings.

Little research has focused on the impact of patient complaints and their outcome on the oral healthcare practitioner. A survey (Bruers et al. 2015, 2016) indicated that 71% of the participants were of the opinion that the legal experience had extensive influence on their practice. Furthermore, 52% felt the same degree of impact on their attitude toward colleagues and patients. In addition, 60% thought their mental and/or physical well-being was affected. In spite of the unpleasant aspects of the overall experience, several practitioners viewed it as "a wake-up call." Complaints by patients have an economic toll as well. In the aforementioned survey, 75% of the practitioner participants unsurprisingly reported loss of the patient due to the conflict. Discords have also produced an effect on commercial structures. Also noteworthy is that multiple complaints from approximately 2000 victims, the media, and DCPs impacted Dentexia, a French oral healthcare organization. Its low-cost centers closed for good as a result.

Conclusion

The structures of the regulatory mechanisms discussed in this chapter were put in place to protect the consumer of oral health care from total dominance of service by DCPs. Recognition or licensing of a DCP serves to ensure that a certain quality of service should be forthcoming. However, as noted, not all DCPs are recognized in every Member State, nor is it ascertained in each one that specific knowledge and skills are to be possessed. CPD requirements relate to the objective of providing superior service based on up-to-date knowledge and competences. An ethical code makes public a profession's commitment to the social welfare, and it also garners community confidence in a profession. In addition, it aids the profession in the maintenance of its monopoly. Fitness to practice procedures and the role of patient complaints indicate that professional authority is not without limits. This trait is expressed in the patient-professional relationship which, in turn, carries professional-community ramifications (Greenwood 1966).

As noted, regulatory mechanisms were developed to ensure certain objectives concerned with the provision of oral health care with superior outcomes. The question to be answered is: Do they achieve their goal? Some studies on the subject have concluded that stringent licensing requirements do not contribute to enhanced outputs. Furthermore, it has been observed that their economic impact contributes to higher prices for patients and increased earnings for practitioners. Lesser regulatory limitations are affiliated with better economic results. Such findings present a negative environment for calls for more stringent licensing practices (Kleiner and Kudrle 2000). Also, in the case of dental hygienists, research results have indicated that rigid entry restrictions to the profession tended to reduce employment rates. In addition, practice limitations reduced productivity as well as stipends. Salary and employment rates have been termed endogenous to each other. Both impact access to care. Thus, decisions concerning entry to a profession and practice regulations must be taken at the same time in order to better access to oral health care. Access is of extreme significance and unfortunately, often, it is limited.

This chapter has highlighted the diversity in the regulatory instruments used for DCPs throughout the EU and the lack of these mechanisms in some Member States for a few DCPs. Differences in the methods adopted for the recognition of professionals impact the labor markets in larger international economic structures, such as the EU (Vollmer and Mills 1966). The spirit of harmonization could be most useful to regulatory instruments in a European framework, given the many purposes for which regulation has been used. As said before, unity can be reached from diversity. Using the open method of coordination for such a delicate project might be useful to achieve agreement.

References

Albreht, T., Brinovec, R. P., Jošar, D., Poldrugovac, M., Kostnapfel, T., Zaletel, M., et al. (2016). Slovenia: Health system review. *Health Systems in Transition, 18*(3), 1–207.

Alexa, J., Rečka, L., Votápková, J., van Ginneken, E., Spranger, A., & Wittenbecher, F. (2015). Czech Republic: Health system review. *Health Systems in Transition, 17*(1), 1–165.

Amariei, C., & Eaton, K. A. (2009). Systems for the provision of oral care in the Black Sea countries: Part 1: Romania. *Oral Health and Dental Management, 8*(1), 3–6.

Analysis of the relationship between national dental associations (NDAs) and dental faculties within the ERO (European Regional Organization) zone (of the International Dental Federation): A NDA-perspective. (n.d.). http://www.erodental.org. Accessed 23 May 2016.

Anell, A., Glenngård, A. H., & Merkur, S. (2012). Sweden: Health system review. *Health Systems in Transition, 14*(5), 1–159.

Azzopardi-Muscat, N., Buttigieg, S., Calleja, N., & Merkur, S. (2017). Malta: Health system review. *Health Systems in Transition, 19*(1), 1–137.

Bailey, S., Bullock, A., Cowpe, J., Barnes, E., Thomas, H., Thomas, R., et al. (2013). Core continuing professional development (CPD) topics for the European dentist. *European Journal of Dental Education, 17*(s1), 23–28.

Barnes, E., Bullock, A. D., Bailey, S. E. R., Cowpe, J. G., & Karaharju-Suvanto, T. (2013). A review of continuing professional development for dentists in Europe. *European Journal of Dental Education, 17*(sl), 5–17.

Bjegovic-Mikanovic, V., Czabanowska, K., Flahault, A., Otok, R., Shortell, S., Wisbaum, W., et al. (2014). *Addressing needs in the public health workforce in Europe*. Copenhagen: World Health Organization and European Observatory on Health Systems and Policies.

Boyle, S. (2011). United Kingdom (England): Health system review. *Health Systems in Transition, 13*(1), 1–486.

Brands, W. G., Bronkhorst, E. M., & Welie, J. V. M. (2011). Professional ethics and cynicism amongst Dutch dental students. *European Journal of Dental Education, 15*(4), 205–209.

Brauer, H. U., Walther, W., Riesen, C., & Dick, M. (2012). Training for legal dental expert witnesses in Germany: An instrument for professional development. *Journal of Dental Education, 76*(5), 656–660.

Bruers, J. J., van Dam, B. A., Gorter, R., & Eijkman, M. A. (2015). The well-being of dentists following a complaint procedure. *Ned Tijdschrift Tandheelkunde, 122*(1), 41–48.

Bruers, J. J. M., van Dam, B. A. F. M., Gorter, R. C., & Eijkman, M. A. J. (2016). The impact of a formal complaint on Dutch dentists' professional practice: A survey study. *BMC Oral Health, 16*, 104. https://doi.org/10.1186/s12903-016-0295-8.

Bullock, A., Firmstone, V., Frame, J., & Thomas, H. (2010). Using dentistry as a case study to examine continuing education and its impact on practice. *Oxford Review of Education, 36*(1), 79–95.

Bullock, A., Bailey, S., Cowpe, J., Barnes, E., Thomas, H., Thomas, R., et al. (2013). Continuing professional development systems and requirements for graduate dentists in the EU: Survey results from the DentCPD project. *European Journal of Dental Education, 17*(Suppl. 1), 18–22.

Charalambous, C., & Theodorou, M. (2013). Systems for the provision of oral health care in the Black Sea countries: Part 13: Cyprus. *Oral Health and Dental Management, 12*(1), 3–8.

CIBG (Dutch Central Health Professions Center, Ministry of Health, Welfare, and Sports). (n.d.). *Explanation of disciplinary measures and criminal penalties*. http://www.bigregister.nl. Accessed 3 Nov 2016.

Cini, R. (2008, August 15). Standards of health care. *Times of Malta*. http://www.timesofmalta.com. Accessed 8 Mar 2017.

Council for the Professions Complementary to Medicine-Malta. (2015). *Council for the Professions Complementary to Medicine-Malta: Annual report 2014*. n.p.: Author. http://www.health.gov.mt. Accessed 28 Jan 2017.

Council of European Dentists. (2013). *CED resolution: Continuing Professional Development of dentists in the European Union*. http://www.cedentists.eu. Accessed 8 Nov 2017.

Council of European Dentists. (2017). *Code of ethics for dentists in the European Union*. http://www.cedentists.eu. Accessed 12 June 2018.

Croatia. (2015). *The health systems and policy monitor* (with modifications since publication of printed version 2015). http://www.hspm.org. Accessed 18 Sept 2015.

Cylus, J. (2015). *Analysis of the health system in Slovenia: Health system expenditure review—Final report*. http://www.mz.govt.si. Accessed 25 Apr 2018.

Cylus, J., Richardson, E., Findley, L., Longley, M., O'Neill, C., & Steel, D. (2015). United Kingdom: Health system review. *Health Systems in Transition, 17*(5), 1–125.

Czech Dental Chamber. (2016). *Annual report*. http://www.dent.cz/en. Accessed 23 May 2016.

Czech Republic. (2018, February). *International Federation of Dental Hygienists eNEWS*. http://www.ifdh.org. Accessed 3 Aug 2018.

Dental Council of Ireland. (2015). *Dental practitioner's CPD: Your guide to the Dental Council's Continuing Professional Development requirements*. http://www.dentalcouncil.ie. Accessed 10 Mar 2017.

DentCPD. (2010). *Harmonisation & standardization of European dental schools' programs of continuing professional development for graduate dentists*. http://www.dentcpd.org. Accessed 16 Nov 2017.

Directive 2005/36/EC of the European Parliament and of the Council of 7 September 2005 on the recognition of professional qualifications.

Directive 2013/55/EU of the European Parliament and of the Council of 20 November 2013 amending Directive 2005/36/EC on the recognition of professional qualifications and Regulation (EU) 1024/2012 on administrative cooperation through the Internal Market Information System (the IMI Regulation).

Džakula, A., Sagan, A., Pavić, N., Lončarek, K., & Sekelj-Kauzlarić, K. (2014). Croatia: Health system review. *Health Systems in Transition, 16*(3), 1–162.

Eaton, K., Brookes, J., Patel, R., Batchelor, P., Merali, F., & Narain, A. (2011). *The impact of continuing professional development in dentistry: A literature review*. http://www.gdc-uk.org. Accessed 20 Jan 2017.

Eaton, K., Garcia, A., Patel, R., & Rincon, V. (2012a). *A practical resource to help in the support of non-UK, EEA qualified dental practitioners practicing in the UK*. http://www.oxforddeanery.nhs.uk. Accessed 17 Jan 2017.

Eaton, K. A., Harris, M., Ross, M. K., & Arevalo, C. (2012b). A survey of dental hygienists in the United Kingdom in 2011. Part 1—Demographics and working patterns as dental hygienists. *British Dental Journal, 213*(10), E18. https://doi.org/10.1038/sj.bdj.2012.1041.

Economou, C. (2010). Greece: Health system review. *Health Systems in Transition, 12*(7), 1–180.

Education & CPD. (n.d.). http://www.gdc-uk.org. Accessed 20 Sept 2019.

Elliott, P. (1972). *The sociology of the professions*. London: The Macmillan Press Ltd.

Enterprise Finland: Ministry of Economic Affairs and Employment. (n.d.). *Dental technician*. http://www.tem.fi. Accessed 12 Feb 2017.

ERO (The European Regional Organisation of the Federation Dentaire Internationale) (International Dental Federation). (2012a). *Report: Working Group women in dentistry*. http://www.erodental.org. Accessed 30 July 2018.

ERO (Europäische Regionale Organisation) (European Regional Organisation-FDI (Fédération Dentaire Internationale) (International Dental Federation). (2012b). *Summary of national reports—Prague 2012*. http://www.erodental.org. Accessed 12 Mar 2017.

European Commission. (2016). *Mutual evaluation of regulated professions. Overview of the regulatory framework in the health services sector—Dental hygienists and related professions. Report based on information transmitted by Member States and discussion in the meeting of 20 April 2015*. GROW/ES- 29 April 2016.

European Economic and Social Committee. (2013). *The state of liberal professions concerning their functions and relevance to European civil society*. http://www.eesc.europa.eu. Accessed 14 Mar 2017.

European Regional Organisation of the Federation Dentaire Internationale (International Dental Federation). (2015a). *Resolution: Dental hygienist profile*. http://www.erodental.org. Accessed 30 July 2018.

European Regional Organisation of the Federation Dentaire Internationale (International Dental Federation). (2015b). *Statement on the continuing medical education in dentistry*. http://www.erodental.org. Accessed 19 June 2016.

Executive Agency for Health and Consumers. (2014). *Study concerning the review and mapping of continuous professional development and lifelong learning for health professionals in the EU: Final report*. http://www.ec.europa.eu. Accessed 10 Nov 2017.

Freidson, E. (1973). Professions and the occupational principle. In E. Freidson (Ed.), *The professions and their prospects* (pp. 19–38). Beverly Hills: Sage.

Gaál, P., Szigeti, S., Csere, M., Gaskins, M., & Panteli, D. (2011). Hungary: Health system review. *Health Systems in Transition, 13*(5), 1–266.

García-Armesto, S., Abadía-Taira, M. B., Durán, A., Hernández-Quevedo, C., & Bernal-Delgado, E. (2010). Spain: Health system review. *Health Systems in Transition, 12*(4), 1–295.

General Dental Council. (2013). *Standards for the dental team*. http://gdc-uk.org. Accessed 20 May 2016.

General Dental Council. (2015). *Annual report and accounts 2014*. http://www.gdc-uk.org. Accessed 20 May 2016.

General Dental Council. (n.d.). *Continuing professional development for dental professionals*. London: Author.

Germany's dental health care system. (2015). *Dental Abstracts, 60*(5), 248–250.

Gough, N. (2012). Do you have no hours of CPD? *Vital, 10*, 34–36.

Gough, N., & Bagnall, S. (2012). Summary of: The impact of General Dental Council registration and continuing professional development on UK dental care professionals: (1) Dental nurses. *British Dental Journal, 213*(2), 70–71.

Government and healthcare in the Czech Republic. (2008). http://www.dent.cz/eng. Accessed 23 May 2016.

Greenwood, E. (1966). The elements of professionalization. In H. M. Vollmer & D. I. Mills (Eds.), *Professionalization* (pp. 9–19). Englewood Cliffs: Prentice-Hall, Inc.

Greenwood, E. (1972). Attributes of a profession. In R. M. Pavalko (Ed.), *Sociological perspectives on occupations* (pp. 3–15). Itasca: F. E. Peacock Publishers, Inc.

Health Care Professionals Act No. 559/1994. http://www.finlex.fi. Accessed 12 Feb 2017.

Health Systems in Transition (HiT) profile of Germany. (Updated 2016, April 26). *The health systems and policy monitor*. http://www.hspm.org. Accessed 5 May 2016.

Healthcare Quality, Complaints and Disputes Act (WKKGZ). (2015). http://www.government.nl. Accessed 29 Mar 2019.

Hiivala, N., Mussalo-Rauhamaa, H., & Murtomaa, H. (2015). Can patients detect hazardous dental practice? A patient complaint study. *International Journal of Health Care Quality Assurance, 28*(3), 274–287.

Hlawacek, S., & Orsulova, M. (2003). *Dental laboratory technician in XXXXX: Comparison with dental laboratory technicians in particular EU member countries*. http://www.ueapme.com. Accessed 30 Oct 2017.

Hofmarcher, M., & Quentin, W. (2013). Austria: Health system review. *Health Systems in Transition, 15*(7), 1–291.

Horsley, T., Grimshaw, J., & Campbell, G. (2010). *How to create conditions for adapting physicians' skills to new needs and lifelong learning*. Copenhagen: World Health Organization on behalf of the European Observatory on Health Systems and Policies.

IFD (International Federation of Denturists). (2016, February). Breaking news: Belgium. *IFD Newsletter*, Edition 2, 8.

Iigűy, M., Iigüy, D., & Oktay, I. (2015). Ethical decision making in dental education: A preliminary study. *BMC Medical Ethics, 16*, 52. https://doi.org/10.1186/s12910-015-0046-4.
International Federation of Dental Hygienists. (2015). http://www.ifdh.org. Accessed 2 Sept 2016.
Irish Dental Association. (n.d.). *IDA (Irish Dental Association) CPD (Continuing Professional Development)*. http://www.dentist.ie. Accessed 24 Oct 2016.
Jaquiery, C. (2012). Dentistry—At the heart of conflict between medicine and technology. *Dentistry, 1*(1), 1–2.
Jenkins, G. H. (1970). Professionals in organizations. In J. A. Jackson (Ed.), *Professions and professionalization* (pp. 53–107). London: Cambridge University Press.
Jevon, P. (2012). Updated guidance on medical emergencies and resuscitation in the dental practice. *British Dental Journal, 212*(1), 41–43.
Johnson, T. J. (1972). *Professions and power*. London: The Macmillan Press Ltd.
Katrova, L. (2009). Systems for the provision of oral health care in the Black Sea countries, Part 2: Bulgaria (2009). *Oral Health and Dental Management in the Black Sea Countries, 8*(2), 3–6.
Kivovics, P. (n.d.). *Oral health in Hungary: 2012*. n.p.: National Center for Healthcare Audit and Improvement.
Kleiner, M. M., & Kudrle, R. T. (2000). Does regulation affect economic outcomes?: The case of dentistry. *Journal of Law and Economics, 43*(2), 547–582.
Koletsi-Kounari, H., Papaioannou, W., & Stefaniotis, T. (2011). Greece's high dentist to population ratio: Comparisons, causes and effects. *Journal of Dental Education, 75*(11), 1507–1515.
Kovács, E., Szócska, G., Török, B., & Ragány, K. (2013). *Why is Hungary the main destination country in dental tourism? Why do patients choose Hungary for dental care? Hungarian case study on dental care and patient flow. ECAB (Evaluating Care Across Borders) project (Grant agreement 242058)*. http://www.semmelweis.hu. Accessed 13 Nov 2015.
Kravitz, A. S., Bullock, A., Cowpe, J., & Barnes, E. (2014). *Council of Dentists manual of dental practice 2014* (5th ed.). n.p.: Council of European Dentists.
Kravitz, A. S., Bullock, A., Cowpe, J., & Barnes, E. (2015). *Council of European Dentists: EU manual of dental practice 2015* (5.1 ed.). Brussels: Council of European Dentists.
Kroneman, M., Boerma, W., van den Berg, M., Groenewegen, P., de Jong, J., & van Ginneken, E. (2016). The Netherlands: Health system review. *Health Systems in Transition, 18*(2), 1–239.
Lai, T., Habicht, T., Kahur, K., Reinap, M., Kiivet, R., & van Ginneken, E. (2013). Estonia: Health system review. *Health Systems in Transition, 15*(6), 1–196.
Larson, M. S. (1977). *The rise of professionalism: A sociological analysis*. Berkeley: University of California Press.
Lithuanian Dental Chamber A. Šeikus. (n.d.). *The accessibility and quality of dental services in Lithuania*. http://www.slideplayer.com. Accessed 28 Aug 2018.
Malamed, S. F. (2015). Medical emergencies in the dental surgery Part 1: Preparation of the office and basic management. *Journal of the Irish Dental Association, 61*(6), 302–308.
Mayol, I. M., Sánchez, M. V. R., Gonzalvo-Cirac, M., & de Ribot, E. (2013). Estudio comparativo de tres modelos occidentales de códigos deontológicos para odontólogos (Comparative study of three Western models of deontological codes for dentists). *Cuadernos de Bioética, 24*(3), 367–376.
Merkur, S., Mladovsky, P., Mossialos, E., & McKee, M. (2008). *Do lifelong learning and revalidation ensure that physicians are fit to practice?* Copenhagen: World Health Organization on behalf of the European Observatory on Health Systems and Policies.
Minervino, B., & Souza, O. T. (2004). Responsabilidade civil e ética do ortodontista (The orthodontist's civil and ethical responsibility). *Dental Press Journal of Orthodontics, 9*(6), 90–96.
Mitenbergs, U., Taube, M., Misins, J., Mikitis, E., Martinsons, A., Rurane, A., et al. (2012). Latvia: Health system review. *Health Systems in Transition, 14*(8), 1–191.
Murauskiene, L., Janoniene, R., Veniute, M., van Ginneken, E., & Karanikolos, M. (2013). Lithuania: Health system review. *Health Systems in Transition, 15*(2), 1–150.

Nash, D. A. (2007). On ethics in the profession of dentistry and dental education. *European Journal of Dental Education, 11*(2), 64–74.

Nash, D. A., Friedman, J. W., & Mathu-Muju, K. R. (2012). *A review of the global literature on dental therapists in the context of the movement to add dental therapists to the oral health workforce in the United States*. http://www.depts.washington.edu. Accessed 11 Sept 2016.

Newsome, P. R. H. (2011). Dental technicians: Regulation and quality assurance. *British Dental Journal, 210*(1), 25–29.

Olejaz, M., Nielsen, A. J., Rudkjøbing, A., Birk, H. O., Krasnik, A., & Hernández-Quevedo, C. (2012). Denmark: Health system review. *Health Systems in Transition, 14*(2), 1–192.

Patients tend to go to court more often nowadays: An interview with Dr. Andy Wolff, Israel. (2015). *Dental Tribune United Kingdom Edition, 9*(4), 14–16.

Regional European Organisation of the FDI (International Dental Federation). (2012). *National report—Spanish Dental Association 2012*. http://www.erodental.org. Accessed 4 Nov 2016.

Ross, M. K., Turner, S., & Ibbetson, R. J. (2012). The impact of General Dental Council registration and continuing professional development on UK dental care professionals: (2) dental technicians. *British Dental Journal, 213*(8), E13. https://doi.org/10.1038/sj.bdj.2012.958.

Sagan, A., Panteli, D., Borkowski, W., Dmowski, M., Domański, F., Czyzewski, M., et al. (2011). Poland: Health system review. *Health Systems in Transition, 13*(8), 1–193.

Sheppard, C. A. (1978). Enforcing continuing competence. In P. Slayton & M. J. Trebilcock (Eds.), *The professions and public policy* (pp. 321–329). Toronto: University of Toronto Press.

Shinberg, B. (2000). The role that licensure plays in society. In I. Smith & C. G. Schoon (Eds.), *The licensure and certification mission: Legal, social and political foundations* (pp. 145–163). New York: Forbes Custom Publishing.

Singh, P., Mizrahi, E., & Korb, S. (2009). A five-year review of cases appearing before the General Dental Council's Professional Conduct Committee. *British Dental Journal, 206*(4), 217–223.

Smatana, M., Pažitný, P., Kandilaki, D., Laktišová, M., Sedláková, D., Palušková, M., et al. (2016). Slovakia: Health system review. *Health Systems in Transition, 18*(6), 1–210.

Sotto, P., & Gaschka, C. (2016, April 26). French court sentences 'horror dentist' who fled to Canada to eight years. *The Globe and Mail*. https://www.theglobeandmail.com/news/world/french-court-sentences-horror-dentist-who-fled-to-canada-to-eight-years/article29758268/. Accessed 30 Oct 2016.

Steel, D., & Cylus, J. (2012). United Kingdom (Scotland): Health system review. *Health Systems in Transition, 14*(9), 1–150.

Stewart, C., & Kinirons, M. (2015). Dentists' requirements for continuing professional development in Ireland: A pilot study conducted at University College Cork. *Journal of the Irish Dental Association, 61*(1), 40–44.

Susskind, R., & Susskind, D. (2015). *The future of the professions: How technology will transform the work of human experts*. Oxford: Oxford University Press.

Swedish Dental Association. (2003). *Dentistry in Sweden*. http://www.mah.se. Accessed 9 Oct 2016.

Tallinn Tervishoiu Kõrgkool. (n.d.). *Estonia: Oral and dental care*. http://www.ttk.ee. Accessed 11 Oct 2016.

The EU Single Market: Regulated professions database. (2018). http://www.ec.europa.eu. Accessed 3 Feb 2018.

Traxlor, F., & Adam, G. (n.d.). *Slovenia: The representativeness of trade unions and employer associations in the hospital sector*. http://www.epsu.org. Accessed 29 Nov 2016.

Turner, S., Ross, M. K., & Ibbetson, R. J. (2012a). The impact of General Dental Council registration and continuing professional development on UK dental care professionals: (1) Dental nurses. *British Dental Journal, 213*(2), E2. https://doi.org/10.1038/sj.bdj.2012.664.

Turner, S., Ross, M. K., & Ibbetson, R. J. (2012b). The impact of registration and CPD (continuing professional development) on dental nurses. *Vital, 9*, 24–31.

Unione Nazionale Igienisti Dentali (National Union of Dental Hygienists). (2012). *Nuovo codice deontologico Unione Nazionale Igienisti Dentali* (The National Union of Dental Hygienists' new deontological code). http://www.unid.it. Accessed 8 Dec 2016.

Vlădescu, C., Scîntee, S. G., Olsavszky, V., Hernández-Quevedo, C., & Sagan, A. (2016). Romania: Health system review. *Health Systems in Transition, 18*(45), 1–170.

Vollmer, H. M., & Mills, D. L. (1966). *Professionalization*. Englewood Cliffs: Prentice-Hall, Inc.

Vrielink, M. O., & van Bockel, J. (2013). Bounded professionalism: Why self-regulation is part of the problem. In M. Noordegraaf & B. Steijn (Eds.), *Professionals under pressure: The reconfiguration of professional work in changing public service* (pp. 179–192). Amsterdam: Amsterdam University Press.

White, W. D. (1979). Why is regulation introduced in the health sector? A look at occupational licensure. *Journal of Health Politics, Policy and Law, 4*(3), 536–552.

Why do dental patients complain? (2013). *British Dental Journal, 215*(8), 386.

Winblad, U., & Ringard, Å. (2009). Meeting rising public expectations: The changing role of patients and citizens. In J. Magnussen, K. Vrangbaek, & R. B. Saltman (Eds.), *Nordic health care systems: Recent reforms and current policy challenges* (pp. 126–150). Maidenhead: McGraw Hill, Open University Press.

Wright, D. T. (1978). The objectives of professional education. In P. Slayton & M. J. Trebilcock (Eds.), *The professions and public policy* (pp. 125–129). Toronto: University of Toronto Press.

Zagoričnik, M. (2011). *Education and training for dental technicians in Europe: Research and results*. http://www.online.scuola.zanichelli.it. Accessed 3 Mar 2017.

Chapter 4
Member States: Healthcare Provision

The Healthcare Delivery System: Its Finances

Important to the operation of any healthcare delivery system are the professionals involved, the organization of their services, and the method of financing, all of which are dependent on the availability of physical, economic, and other resources, as well as support services. Diverse has been the descriptor used to describe the education and regulation of the dental team within the framework of the European Union (EU). The same word applies to the nature of the healthcare systems in the Member States and their benefits. These European structures are quite different from the American ones and often from each other.

A hallmark of many of these systems is that they feature compulsory social health and/or public health insurance. The Member States which fall within these categories are almost all. In fact, in some nations, such as Hungary, Italy, Lithuania, Poland, Romania, and Spain, it is not possible to opt out of the public healthcare delivery system. In the last noted nation, only civil servants are allowed to choose fully private healthcare services (Donatini 2016; Eaton et al. 2012; Gaál et al. 2011; García-Armesto et al. 2010; Murauskiene et al. 2013; Sagan et al. 2011; Vlădescu et al. 2016). However, if in Malta and other Member States, as well, an individual selects only private health care over that of the National Health Service, she/he still has to pay the subscription fee to the latter organ (Azzopardi-Muscat et al. 2017).

Several Member States have healthcare delivery systems, for the most part, financed by taxation of one kind or another. These nations include Ireland, Italy, Latvia, Portugal, Spain, Sweden, and the United Kingdom (García-Armesto et al. 2010; Mitenbergs et al. 2012; Simões et al. 2017).

Italy relies primarily on corporate taxation, and the subnational regions generate additional funds on their own (Bindi et al. 2017; Donatini 2016). In addition to general taxation, Portugal taxes alcoholic, sweetened, and added sugar drinks. Taxes in Spain used for health care relate to gifts, inheritances, properties, property

S. Z. Koff, *The Dental Team in the European Union*,
https://doi.org/10.1007/978-3-030-72232-6_4

transfers, gambling, personal income, VAT (value-added tax), hydrocarbon-based products, retail sales, tobacco, alcoholic drinks, and electricity. Some private financing also contributes to Spanish healthcare delivery. Its biggest private source results from copayments related to pharmaceutical prescriptions (García-Armesto et al. 2010; Hogan Lovells International 2014). In addition to national income taxes and indirect ones, the Swedish healthcare delivery system is also supported by municipal proportional income taxes, other local taxes, State grants, and subsidies. Employer payroll taxes are also significant (Anell et al. 2012; Glenngård 2016; Pälvärinne et al. 2018).

The national healthcare systems in Ireland, Latvia, and the United Kingdom, for the most part, are based on general tax finances. In fact, 98.8% of the National Health Service funding in the United Kingdom has come from this source. Finances also mainly result from noncitizens who use the National Health Service as private patients and, thus, have to pay for its services. In addition, other user charges and private health insurance provide revenue (Boyle 2011). Payments by employees and employers via a payroll tax are also used in Latvia. They represent a percentage of gross stipends (Lace 2017; Mitenbergs et al. 2012).

In several Member States, the national health insurance fund relies on regular contributions from employees, employers, and the self-employed in the form of this payroll tax. In this situation, health insurance payments are related to a percentage of income. This occurs in Austria where funding via sickness funds covers the majority of healthcare expenditures. Payments by employees and employers to these structures are based on the incomes of the insured. These contributions have provided 59% of the necessary healthcare funds. The difference is made up by retention fees, government subsidies, voluntary health insurance contributions, and out-of-pocket copayments for some services received (Hofmarcher and Quentin 2013). People with communicable diseases and households with low incomes are excluded from contribution requirements to the social health insurance program.

Belgium utilizes a payroll tax as well. Contributions to the national health insurance fund are 7.35% of gross stipend. 3.55% is deducted from one's salary, and 3.80% is contributed by the employer. Obviously, self-employed individuals are responsible for the total tax. In this particular Member State, these compulsory payments provide insurance for the payer and her/his family.

In different style, Bulgarians are liable for a consumer tax detailed in Article 37 of the Health Insurance Act. It amounts to 1% of the national minimum wage, and it is to be paid at every outpatient healthcare appointment. For each day as an inpatient in a hospital, the payment is based on 2% of the national minimum wage. Payment of this tax is limited to 10 days annually. The amount of the aforementioned payments is established by a decree of the Council of Ministers, an executive organ. Also, employers and employees are equally responsible (50% each) for social insurance contributions since 2010. In addition, the self-employed and unemployed must submit their income-related payments. Taxation transfers from State and municipal budgets, corporate donations, out-of-pocket and voluntary health insurance payments, as well as gifts contribute to the financial status of the national health insurance fund.

Differences pertaining to the financing of healthcare systems frequently relate to the amount of the payroll tax. In Croatia, the percentage of contribution is 15.5% of the employee's gross salary (Jolena 2017). In this particular Member State, retired persons must pay a mandatory percentage of their pensions for health insurance (Džakula et al. 2014). Also, employers' payments as well as general taxation help support efforts in public sector health care (Sobol and Vochelle 2016).

Cyprus, in terms of health insurance payments, is similar to other Member States in that employees, employers, the self-employed, and pensioners are obliged to assume these contributions to the fund of the National Health Service. As of 2017, employees and pensioners pay 2.65% of earned income. Employers on behalf of their employees pay 2.9% of their salaries. The self-employed are to transfer to the fund 4% of their earnings. Then, the State also remunerates the fund 4.7% of income for each beneficiary (Agreement on contributions to the NHS (National Health Service) 2017).

To cover the cost of healthcare expenditures, the Czech Republic has enacted compulsory wage-based payments as well. One-third of the premium is paid by the employee, and the employer assumes responsibility for the remainder. As in other Member States, self-employed individuals also contribute. The State pays on behalf of children up to age 18 or age 26, if they are enrolled as students, retired persons, economically inactive individuals, mothers on maternity leave, or those who take full-time care of one child up to age 7 or two children up to age 15, national service people, and prisoners, to mention a few groups (Alexa et al. 2015; The Czech Republic n.d.; Hogan Lovells International 2014).

Denmark is another nation whose healthcare structure is heavily financed by general taxation (Vrangbaek 2016). Part of the general tax structure is a health contribution tax which has consisted of 8% of taxable income. This source finances 77% of healthcare activities. It is supplemented by block grants from the national government, reimbursements, equalization schemes, and municipal contributions in the form of local activity-based payments (Ministry of Health 2017). The statutory health insurance system in Estonia is funded via a general addition to a social payroll tax. Much of the revenue is funded by patients as 96% comes from the private sector (Kravitz et al. 2015). In fact, Estonia stands out among the Member States because it is known as a nation in which oral health care is least supported by the State (Lai et al. 2013; Regional European Organisation of the FDI 2011).

Tax-based revenues are important to the Finnish healthcare delivery system. The two sources of public financing consist of municipal taxes and the national health insurance fund supported by insurance fees. Primarily, taxes finance the provision of health care. National health insurance is supported by employees' and State fees collected at the same time as taxes (Vuorenkoski et al. 2008). Private health insurance, benefit societies, and municipalities are also involved in financial support. All in all, the public sector has financed 76% of Finnish total healthcare expenditures.

Multiple taxes in France help support the provision of health care. There are personal income taxes whose role in the healthcare system was enhanced in order to countervail the relative decrease of wage income, to restrict price distortions in the labor market, and to distribute impartially among citizens the needs of the system's financing. Contributions have augmented. Financial pressures came to the fore and reimbursement levels were reduced. Social health insurance is financed by employer and employee contributions in the form of payroll taxes. Additional tax structures relate to tobacco, alcohol, and other products that can potentially harm individuals (Chevreul et al. 2015; Durand-Zaleski 2016). In addition, there are taxes on the pharmaceutical industry. State subsidies and voluntary health insurance also contribute to healthcare delivery.

In Germany, the statutory health insurance system, as in other nations, derives funds from income-related payments and grants from taxes. The income-related payments, a percentage of gross wages up to a ceiling, are mandatory. If an individual earns less than a set amount per year, she/he is automatically insured along with any nonearning family members (Blümel and Busse 2016; Hogan Lovells International 2014). Employers, as in other Member States, must also contribute. Unemployed individuals donate in proportion to their unemployment entitlements. If a person is experiencing long-term unemployment, the government assumes their payments.

Greek social insurance funds have a prominent role in healthcare delivery. The funds which require compulsory membership are supported by payments from employees, employers, and the State as an employer. Overall, sources of finance of the Greek healthcare system are represented by the aforementioned social insurance and taxation. In addition, revenue is derived from state subsidies, private health insurance, and out-of-pocket payments (Eaton et al. 2012; Economou 2010). An economic crisis has had a devastating impact on Greek citizens. Many were unable to meet the mandatory contributions for health care, primarily as a result of unemployment. They became uninsured. To rectify this situation, all Greek citizens were given the right to access the healthcare delivery system.

Hungary features universal mandatory health insurance as well. However, the percentage of gross salary payments is different. Employers, for their contributions, are responsible for 2% of the employee's gross stipend, and the employee pays 6% of her/his gross wages (Boncz n.d.; Gaál et al. 2011; Hungary: Country overview 2016). In Lithuania, the financial system is similar to others. Payments are divided between the employee and employer. As in Hungary, the former contributes 6% of her/his gross wages and the latter 3%. A self-employed individual pays the entire 9%. Contribution rates are decided annually by the Lithuanian Parliament. This revenue is supplemented by State payments for the unemployed, fragile groups and their carers, those eligible for social assistance, individuals under age 18, students, women on maternity leave, and single parents. The contributions for the first two cited groups are based on the individual's average salary levels over the last couple of years (Baliukevičius and Sabalienė 2017; World Health Organization. Regional Office for Europe and European Observatory on Health Systems and Policies 2000; Murauskiene et al. 2013).

Luxembourg follows nations in which employees and employers make compulsory payments to the health fund. Employees on average pay 5.44% of their gross salary with a capped maximum contribution. Half of this sum is paid by the employer. In addition, the State makes payments to the social security system

(Berthet et al. 2015). The Maltese health system receives most of its finances (65%) from direct and indirect taxation. In Malta, insurance contribution rates vary as in other Member States, according to income. In addition, pensioners and the unemployed are released from these compulsory payments (Azzopardi-Muscat et al. 2017). These sources have additional support from private financing that results from out-of-pocket patient payments and voluntary health insurance (PwC 2012). In the Netherlands, all persons pay the same nominal premium for basic health insurance. In addition, the insured are required to contribute an income-related sum, and the employer must make a similar payment (Hogan Lovells International 2014; Kroneman et al. 2016).

Poland, like other Member States, relies on multiple sources to finance healthcare delivery. As in other cases, the principal origin of the National Health Fund's revenue is the citizens' premium payments for public health insurance. The statutory premium rate has been set at 9% of gross salary. This payment is to be made every month, and it is indivisible, meaning that the contribution is not divided between employee and employer. For the payer, it can, in part, be deducted from income taxes up to 7.75%. Premiums for those on disability and pensioners are based on the financial amounts of their benefits (Skica and Rodzinka 2014). Other funds are obtained from the national government and local ones. The amount of finances received from resources in the public sector is one of the lowest in Europe. A large portion of money derives from the well-established private sector with its commercial basis. As in Slovenia, the economic challenge is great (Malkiewicz et al. 2016; Nieszporska 2017). In Romania, the social health insurance contribution rate is 10.7% of gross stipend of which the employer pays 5.2% and the employee 5.5%. The self-employed contribute 5.5% of their earnings (European Commission 2016a). The fixed amount of salary is to be paid monthly.

The State health insurance premium in Slovakia is equal to 14% of an income-related base. Employees pay 4% of basic monthly income earned, and employers contribute 10%. For employees, the maximum base premium has been 300% of average wages 2 years before. This figure has been judged as very low (Nemec et al. 2013). Self-employed individuals pay a minimum base that is 44% of an average wage 2 years previously. These people are responsible for the 14% contribution which is figured as 14% of an assessment base for income tax divided by a predefined coefficient. This method has been evaluated as biased in favor of persons with a high income. The self-employed and employees who are seriously and permanently differently abled receive up to a 50% discount on their payroll tax contributions. The same is available to the latter group's employers. The voluntarily unemployed are required to make the same aforementioned 14% contribution. Also, there is a cap on earnings. If it is reached, the payer contributes no more money. For those folks lacking a regular income, the State makes mandatory contributions on their behalf. This category includes, for example, young children, students up to age 26, the unemployed, retired persons, those taking care of children up to age 3, and the differently abled. However, it has been asserted that the State never contributed the full amount which has been 3 to 5% of the minimum wage (Nemec et al. 2013). Presently, the rate has been set at 4.2% of the average salary 2 years previously.

Lastly, dividends aid healthcare delivery in Slovakia. Payments from this source are calculated at 14% with a maximum assessment base established at 60 times the average industry income from 2 years previously (Albreht et al. 2016; Nemec et al. 2013; Smatana et al. 2016).

Slovenia has adopted employer and employee payroll taxes that differ from other Member States in terms of payment percentages. The employer has been obliged to pay 7.09% of gross salary and the employee 6.36%. Self-employed people are required to pay as well. Additional resources are secured from State and local budgets and non-tax sources, such as proceeds from the sale of goods and services. As in other cases, funds are realized from out-of-pocket payments and private health insurance. It is noteworthy that with the economic crisis, unemployment increased greatly. Thus, the result was a large decrease of individual compulsory contributions (Albreht et al. 2016; Cylus 2015; Nemec et al. 2013).

Public Healthcare Programs

The public healthcare programs in the Member States are quite different from one another. Their service baskets, for the most part, cover, if not wholly, at least partially, primary health care defined as "care for individuals, families and the community at large through programmes including health promotion, prevention, curative care and rehabilitation" (García-Armesto et al. 2010, p. 113). Theoretically, such a package should include an array of dental care provision in every Member State, but such does not occur.

Primary health care includes oral healthcare providers, as it should, in all Member States, except Greece, Portugal, and Romania (Lember et al. 2015). Even though several Member States include dental treatment in their benefits, often, the services offered are very restricted and subject to high levels of copayments. For example, in Austria, public insurance covers a specific number of conservative and surgical oral healthcare procedures and a specific set of orthodontic and prosthodontic treatments. The former total 41 and the latter 11 (Hofmarcher and Quentin 2013). Being minimally covered by the state insurance plan, oral healthcare services are restricted as well in France (Chevreul et al. 2015; Durand-Zaleski 2016). In Italy, the National Health Service offers oral health care, but it has provided only 5–8% of total dental treatments, even though a minimum set of dental services are included in public benefits. The cited percentages vary from one subnational unit to another. However, they are always quite scarce (Bindi et al. 2017; Ferré et al. 2014). Public oral health care in the Netherlands is reserved to young folks and individuals with special needs. Otherwise, no separate general public dental service exists. Significant copayments are involved with dentistry benefits in several Member States.

Payments for dentistry account for almost 20% of all out-of-pocket expenses in the Member States. In fact, in Denmark, Estonia, and Spain, the percentage climbs to 30% and even higher. Lithuania and Slovenia are other Member States that have high out-of-pocket payments. The impact on household finances can be devastating.

These costs result from a lack of coverage for dental treatment and prostheses by public and secondary insurance programs (Murauskiene et al. 2013; OECD/EU 2016). They generate concern because they could increase barriers to oral healthcare access for vulnerable and other groups.

Dental care out-of-pocket payments in the United States present the highest level of financial barriers compared to other types of healthcare services. The same applies to several Member States. This situation must be rectified. A Swedish study (Franzén 2015) reveals that dentistry programs can and do develop practitioners that are of the opinion that the economic facets of the profession can be congruent with professional ethical values. Large profits are not the ultimate goal.

Out-of-pocket expenses also consist of cost-sharing and other expenditures, such as informal payments or "under-the-table" compensation. Unfortunately, they are well-rooted in Bulgaria (Dimova et al. 2012), Croatia (Džakula et al. 2014; United Nations Office of Drugs and Crime 2011), Greece (Souliotis et al. 2016; Thomson et al. 2019), Hungary (Kovács et al. 2013; Thomson et al. 2019), Latvia (Mitenbergs et al. 2012), Lithuania (Murauskiene et al. 2013), Poland (Thomson et al. 2019), Romania (Vlădescu et al. 2016), and Slovakia (Smatana et al. 2016). These countries, primarily located in East-Central Europe, are newer Member States. In many of these nations, as in Croatia, people rank corruption as the most significant challenge after unemployment and poverty (United Nations Office of Drugs and Crime 2011).

Informal payments reflect failures in the governance of a healthcare delivery system. Usually, they are found in situations where the available services are quite sparse (Thomson et al. 2019). These payments are made to healthcare providers, including dental personnel as well as institutions. They are offered as gratitude gifts or to ensure superior treatment, faster appointments, and so forth. All such payments are not always voluntary. Often, they are demanded. Moreover, they assume forms other than money. They also include food, drink, other gift items, exchange of services, etc. (Smatana et al. 2016; United Nations Office of Drugs and Crime 2011). It has been found that females are more likely to make these payments (Williams et al. 2016). Obviously, such practices must be obliterated and replaced with transparency and accountability.

It is noteworthy that Malta's public healthcare system features an excellent endeavor, a Mobile Dental Unit in which practitioners offer free examinations and advice to various communities (Azzopardi-Muscat et al. 2017). Also noteworthy is the Spanish practice whereby the public system offers dental treatment, but not that involving braces, to children and adolescents up to ages 14 or 18 depending on their region of residence. A broad set of services is available (Bravo et al. 2015; García-Armesto et al. 2010). Austrian youths are provided free dental braces up to age 18 (Reinbacher 2014). And in Sweden, individuals under age 21 (and in the near future up to age 24) enjoy free access to dental care that includes all specialist treatments (Glenngård 2016; Pälvärinne et al. 2018). Such generally takes place in several Member States, although the ages of beneficiaries differ. These are not unusual practices in insurance systems of this type. For Americans, they are. Of note, also, is the fact that in Hungary, people may choose their primary care physician, but not their primary care dentist (Gaál et al. 2011). Furthermore, it is interesting that in Belgium, in order to maintain public sector coverage of oral health care, one must undergo at least one annual dental checkup. Such a practice highlights the significance of prevention.

Secondary Sources of Healthcare Coverage

In this presentation concerning the financing of the Member States' healthcare delivery systems, the terms private health insurance and voluntary health insurance have been used. These labels refer to the same concept, secondary sources of coverage. Such policies are virtually available in every Member State, but being of various types, they cover diverse items and, thus, have different objectives. Their role is obviously related to the nature of the particular healthcare delivery system. There are three basic sorts of this insurance: duplicate, complementary, and supplementary. Each kind performs a different function.

One sort offers duplicate coverage. In other words, it covers the same services as the particular public health insurance. However, many of these policies offer access to diverse providers of service who are not eligible for payment under existing public arrangements. Furthermore, they also often afford the patient an opportunity to "jump the line" and, thus, achieve faster access to service. Also, many such policies require lower cost-sharing payments. Duplicate coverage is found in Denmark, Finland, Greece, Ireland, Italy, Latvia, Luxembourg, Poland, Spain, Sweden, and the United Kingdom (Alexandersen et al. 2016; García-Armesto et al. 2010; Paris et al. 2016; Sagan and Thomson 2016).

Voluntary health insurance is also termed complementary. As is evident from its name, this type complements public health insurance. For example, many policies of this sort cover costs, such as copayments or cost-sharing payments, that are not normally reimbursed by the public insurance system. Such a scheme exists in many Member States. It is found in Austria, Belgium, Croatia, Denmark, Estonia, Finland, France, Germany, Greece, Ireland, Italy, Latvia, Lithuania, Luxembourg, Malta, the Netherlands, Poland, Portugal, Romania, Slovenia, Sweden, and the United Kingdom (Albreht et al. 2016; Berthet et al. 2015; Chevreul et al. 2015; Cylus 2015; Donatini 2016; European Commission 2016b; Odeyemi and Nixon 2013; Paris et al. 2016; Sagan and Thomson 2016; Vuorenkoski 2016). The list is lengthy.

Private health insurance may also be termed supplementary, meaning it includes services not found in public arrangements, such as dental care or payments for pharmaceuticals. It might also offer superior amenities in hospitals, such as single rooms, etc. The list of Member States featuring this type of private health insurance is even longer than that for the complementary sort. It includes all nations in the EU (Alexandersen et al. 2016; Blümel and Busse 2016; Dimova et al. 2012; Donatini 2016; Gaál et al. 2011; Hofmarcher and Quentin 2013; Hogan Lovells International 2014; Kontopoulos and Kontopoulou 2014; Odeyemi and Nixon 2013; Paris et al. 2016; PwC 2012; Sagan and Thomson 2016; Vuorenkoski 2016).

In a few Member States, it is noteworthy that voluntary or private health insurance may be substitutive. This occurs in Estonia and Germany. In the former nation, those that do not qualify for the public scheme, such as the unemployed spouses of persons covered by public schemes, may take advantage of private health insurance. In Germany, individuals under 55 and with an income over an established threshold may opt out of the obligatory statutory public structure in favor of substitutive private health insurance coverage. If their income eventually falls below the threshold, they may rightfully reverse their original decision and join the public scheme (Sagan and Thomson 2016).

In some Member States, both the public and private insurance arrangements must accept any applicant, and the premium should not be based on her/his health risk profile. Also, in EU nations, for the most part, as a general rule, and as in Croatia, private health insurance is optional (Jolena 2017). However, in Poland and Flanders, a noted part of Belgium, it is mandatory. Furthermore, across the EU, it may be obligatory for some employees as part of their work contract (Skica and Rodzinka 2014).

The decision to purchase voluntary health insurance is conditioned by several factors. Obviously, the cost and ability to pay for treatment and private health insurance are important to the decision. Other matters related to the choice concern an individual's perceptions of the functional and aesthetic status of treatment and evaluation of the necessity for treatment. Moreover, the impact of the expenditure and clinical relationships are significant to a decision (Exley et al. 2012). Other factors impact the choice of whether to purchase private health insurance or not. These include the individual's age, education, the typology of her/his national healthcare structure, the nature of its benefit basket, effective access to covered care, and governmental incentives and disincentives related to the matter (Odeyemi and Nixon 2013; Paris et al. 2016).

Who are the principal procurers of these secondary sources of healthcare coverage whose benefit packages differ from nation to nation? Several Member States report their voluntary health insurance is usually procured by the higher social classes with elevated incomes, as in Cyprus and Latvia (Agreement on contributions to the NHS 2017; Kravitz et al. 2015). As aforementioned, in Germany, private health insurance is available to those persons with incomes above an established threshold. In Malta, mostly families, not individuals, purchase secondary healthcare coverage (Sagan and Thomson 2016). Usually those with higher education, residents in urban areas, and the employed in large and medium firms as skilled workers or in another superior capacity buy these policies.

Polish, Portuguese, and Danish employers are also procurers of private health insurance as a fringe benefit for their employees. This practice is common. In some Member States, such as Lithuania and Malta, this type of coverage is primarily bought by companies and on a group basis by multinationals or large national firms, again for their employees. On the other hand, the result is that there are few individual buyers of private health insurance policies, particularly in Lithuania (Sagan and Thomson 2016).

In several Member States, voluntary or private health insurance has not been very popular, and thus, its role on the healthcare stage has been minor or quite limited. These nations include Bulgaria, Croatia, Cyprus, the Czech Republic (Alexa et al. 2015), Estonia, Hungary (Gaál et al. 2011), Italy (Donatini 2016), Latvia (Mitenbergs et al. 2012), Lithuania (Murauskiene et al. 2013), Slovakia, and Sweden (Alexandersen et al. 2016). It is noteworthy that in some of these nations, the attractiveness of this type of coverage is increasing and in a few, such insurance is struggling to develop a role that is more than minor or negligible. The function of this type of secondary coverage differs from one Member State to another, and the percentage of the population in each one that has purchased voluntary health insurance is diverse.

In England, only 10.6% of the population availed itself of secondary coverage (Collinson 2017). In Spain, 13.4% of the inhabitants have procured these policies (OECD 2015). Fifteen percent of Greek residents have bought private health insurance, and approximately 20% of the Finns have found voluntary health insurance attractive enough to purchase (Alexandersen et al. 2016). In Malta, 22% of the residents have a private source of coverage (Azzopardi-Muscat et al. 2017), and the proportion is higher in Portugal where 25% of the population enjoys such a benefit. The percentage climbs in Germany where it reaches 33% and in Austria it arrives at 35.2% (OECD 2015). In Denmark, 40% of the people are privately insured (Boslaugh 2013), and in Ireland, 44.5% have selected the same choice (OECD 2015). Approximately 56% of the Luxembourgish has identical coverage (Berthet et al. 2015). The percentages really jump when it comes to Belgium and the Netherlands. They seem magnetic. In the former Member State, 81.3% has been attracted by this secondary coverage, and in the latter nation, 86% felt the same way (OECD 2015). Voluntary health insurance is even more popular in France and Slovenia. The percentage is the same for both Member States. It stands at 95% (Albreht et al. 2016; Cylus 2015). It is noteworthy that no data is available for Poland and Romania. In the case of the former Member State, it has been reported that there is an absence of a formal private health insurance system (OECD 2012), and in reference to the latter nation, it has been noted that the source of secondary insurance is still in its infancy (Vlădescu et al. 2016).

How do people utilize their secondary insurance? For what purposes? The response is for several and various ends. Coverage of hospital care has been of primary importance to Austrians and the Danish (Alexandersen et al. 2016; Hofmarcher and Quentin 2013). Croatians, Germans, Romanians, and individuals in the United Kingdom have used this type of insurance mainly to cover the cost of superior amenities in hotel and hospital accommodations. Evidently, the care environment matters for these folks (Blűmel and Busse 2016; Jolena 2017; Sagan and Thomson 2016) who desire more comfortable quarters and believe they contribute to a higher standard of care.

Voluntary health insurance has been relied on by many individuals in Finland, Spain, Sweden, and the United Kingdom to guarantee more ample choice of service providers and preferential access to these professionals. Very often, there is a waiting list for appointments with a particular provider, and by using a secondary insurance source, these people are frequently able to "jump the line." Also, these policies are used to access services, such as dentistry, that are limited in a particular public benefits basket (Alexandersen et al. 2016; García-Armesto et al. 2010; Sagan and Thomson 2016; Vuorenkoski 2016).

As noted, voluntary insurance often covers what is not available in the public sector. For example, the National Health Service in the United Kingdom fails to cover alternative and complementary therapies. For this reason, some people use their secondary policies to pay for the so-called nonessential services in public arrangements. This has been considered important to Germans, Luxembourgers, Romanians, and people in the United Kingdom (Blümel and Busse 2016; Sagan and Thomson 2016).

Most pertinent to this discussion is that utilization of voluntary health insurance has often served to cover copayments charged by service providers, in this case, the dental squad. In particular, such use has been related mainly to dental services in Denmark, France, Germany, Luxembourg, and the Netherlands (Alexandersen et al. 2016; Blümel and Busse 2016; Chevreul et al. 2015). In Luxembourg, if a person wants full reimbursement, she/he must have visited the dentist annually during the 2 years prior to treatment. If not, the reimbursement will definitely be less than the copayment (Kravitz et al. 2015). This practice resembles the aforementioned one in Belgium, and obviously, it has a similar objective. In Finland and the Netherlands, this secondary insurance is mainly used to cover copayments for pharmaceuticals (Nash et al. 2012; Vuorenkoski 2016; Wammes et al. 2016). On the other hand, Croatians, Romanians, and Slovenians have used this coverage in relation to copayments in general and not specific ones (Albreht et al. 2016; Jolena 2017).

In several Member States, secondary sources of insurance coverage have been utilized to redeem some dental costs. This is not an easy task. It has been undertaken in Austria (Hofmarcher and Quentin 2013), Greece, Ireland (Eaton et al. 2012), Luxembourg (Berthet et al. 2015), Malta (Azzopardi-Muscat et al. 2017), Portugal (Simões et al. 2017), and Spain (García-Armesto et al. 2010). The task is especially difficult in Greece where it has been stated that the insurance for oral health care is equal to zero. As noted, in Luxembourg, a condition is attached to reimbursement. Furthermore, in Malta, few secondary insurance schemes cover dental care, and, if they do, they relate to a very restricted number of dental procedures. The Irish situation is similar to the Maltese. It is much worse in Estonia and Lithuania where private insurance for oral health care is not available (Azzopardi-Muscat et al. 2017; Eaton et al. 2012; Kravitz et al. 2015.

Conclusion

This presentation focusing on the financing of public and secondary insurance coverage and their provisions within the framework of the EU again reveals diversity. Some structures rely on taxation more heavily than others. Also, tax structures are not congruent. Although most systems utilize a payroll tax, the percentages related to contribution amounts and the parties involved differ. The role of the State, particularly in reference to safety nets and protection of the fragile and other groups, is disparate as well. Also, municipalities differ in terms of their use of budgets. Funds derived from private or voluntary health insurance were noted in reference to several Member States. In these areas, the border between the public and private healthcare sectors is obscured. In reference to the financing and provision of public healthcare coverage, especially in terms of dentistry, and the role of and participants in secondary protection, the principal descriptor still remains diversity. Even though the same structures are often utilized, they have been implemented diversely within the Member States, and the particulars frequently differ. The consequences of this diversity in some Member States for some inhabitants are especially severe.

In a position paper, the Council of European Chief Dental Officers (2012) asserted that oral health care should be included in an integrated healthcare system. In other words, oral health care should be a part of primary care. After all, the state of oral health has an important relationship to general health. Furthermore, it was stated that oral health treatment should be available to all individuals with special medical and social needs and that care should be provided without cost for the relief of oral pain and life-threatening conditions. Realization of these objectives lies with public officials. After all, access to health care, including oral health care, is a basic human right.

References

Agreement on contributions to the NHS (National Health Service). (2017, May 17). Health *Systems and Policy Monitor*. http://www.hspm.org. Accessed 25 Apr 2018.

Albreht, T., Brinovec, R. P., Jošar, D., Poldrugovac, M., Kostnapfel, T., Zaletel, M., et al. (2016). Slovenia: Health system review. *Health Systems in Transition, 18*(3), 1–207.

Alexa, J., Rečka, L., Votápková, J., van Ginneken, E., Spranger, A., & Wittenbecher, F. (2015). Czech Republic: Health system review. *Health Systems in Transition, 17*(1), 1–165.

Alexandersen, N., Anell, A., Kaarboe, O., Lehto, J. S., Tynkkynen, L.-K., & Vrangbaek, K. (2016). The development of voluntary private health insurance in the Nordic countries. *Nordic Journal of Health Economics, 4*(1), 68–83.

Anell, A., Glenngård, A. H., & Merkur, S. (2012). Sweden: Health system review. *Health Systems in Transition, 14*(5), 1–159.

Azzopardi-Muscat, N., Buttigieg, S., Calleja, N., & Merkur, S. (2017). Malta: Health system review. *Health Systems in Transition, 19*(1), 1–137.

Baliukevičius, A., & Sabalienė, J. (2017). *Compulsory health insurance in Lithuania*. Riga: National Health Insurance Fund.

Berthet, F., Calteux, A., Wolter, M., Weber, L., van Ginneken, E., & Spranger, A. (2015). *Health systems in transition: HiT in brief: Luxembourg*. n.p.: World Health Organization.

Bindi, M., Paganelli, C., Eaton, K. A., & Widström, E. (2017). The healthcare system and the provision of oral healthcare in European Union member states. Part 8: Italy. *British Dental Journal, 222*(10), 809–817.

Blümel, M., & Busse, R. (2016). The German health care system, 2015. In E. Mossialos, M. Wenzl, R. Osborn, & D. Sornak (Eds.), *2015 international profiles of health care systems* (pp. 69–76). New York: The Commonwealth Fund.

Boncz, I. (n.d.). *Financing of the Hungarian health care system*. http://www.rafeehs.com. Accessed 23 Apr 2018.

Boyle, S. (2011). United Kingdom (England): Health system review. *Health Systems in Transition, 13*(1), 1–486.

Bravo, M., San Martin, L., Casals, E., Eaton, K. A., & Widström, E. (2015). The healthcare system and the provision of oral healthcare in European Union member states. Part 2: Spain. *British Dental Journal, 219*(11), 547–551.

Chevreul, K., Brigham, K. B., Durand-Zaleski, I., & Hernández-Quevedo, C. (2015). France: Health system review. *Health Systems in Transition, 17*(3), 1–218.

Collinson, P. (2017, January 15). Private health insurance sales surge amid NHS (National Health Service) crisis. *The Guardian*. http://www.theguardian.com. Accessed 20 Aug 2019.

Council of European Chief Dental Officers. (2012). *CECDO position paper on public-private mix*. http://www.cecdo.org. Accessed 14 June 2017.

Cylus, J. (2015). *Analysis of the health system in Slovenia: Health system expenditure review – Final report*. http://www.mz.govt.si. Accessed 25 Apr 2018.

Dimova, A., Rohova, M., Moutafova, E., Atanasova, E., Koeva, S., Panteli, D., et al. (2012). Bulgaria: Health system review. *Health Systems in Transition, 14*(3), 1–186.

Donatini, A. (2016). The Italian health care system, 2015. In E. Mossialos, M. Wenzl, R. Osborn, & D. Sornak (Eds.), *2015, international profiles of health care systems* (pp. 97–106). New York: The Commonwealth Fund.

Durand-Zaleski, I. (2016). The French health care system, 2015. In E. Mossialos, M. Wenzl, R. Osborn, & D. Sornak (Eds.), *2015 international profiles of health care systems* (pp. 59–68). New York: The Commonwealth Fund.

Džakula, A., Sagan, A., Pavić, N., Lončarek, K., & Sekelj-Kauzlarić, K. (2014). Croatia: Health system review. *Health Systems in Transition, 16*(3), 1–162.

Eaton, K., Garcia, A., Patel, R., & Rincon, V. (2012). *A practical resource to help in the support of non-UK, EEA qualified dental practitioners practicing in the UK*. http://www.oxforddeanery.nhs.uk. Accessed 17 Jan. 2017.

Economou, C. (2010). Greece: Health system review. *Health Systems in Transition, 12*(7), 1–180.

European Commission. (2016a). *Mutual evaluation of regulated professions. Overview of the regulatory framework in the health services sector--Dental hygienists and related professions. Report based on information transmitted by Member States and discussion in the meeting of 20 April 2015*. GROW/ES- 29 April 2016.

European Commission. (2016b). *Romania: Health care & long-term care systems*. http://www.ec.europa.eu. Accessed 20 Apr 2018.

Exley, C., Rousseau, N., Donaldson, C., & Steele, J. G. (2012). Beyond price: Individuals' accounts of deciding to pay for private healthcare treatment in the UK. *BMC Health Services Research, 12*, Article number 53. https://doi.org/10.1186/1472-6963-12-53.

Ferré, F., de Belvis, A. G., Valerio, L., Longhi, S., Lazzari, A., Fattore, G., et al. (2014). Italy: Health system review. *Health Systems in Transition, 16*(4), 1–168.

Franzén, C. (2015). Balancing costs and patients' health: Dental students' perception of economics in dentistry. *Professions and Professionalism, 5*(3). https://doi.org/10.7577/pp.927. Accessed 1 Aug 2016.

Gaál, P., Szigeti, S., Csere, M., Gaskins, M., & Panteli, D. (2011). Hungary: Health system review. *Health Systems in Transition, 13*(5), 1–266.

García-Armesto, S., Abadía-Taira, M. B., Durán, A., Hernández-Quevedo, C., & Bernal-Delgado, E. (2010). Spain: Health system review. *Health Systems in Transition, 12*(4), 1–295.

Glenngård, A. H. (2016). The Swedish health care system, 2015. In E. Mossialos, M. Wenzl, R. Osborn, & D. Sornak (Eds.), *2015 international profiles of health care systems* (pp. 153–160). New York: The Commonwealth Fund.

Hofmarcher, M., & Quentin, W. (2013). Austria: Health system review. *Health Systems in Transition, 15*(7), 1–291.

Hogan Lovells International. (2014). EU pricing and reimbursement: Pricing and reimbursement in major European countries. http://www.hoganlovells.com. Accessed 18 Apr 2018.

Hungary: Country overview. (2016). *Dental World*. http://www.english.dentalworld.hu. Accessed 18 Sept. 2016.

Jolena, R. (2017). *Drug reimbursement–Croatia*. http://www.cddf.org. Accessed 21 Apr 2018.

Kontopoulos, A., & Kontopoulou, E. (2014). The place of private health insurance in Cyprus and its prospects. *International Journal of Caring Sciences, 7*(2), 390–405.

Kovács, E., Szócska, G., Török, B., & Ragány, K. (2013). *Why is Hungary the main destination country in dental tourism? Why do patients choose Hungary for dental care? Hungarian case study on dental care and patient flow*. ECAB (Evaluating Care Across Borders) project (Grant agreement 242058). http://www.semmelweis.hu. Accessed 13 Nov 2015.

Kravitz, A. S., Bullock, A., & Cowpe, J. with Barnes, E. (2015). Council of European Dentists: EU manual of dental practice 2015. (5.1. Brussels, Council of European Dentists.

Kroneman, M., Boerma, W., van den Berg, M., Groenewegen, P., de Jong, J., & van Ginneken, E. (2016). The Netherlands: Health system review. *Health Systems in Transition, 18*(2), 1–239.

Lace, T. (2017). *Changing the funding of the Latvian compulsory healthcare system: For better or for worse?* http://www.ec.europa.eu. Accessed 5 Oct 2018.

Lai, T., Habicht, T., Kahur, K., Reinap, M., Kiivet, R., & van Ginneken, E. (2013). Estonia: Health system review. *Health Systems in Transition, 15*(6), 1–196.

Lember, M., Cartier, T., Bourgueil, Y., Dedeu, T., Hutchinson, A., & Kringos, D. (2015). Structure and organization of primary care. In D. S. Kringos, W. G. W. Boerma, A. Hutchinson, & R. B. Saltman (Eds.), *Building primary care in a changing Europe* (pp. 41–66). Copenhagen: World Health Organization on behalf of the European Observatory on Health Systems and Policies.

Malkiewicz, K., Malkiewicz, E., Eaton, K. A., & Widström, E. (2016). The health care system and the provision of oral healthcare in European Union member states. Part 6: Poland. *British Dental Journal, 221*(8), 501–507.

Ministry of Health. (2017). *Healthcare in Denmark: An overview*. Copenhagen: Author.

Mitenbergs, U., Taube, M., Misins, J., Mikitis, E., Martinsons, A., Rurane, A., et al. (2012). Latvia: Health system review. *Health Systems in Transition, 14*(8), 1–191.

Murauskiene, L., Janoniene, R., Veniute, M., van Ginneken, E., & Karanikolos, M. (2013). Lithuania: Health system review. *Health Systems in Transition, 15*(2), 1–150.

Nash, D. A., Friedman, J. W., & Mathu-Muju, K. R. (2012). *A review of the global literature on dental therapists in the context of the movement to add dental therapists to the oral health workforce in the United States*. http://www.depts.washington.edu. Accessed 11 Sept 2016.

Nemec, J., Cankar, S. S., Kostadinova, D., Maly, I., & Darmopilova, Z. (2013). Financing health care: What can we learn from CEE (Central and East European) experience? *Administrative Culture, 14*(2), 212–232.

Nieszporska, S. (2017). Priorities in the polish health care system. *The European Journal of Health Economics, 18*(1), 1–5.

Odeyemi, I. A. O., & Nixon, J. (2013). The role and uptake of private health insurance in different health care systems: Are there lessons for developing countries? *ClinicoEconomics and Outcomes Research, 5*, 109–118.

OECD (Organization for Economic Cooperation and Development). (2012). OECD economic surveys: Poland., *2012*(7). https://doi.org/10.1787/eco_surveys-pol-2012-en. Accessed 20 Aug 2018.

OECD (Organization for Economic Cooperation and Development). (2015). Coverage for health care. In *Health at a glance 2015: OECD indicators*. Paris: OECD Publishing.

OECD/EU (Organization for Economic Cooperation and Development/ European Union). (2016). *Health at a glance: Europe 2016 – State of health in the EU cycle*. Paris: OECD Publishing.

Pälvärinne, R., Widström, E., Forsberg, B. C., Eaton, K. A., & Birkhed, D. (2018). The healthcare system and the provision of oral healthcare in European Union member states: Part 9: Sweden. *British Dental Journal, 224*(8), 647–651.

Paris, V., Hewlett, E., Auraaen, A., Alexa, J., & Simon, L. (2016). *Healthcare coverage in OECD countries in 2012* (OECD Health working papers, No. 88). Paris: OECD Publishing.

PwC (PricewaterhouseCoopers). (2012). *Healthcare delivery in Malta*. http://www.pwc.com/mt. Accessed 23 Apr 2018.

Regional European Organisation of the FDI (International Dental Federation). (2011). *National report—Estonia 2011*. http://www.erodental.org. Accessed 13 Oct 2018.

Reinbacher, C. (2014). *Austria: Free dental braces for children as of 2015*. http://www.s-ge.com. Accessed 7 Oct 2015.

Sagan, A., & Thomson, S. (Eds.). (2016). *Voluntary health insurance in Europe: Country experience*. Copenhagen: European Observatory on Health Systems and Policies.

Sagan, A., Panteli, D., Borkowski, W., Dmowski, M., Domański, F., Czyzewski, M., et al. (2011). Poland: Health system review. *Health Systems in Transition, 13*(8), 1–193.

Simões, J., Augusto, G. F., Fronteira, I., & Hernández-Quevedo, C. (2017). Portugal: Health system review. *Health Systems in Transition, 19*(2), 1–184.

Skica, T., & Rodzinka, J. (Eds.). (2014). *Financing of health care system in Poland*. Rzeszow: The Institute for Financial Research and Analyses.

Smatana, M., Pažitný, P., Kandilaki, D., Laktišová, M., Sedláková, D., Palušková, M., et al. (2016). Slovakia: Health system review. *Health Systems in Transition, 18*(6), 1–210.

Sobol, L., & Vochelle, D. (2016). *Health care and medical equipment in Croatia*. http://www.awex-export.be. Accessed 13 Mar 2017.

Souliotis, K., Golna, C., Tountas, Y., Siskou, O., Kaitelidou, D., & Liaropoulos, L. (2016). Informal payments in the Greek health sector amid the financial crisis: Old habits die last. *The European Journal of Health Economics, 17*(2), 159–170.

The Czech Republic. (n.d.). http://www.dent.cz Accessed 1 Sept 2016.

Thomson, S., Cylus, J., & Evetovits, T. (2019). *Can people afford to pay for health care? New evidence on financial protection in Europe*. Copenhagen: World Health Organization Regional Office for Europe.

United Nations Office of Drugs and Crime. (2011). *Corruption in the western Balkans: Bribery as experienced by the population*. http://www.unodc.org. Accessed 1 July 2017.

Vlădescu, C., Scîntee, S. G., Olsavszky, V., Hernández-Quevedo, C., & Sagan, A. (2016). Romania: Health system review. *Health Systems in Transition, 18*(45), 1–170.

Vrangbaek, K. (2016). The Danish health care system, 2015. In E. Mossialos, M. Wenzl, R. Osborn, & D. Sornak (Eds.), *2015 international profiles of health care systems* (pp. 39–47). New York: The Commonwealth Fund.

Vuorenkoski, L. (2016). *Finland: Voluntary health insurance in Europe* (Observatory Studies Series, No. 42). http://www.nih.gov. Accessed 27 Apr 2018.

Vuorenkoski, L., Mladovsky, P., & Mossialos, E. (2008). Finland: Health system review. *Health Systems in Transition, 10*(4), 1–168.

Wammes, J., Jeurissen, P., & Westert, G. (2016). The Dutch health care system, 2015. In E. Mossialos, M. Wenzel, R. Osborn, & D. Sornak (Eds.), *2015 International profiles of health care systems* (pp. 115–122). New York: The Commonwealth Fund.

Williams, C. C., Horodnic, I. A., & Horodnic, A. V. (2016). Who is making informal payments for public healthcare in East-Central Europe? An evaluation of socio-economic and spatial variations. *Eastern Journal of European Studies, 7*(1), 49–61.

World Health Organization. Regional Office for Europe & European Observatory on Health Systems and Policies. (2000). *Health care systems in transition*. Lithuania: World Health Organization. Regional Office for Europe. https://apps.who.int/iris/handle/10665/108334. Accessed 29 Oct 2020.

Chapter 5
The Dental Squad

Dentists

The dental team was born in several Member States, particularly, in Finland and the United Kingdom, because of a scant workforce and a high level of disease. Development did not take place, for example, in Greece and Belgium, due to a perceived lack of necessity (Kravitz and Treasure 2007). As aforementioned, different regulatory approaches are found across the European Union (EU) in reference to members of the dental squad. Each dental care professional (DCP) group has a diverse scope of practice corresponding often to national legislation, and, as time passes, there have been changing boundaries between these clusters. Moreover, the formal composition of the dental team often varies from one Member State to another, as noted. In spite of this recognized diversity, the Council of European Dentists (2009) has officially held, as noted, that the leader of the dental squad with the sole role of diagnosis and treatment is the dentist.

According to the International Labour Organization's International Standard Classification of Occupations (ISCO 08 Code 2261), dentists, as the primary providers of oral health care, utilizing their acquired skills, "…diagnose, treat and prevent diseases, injuries and abnormalities of the teeth, mouth, jaws, and associated tissues. They restore oral function using a broad range of specialized diagnostic, surgical, and other techniques to promote and restore oral health"[1] (International Labour Organization 2012, p. 133). Many tasks relate to this charge of restoring and promoting oral health. These, among others, involve undertaking oral healthcare prevention, restoration, and surgical procedures; administering anesthetics; issuing pharmaceutical prescriptions; taking impressions; providing prosthodontic appliances, depending on the composition of the dental squad; engaging in the diagnosis of diseases with oral implications and patient education; and serving as the prime

[1] Copyright © International Labour Organization 2012.

S. Z. Koff, *The Dental Team in the European Union*,
https://doi.org/10.1007/978-3-030-72232-6_5

decision-maker and coordinator (International Labour Organization 2012; Rowbotham et al. 2009). In addition, these professionals can carry out all of the tasks within the scope of practice of each group in the dental squad.

Obviously, the number of dentists varies from Member State to Member State. However, databases often do not agree on the quantity in each EU nation. This is due to the procedures used in collecting and reporting the data. Unfortunately, there is not a uniform system. Dentists may be counted according to different groupings: practicing, professionally active, and licensed to practice. The first-named category designates those professionals that provide dental services to patients. The second group refers to those professionals that do not have direct contact with patients and may be involved in research, administration, the commercial world, etc. The third cluster concerns those that earned a dentistry degree and sought a license to practice. Then, there is the question of whether dentists in both the public and private sectors and hospital services are included in the count. Also, some professionals might possess more than one title. They could be registered more than once, but only use one title, if that, for their employment (Boyle 2011).

Some Member States provide databases information for individuals that are engaged in their profession, and others report data concerning those persons licensed to practice or who are professionally active (Healthcare personnel statistics 2016). The EU Open Data Portal asserts that data concerning dentists should only relate to those professionals that provide dental services directly to patients. These various matters impede cross-national comparisons. A uniform procedure should be developed and accepted by the Member States for purposes of cross-national and national policy development.

The number of professionals in each nation is contingent on many factors, some of which relate to the type of healthcare delivery system in a nation, the dentistry education program, population statistics, insurance type(s) and its (their) availability, etc. In 2015, approximately 345,000 dentists were practicing in the Member States (Dental Tribune International 2017). Germany claims the most practicing dentists in the EU. It is also the largest nation in terms of population (Ziller et al. 2015). Spain features a plethora of practicing dentists, but, as aforementioned, a *numerus clausus* does not exist, even though efforts have been made to obtain one. Also, it is noteworthy that of the number of dentists cited for Romania, 616 were also registered with the General Dental Council in the United Kingdom (Oancea et al. 2016). Such an occurrence could result from an overproduction of dentists which obviously impacts the employment environment. Duplicate registration offers additional opportunities. On the other hand, dentists are needed in other Member States, particularly in Scandinavia where it is claimed well-qualified dentists with experience are a necessity (Global migrants: Which are the most wanted professions? 2013).

Achieving the appropriate dentist-to-population ratio is a matter all nations must confront. Some Member States have too many dentists for their population and some too few. In terms of the number of practicing dentists per 100,000 inhabitants, Greece led the way in 2015 with 123, followed by Bulgaria and Cyprus with 105 and 103, respectively. Estonia (94), Portugal (91), and Lithuania (91) featured numbers in the 90s. Luxembourg (89), Germany (86), the Czech Republic (80), Sweden (80), and Croatia (80) displayed numerals in the 80s. Italy and Romania followed with 78 each, and Spain and Denmark each claimed 75. Belgium (74), Finland (72), and Latvia (72) also had units in the 70s. Those who featured figures in the 60s were Slovenia (67), France (64), Ireland (61), and Hungary (60). Austria (57), the United Kingdom (53), and the Netherlands (51) were linked in a group with numbers in the 50s. Slovakia (49), Malta (48), and Poland (33) found themselves at the bottom of the continuum.

In the Member States, the number of practicing dentists per 100,000 inhabitants, for the most part, was not greatly modified between 2010 and 2015. However, some nations improved their ratios. This occurred in Lithuania, Romania, Hungary, Italy, Spain, and Bulgaria, who gained 30%, 29%, 28%, 24%, 23%, and 13%, respectively. On the other hand, the opposite took place in Greece, Denmark, and France, each one of which experienced a 4% decline. In Cyprus, according to a commentator, the increased number of practicing dentists and the high dentist-to-population ratio raise concerns about the sustainability of the dental profession (Charalambous and Theodorou 2013). Bulgaria has had the highest density of dentists in Europe, approximately 25% higher than the EU average of 67 per 100,000 inhabitants. It is also noteworthy that Greece with its high dentist-to-population ratio has grave problems concerning access to oral health care (Damaskinos and Economou 2012; Damaskinos et al. 2016; Dimova et al. 2012; Koletsi-Kounari et al. 2011).

On the other hand, the Maltese ratio is below the EU average. Of note is the fact that the University of Malta, the one dentistry faculty in the nation, with its *numerus clausus* only admits eight dental students per year (Azzopardi-Muscat et al. 2017). The ratio in the United Kingdom, being only higher than that of the Netherlands, Slovakia, Malta, and Poland, has generated concern in light of the Brexit decision to withdraw from the EU. Almost 20% of the dentists registered with the General Dental Council in that area are from other Member States. The dentistry workforce is understaffed and could become more so depending on the terms of withdrawal from the EU. It is feared that many of these latter professionals could depart from the United Kingdom. A survey found that four of ten dentists trained in the EEA nations are open to moving elsewhere after Brexit is completed.

Women, in the last decades, have invaded the dentistry profession in the EU Member States. Medicine can lay claim to Elizabeth Blackwell and nursing to Florence Nightingale. Dentistry can do the same with Lucy Taylor Hobbes (1833–1910) and Henriette Hirschfeld (1834–1911). The former was the first American female graduate with a dentistry degree, and the latter claimed fame as the first female dentist in Germany. After these women made their mark, males, for a century, continued to compose a majority of the profession. Females were present, but in small numbers. Women's numbers continued to increase, and it was predicted that by 2020 the majority of all practicing dentists would be female (Parkash et al. 2006). In 2012, in Europe, more than 60% of dentists were women. The cited prediction has also already taken place in several Member States as well. These nations include Latvia (87%), Estonia (87%), Lithuania (83%), Poland (75%), Finland (69%), Romania (68%), Bulgaria (66%), Croatia (65%), Cyprus (65%), the Czech

Republic (65%), Slovenia (63%), Slovakia (61%), Hungary (57%), Portugal (57%), Spain (52%), and Sweden (52%) (ERO 2012; Kravitz et al. 2015; Malkiewicz et al. 2016).

The role of females was transformed, among other things, due to the rise of the women's liberation movement and women's rights organizations linked with birth control, which opened the gates to a professional career for women in dentistry and other professions. These factors allowed females to combine family and career. The modified demography of dentistry has raised discussion concerning work patterns, practice models, earnings, specialty education and practice, and professional leadership, to name some topics. Females might have acquired numbers, but, unfortunately, not power or authority within the workplace and the profession and its organs. Their impact on professional politics has been less than that of their male colleagues. The quantity of women in executive positions is limited. In addition, their access to dentistry subfields is of the same nature. Moreover, in the world of work, they are less likely than male professionals to own a practice. In terms of research, particularly in Spain, fewer projects are led by females, and the gender gap is even larger concerning funded projects (Gross and Schäfer 2011; del Mar García-Calvente et al. 2015).

Females in dentistry still have to pass through the so-called glass ceiling. Their role and position are distinguished from their male colleagues by demographic data, income, career patterns, retirement practice, and positions within professional structures and the workplace. In reference to the latter, the more senior the position, the larger the imbalance (Whelton and Wardman 2015). Female dentists still have to continue their battle. If they are successful, the profession will undergo more change. Dentistry, according to some researchers (Furtinger et al. 2013), will abandon its dominant technical approach in favor of one featuring communication and understanding. The promotion of health as well as preventive treatments and dental esthetics and cosmetics will continue to unfold. Furthermore, part-time employment, it is predicted, will become more popular. Twenty-five percent of the participants in a survey of women in dentistry in England worked part-time due to childcare problems. These issues presented a cause for stress for many female dentists. Moreover, 25% asserted they were planning to withdraw from the profession within the next 10 years for reasons other than retirement (Minford Chartered Accountants 2016).

In the Member States, dentists, when they are ready to face the world of work, have an ample field to explore that includes private or public practice, academia, a hospital staff, the military, employment in research or administrative positions, and those in the commercial world. In England, this field even contains a supermarket. More than 10 years ago, the United Kingdom was experiencing a dentistry crisis. To aid in its relief, the nation's first in-store dental clinic was opened. Shoppers were and are welcomed on a "first-come, first-served" basis. Checkups as well as general and cosmetic dentistry are available (DrBicuspid Staff 2008).

Diverse places for employment of the dental team have been indicated. Most recently, the European Dental Students' Association has expressed interest in the appearance of dental networks. Practice sharing and partnerships positively impact providers of services and patients. Benefits for the former include use of modern equipment without succumbing to large personal investment. Moreover, these professionals can procure flexible work agreements featuring lesser commitment than ownership of a solo practice. Patients, like DCPs, can enjoy a modern dentistry unit with confidence.

On the other hand, the student organization has a doubt related to these structures. Such practice chains account for a multitude of dentistry units, and the possibility of competing with them may no longer be an option. Their size and finances from external investors could lead to a management design in which patients do not rank number one. The European Regional Organisation of the International Dental Federation is of the same opinion (EDSA 2016).

After reviewing the nature of the healthcare delivery systems in the Member States, it is most surprising to discover that, for the most part, in the majority of these nations, dental practitioners work in independent practices. Private practice has been most attractive. It is possible to work shorter hours and also to set one's own work schedule. It has offered better wages as well as the opportunity to choose one's patients (Widström et al. 2009). In Cyprus, there has been higher productivity in private sector dentistry than that in the public sector (Charalambous et al. 2013). The exception is provided by Luxembourg which is unique. All dental practitioners must work for the State system, and thus, private or independent practice does not exist. In other systems, often private practitioners provide the bulk of dental consultations and oral healthcare treatments. In several Member States, such as Germany, Croatia, and the United Kingdom, private practitioners contract with the publicly funded system (Boyle 2011; Džakula et al. 2014; Ziller et al. 2015). However, in Slovenia, one cannot combine employment in a purely private practice with a public provider (Albreht et al. 2016).

In Austria, the government wants to replace independent dental offices with primary health centers occupied by more than a single practitioner. Moreover, it says the centers can be owned by investors, not necessarily, dental practitioners. The Austrian Dental Chamber does not view this transformation with favor and plans to formally oppose it.

Recently graduated dentists in the Netherlands were surveyed as to their employment hopes. The majority wanted to pursue a specialization and to own their practice. This notion was more prevalent among males than females. The concept of the dental team with delegation of tasks was heartedly accepted. In fact, respondents took the notion for granted (van Dam et al. 2009).

Academia for dentistry, as noted, has faced a recruiting challenge. A survey was undertaken (Goldacre et al. 2000), in the United Kingdom, to examine this problem. Participants were quite pleased with their employment. They enjoyed teaching and the variety of work in their careers. However, problems related to obtaining research funds and pressures resulting from service work, research, and teaching were disquieting. Several respondents preferred to allocate more time to research and less to service work and teaching. Also, they were concerned about the time needed for training and its quality. In addition, they were not satisfied with their amount of free time. In several Member States, dentists employed as academics, often with permission from their institution, can also work elsewhere, usually in a private practice.

The employment situation for dentistry has been uncertain and dismal in Greece, Spain, Germany, Italy, and Finland (Damaskinos et al. 2016; Dominguez 2012; Koletsi-Kounari et al. 2011). In these countries, the status of the profession is very prestigious, and production of these professionals is more than needed. Also, workforce planning presents difficult challenges. In Spain, in 2009, 24% of dentistry graduates went to other EU Member States to find employment. The percentage doubled in 6 years. Also, many dentists, as in 2012, find other employment, such as professors of foreign languages, dental hygienists, receptionists, and sales promoters (Dominguez 2012).

In Greece, students, who do not gain admission to Greek faculties, study abroad and return to Greece hoping to practice (Koletsi-Kounari et al. 2011). Unemployment is often the result. Employment is usually sought in the two largest urban areas and not where it is really needed. In fact, over 600 Greek dentists have been registered for practice in the United Kingdom (Damaskinos et al. 2016; Janulyte et al. 2014).

Lithuania presents another problem: an insufficient number of patients. Due to this situation, practitioners plan to work beyond retirement age and/or emigrate. The majority of these professionals work in the private sector (Janulyte et al. 2014).

In most Member States, the fees of dentists practicing in the private sector are freely determined by the providers themselves. Such occurs in the Czech Republic, Denmark, Hungary, Latvia, Slovenia, the United Kingdom, Sweden, the Netherlands, and Portugal with the intervention of the Portuguese Dental Association, to cite a few countries (Albreht et al. 2016; Alexa et al. 2015; Eaton et al. 2012a; Kravitz et al. 2014; Mitenbergs et al. 2012; Simões et al. 2017; Vrangbaek 2016). The Irish Dental Council's Code of Practice obliges dental practitioners to display their private fees in such a manner that patients can consult them before their appointment takes place.

Patients in most Member States exercise free choice of their primary care dentist and physician with minor exception. Wanting to know what factors influence selection of a dentist, a survey was completed in which participants were confronted with practitioner nationality, experience, and gender as each relates to selection of a provider of dental services (Swami et al. 2011). In terms of nationality, British was preferred over Eastern European. Female was favored over male as was much experience over moderate activity. The gender factor did not generally impact one's preferences. Important considerations in the choice of a dental practitioner are several. These relate to pain management and communication skills, qualifications, respect for patients' rights, fees, and being able to control stressful circumstances (Puriene et al. 2008).

Sometimes a challenge for dentists is juvenile anxiety related to a dental appointment. Evidently, one's apparel is important to a child in the creation of an amiable rapport. Research has focused on children's views in reference to dental practitioners' dress. The traditional white coat and name badge have been accepted along with the use of a plain mask and white gloves. Negative opinions have been assigned to protective eyewear and the use of caps. Also, approval has been given to wrist watches and closed shoes, but not to jewelry (Panda et al. 2014).

Gender-based assumptions, it has been found (Smith and Dundes 2008), do have an impact on the patient-dentist relationship. Evidently, female dentists are better communicators, more likely to take the time needed to discuss matters, and less likely to manifest the power and authority of their profession, and they are generally more amiable and understanding.

Nowadays, emphasis has been placed on a preventive approach to dentistry. It is interesting that in a recent British survey (Yusuf et al. 2015), participants demonstrated limited knowledge of important matters related to preventive care, but their attitude toward the concept was most positive. Younger and female practitioners were more likely to engage in a range of preventive activities than their older and male colleagues. Moreover, many respondents claimed to have undertaken preventive measures, but certain organizational factors, such as time pressures, insufficient remuneration, as well as poor patient compliance, presented barriers.

Service provider evaluations via the Internet have become common procedures across Europe. While such opinions may be useful to diverse parties, the Council of European Dentists (2014) has expressed some concerns related to the lack of control over websites that would guarantee that the facts provided are fair and accurate. Suggestions were offered to protect the abuse of online evaluations and the parties involved. National dental associations were urged to develop implementation mechanisms. It so happens that there is usually concordance between the patient's degree of satisfaction and the dentist's perspective. In cases of dissatisfaction with practitioners, she/he was not always aware of this possible evaluation. Such means that these professionals should be cognizant of the methods that patients utilize to evaluate services (Riley et al. 2014).

There are several factors that impinge on a dental practitioner's performance. These influence job satisfaction as well as the quality of clinical work undertaken. They include gender, health of the practitioner, smoking engagement, use of drugs and alcohol, psychological factors, education and training, work-related elements, and the country's leadership in dentistry, to cite a few.

As aforementioned, females have permeated the dental profession across the EU. Gender differences are reflected in career patterns. Women are more likely to work part-time and to take advantage of career breaks, mainly for family reasons. An early study indicated that only one-half of female practitioners returned to their profession after such an interruption. Female communication skills have been found to be superior, and there are significant differences between male and female dentists in reference to psychomotor performance and cognitive function. In addition, there is diversity in leadership style. For both genders, back, neck, shoulder, and hand/wrist aches, as well as other types of maladies, such as mental health issues that are work-related, have a significant impact on their performance. As with any occupation, personality and other individual characteristics relate to performance. Of vital significance are flexibility and the capacity to react to change. As noted, continuing professional development (CPD) contributes to the enhancement of the practitioner's skills and keeping them up-to-date. The work environment, its culture and available support, and formal and informal professional networks, including the chemistry of the dental team, all have a role in the dentist's performance. Influential factors are multiple (NHS, National Patient Safety Agency, and National Clinical Assessment Service 2011).

Dental Hygienists and Dental Hygienists-Therapists

In 1913, in the United States, in Bridgeport, Connecticut, a new profession was born with the creation of the first educational program for dental hygienists by Dr. Alfred C. Fones. The same activity was initiated on the European stage in Norway in 1924. It continued, thereafter, to be repeated in several countries. Dental hygienists, whose professional activities were transformed since the profession's birth from a concentration on the prevention of caries to the rapport between oral and general health and well-being (Jongbloed-Zoet et al. 2012), are important members of the oral healthcare squad.

Basically, these DCPs carry out preventive and prophylactic services, as well as oral health education for individuals of all ages defined as "all the educational activities directed to patients, including aspects of therapeutic education, health education and clinical health promotion" (Visser et al. 2001, p. 4). As aforementioned, this profession is not recognized across the Member States. In one such nation, France, half of the dental practitioners are attempting to change the law. The other half is of the opinion that hygienists are costly and that they themselves can better perform hygiene activities (O'Hehir n.d.).

Once again, diversity becomes the principal descriptor associated with a dental care profession, not only in terms of recognition but also in reference to scope of practice and other factors. Some Member States do not regulate dental hygienists, as noted. Others regulate their activities always under the supervision of a dentist, and still others allow fully autonomous practice. Also, Member States have differed as to additional requirements, such as those concerned with liability insurance, as well as the conditions for reimbursement of dental hygiene services. In some cases, a dentist's prescription is needed. Some basic diversities between the Member States in terms of dental hygienists' permitted activities relate to dental prescription, dental supervision, radiographs, administration of local anesthesia, independent practice, and direct access.

In some Member States, such as Germany, Hungary, Ireland, Italy, Latvia, Lithuania, Malta, Poland, Portugal, Slovakia, and Spain, dental hygienists work under clinical supervision, that of a dentist. In Poland and Spain, the physical presence of the dentist on site is required when the dental hygienist is carrying out professional activities (Eaton et al. 2012b; European Commission 2016). The Czech Republic had this requisite as well. However, after 7 years of negotiation, these professionals, in 2018, received permission to work without oversight (The Czech Republic 2018). In the Nordic Member States, Denmark, Finland, and Sweden, and in the United Kingdom, the Netherlands, and Slovenia as well, dental hygienists are permitted to work autonomously. In a few cases, these DCPs must work only under prescription of a dentist, as in Ireland, Italy, and Spain. In Lithuania, dental hygienists may diagnose and plan treatment for patients under a dentist's prescription (Eaton et al. 2012b; European Commission 2016).

In some Member States, these professionals are permitted to take radiographs. In Ireland, this is possible, if one has completed a radiography course approved by the Irish Dental Council. However, it is reported that there is no validation of this training. Panoramic radiographs may be taken by these DCPs in the Netherlands, provided that appropriate training has been received and the professional is in possession of a dentist's prescription. The same holds for Poland. In Slovakia, one needs permission from the Public Health Authority of the Slovak Republic. Dental hygienists in Denmark, Finland, and the United Kingdom may take radiographs as well (Eaton et al. 2012b).

Local anesthesia may only be administered by these DCPs, in Austria and the Czech Republic with permission of the dentist. On the other hand, such administration may take place by injection or infiltration in the Netherlands. In the United Kingdom, use of local and nerve block analgesia is allowed, and in Denmark, Finland, Lithuania, Sweden, and Ireland, dental hygienists may deliver local anesthesia. In the last mentioned Member State, this may be done only under the direct supervision of a dentist. When dental hygienists treat patients under conscious sedation or general anesthesia in Ireland and Malta, a dentist must be present throughout the entire treatment (Eaton et al. 2012b). It is most obvious that several EU members are absent from this list.

There are certain practices that are common to this DCP's role in most Member States. These activities relate to patient examination; dental hygiene treatment planning; cleaning and polishing of teeth; scaling; topical application of appropriate medicaments, solutions, varnishes, gels, and fissure sealants; tasks of re-cementing; and oral hygiene education. These activities are congruent with the five competence domains of the dental hygienist which are (1) professionalism, ethics, and communication; (2) knowledge base and information literacy; (3) primary prevention, oral health promotion and the prevention of oral diseases; (4) secondary prevention, screening, clinical examination, diagnosis, and treatment planning; and (5) secondary and tertiary prevention, therapy and maintaining oral health (European Dental Hygienists Federation 2016).

As noted, specifics related to professional activities vary across the EU. Finnish academics have assessed the role of dental hygienists. They were of the opinion that these professionals should be more active in the field of orthodontics and preventive care. In terms of the latter, they envisioned a role related to tobacco use and nutrition. Basically, the new role of dentistry and that of these professionals were not congruent (Virtanen et al. 2016). It is interesting that an extended scope of practice for dental hygienists in a literature review was viewed positively by a majority of dentists and members of the hygiene profession. However, independent dental hygiene practice was opposed by a majority of dentists and, as one would expect, favored by the same amount of dental hygienists (Reinders et al. 2017). It is obvious that this DCP's scope of practice throughout the EU is not congruent with the recent policy of the International Federation of Dental Hygienists, which reads:

> The IFDH supports dental hygienists as health care professionals who are key providers of primary oral health care preventive and maintenance services. Dental hygienists may work autonomously and participate with interdisciplinary health care teams to provide total health care to the public across the life span. (International Federation of Dental Hygienists 2019)

It is noteworthy that a more autonomous scope of practice for dental hygienists has had a positive impact on individuals' oral health (Langelier et al. 2016).

A Finnish study of dental hygienists' willingness to undertake new treatment measures found these professionals receptive to the notion of performing new procedures related to orthodontics, local anesthesia, clinical photographing, glass-ionomer and composite fillings, and tooth bleaching. Obstacles to doing so were their perceived incompetency, the homogeneity of their patients, and the traditional method of delegating tasks in their places of employment. The environment in their workplace had a significant impact on their attitude toward undertaking new treatment procedures, as one would expect (Virtanen et al. 2011). The activities of any profession must be congruent with the nature of the broader field. After all, times change and professions, like any individual, must be flexible. In the same vein, research (Hach et al. 2017) has revealed that Danish dental hygienists are carrying out a broader range of activities that include many traditional duties of a dentist. Curricula and CPD programs must reflect such transformations.

In the Netherlands, the Minister of Health is experimenting with the dental hygienist profession for a period of 5 years with the hope of bettering its efficiency and effectiveness. These professionals have permission to undertake all treatments except restricted ones (administering local anesthesia, ordering and taking radiographs, and treatment of primary cavities) that require a dentist's prescription. After the 5-year experiment, new regulations might be advanced. Dutch dentists, in general, do not have a favorable opinion of this change. Meanwhile, the Dutch Dental Hygienists Association is busy developing training to acquire the necessary skills for a possible new scope of practice.

Dental hygienists can take advantage of multiple possible places of employment. Included in these possibilities are independent practice which, as noted, is permitted in some Member States, general or specialized dental practices, hospitals or other healthcare institutions, schools, nursing homes, prisons, dental care-related organizations, academia, the armed services, research structures, social health services, special needs agencies, and the commercial world, to name some facilities. These professionals may be self-employed and an employer, in some cases, an employee, or a freelancer. They may choose between the public and private sectors, a full-time or part-time position, and the roles of clinician, educator, administrator, and consultant. In theory, the possibilities are many. Unfortunately, reality sometimes differs.

For example, in the Netherlands, dental hygienists may engage in independent practice with direct access. However, challenges exist. Supervision and a written prescription are obligatory for radiography, as aforementioned. Further obstacles are evident that impinge on periodontal and restorative activities, some of which again require a written prescription. Furthermore, a dental hygienist is not allowed to own an X-ray machine. Needless to say, self-employment without being able to freely undertake radiographs is an enormous problem (Slot 2013). Also, of note is the fact that a significant complaint among Portuguese dental hygienists is the lack of employment and other opportunities for young members of this profession (Araújo 2013).

Basically, dental therapy is a subset of dental care as is dental hygiene. Members of both professions claim a double role. One relates to clinical activities and the other to those that are health promotional. In addition to being able to assume dental hygienists' responsibilities because of the combined educational programs in some places, dental therapists can also perform some restorations, install preformed crowns, and undertake pulp treatments in deciduous teeth. These professionals are able to offer the basic dental care that a dentist does. Their work includes patient examination, diagnosis, design of treatment plans, radiography, oral health education, preventive services, taking impressions, tooth whitening, preparation of cavities in primary and permanent teeth, restorative services, and tooth extraction under local infiltration analgesia. Currently, the British Society of Dental Hygiene and Therapy and the British Association of Dental Therapy are in the process of applying for prescribing rights with exemptions. For many years patients of these professionals were children and adolescents, but now, they include adults as well (Nash et al. 2012; Rowbotham et al. 2009).

Like dental hygienists, dental therapists may be employed in diverse settings. In fact, the list for both professions is the same. Dental therapists are especially used in the Netherlands and the United Kingdom. There are also orthodontic therapists. As is evident from the name of this professional title, the individual works in orthodontics and undertakes certain treatments via the prescription of an orthodontist. In Ireland, all work performed by this professional must be inspected and approved by the orthodontist before the patient is discharged from the practice. Research has noted that the quality of orthodontic treatment has not been modified since the introduction of these professionals (Rooney et al. 2016).

It has been suggested that much of the work in a general dental practice is of the type that can be delegated to dental therapists. If such happened and more was assigned to these DCPs, it has been asserted that the cost savings would be enormous. An increase in the number of dental team members would be necessary. Moreover, with such a role enhancement, only about 30% of the present-day registered dentists would be needed (Nash et al. 2012; Wanyonyi et al. 2015). Research has revealed that when tasks have been delegated to these professionals, patients' views have been most positive (Dyer et al. 2013).

Of note is that dental therapists' patients in the United Kingdom have manifested a significantly higher level of satisfaction than patients treated by dentists. Moreover, the quality of their technical care has been found to be comparable to that of dental practitioners and, in some cases, superior. This same positive attitude has been reconfirmed. It has also been aligned with trust due to treatment delegation. Research involving a test for the accuracy of therapists' screening for dental diseases affirmed their competency. Needless to say, such an outcome has significant implications for the dental service arrangements of healthcare systems, especially the public ones (Macey et al. 2015).

Not all practices in the Member States that recognize the dental hygienist and the dental therapist include these DCPs in their staffs. As noted, some dental practitioners are convinced that these DCPs are too costly. Furthermore, some believe that they can better perform their functions. It is noteworthy that prices, especially for routine dental hygiene services, are lower than those for restoration. Thus, when a dental practitioner provides hygiene procedures, practice production declines. Moreover, a large percentage (40–85%) of dentist appointments fixed in a practice result from its dental hygienist (O'Hehir n.d.).

A major advantage of including one or both of these DCPs in the staff of a dental office is that access to it and oral health care are generally enhanced for children, adolescents, and adults, many of whom come from underserved groups and communities. It has been found that both the dental hygienist and the dental therapist promote greater access to and utilization of oral healthcare services. They not only promote these items, but they see results. Furthermore, patient satisfaction is high, as aforementioned, and dental anxiety is low among their patients (Turner et al. 2012). Having these DCPs among practice personnel offering high-quality, safe, and cost-effective care also allows for task delegation. It affords the dentist more time to focus on complex dental procedures and to increase income. Dental hygienists and dental therapists represent a win-win situation for all—professionals, consumers, and societies (Koppelman et al. 2016; O'Hehir n.d.; Slot 2013).

Chair-Side Assistants/Dental Nurses

The dental chair-side assistant/dental nurse is another member of the dental team whose responsibilities relate to primary prevention, organization of the practice, and offering support and assistance to the dentist and dental hygienist (Nash et al. 2012). This assistance aids in preventive, diagnostic, and therapeutic procedures. More specifically, this DCP helps the dentist in the four-hand method of delivering dental care and usually works under her/his supervision. In Ireland, if this figure has completed a dental radiography course, the taking of radiographs, according to a dentist's prescription, is permitted. This person usually prepares the patient for treatment, assists during treatment, and, after it has taken place, is responsible for preparing the office for the next dental procedure. Obviously, these tasks involve infection control activities, such as sterilization of instruments and equipment. Also, this professional participates in oral health promotion activities and assumes administrative and clerical tasks, as well (Education and Culture DG 2006; European Commission 2016).

In some Member States, dentists are required to exercise their profession working with a chair-side assistant/dental nurse. This takes place in Poland, Hungary, and Slovakia (Eaton et al. 2012b). Also, this profession's growth in Scotland in recent years is noteworthy. In a 5-year period, it experienced more than a 65% increase in its numbers. A similar augment in quantity took place in the dental technician profession (Dental nurse boom in Scotland 2013).

Dental Technicians and Clinical Dental Technicians

Although the dental technician, sometimes referred to as a dental craftsman, dental mechanic, or dental technologist, is not a part of the practice staff of the dental squad, this DCP is formally a member. She/he designs, prepares, modifies, and repairs dental prostheses, using appropriate products, techniques, and procedures, upon prescription of a dentist or, in some cases, a denturist or clinical dental technician. The dental devices this figure produces include inlays, crowns, onlays or partial crowns, bridges, full or partial dentures, veneers, space maintainers, retainers, and labial or lingual arch wires, and other items. This DCP also undertakes various technical repairs and restorations of prostheses constructions. Basically, the products of their activities aid dental patients' speech and chewing facility as well as their appearance. In carrying out their activities, dental technicians adopt a wide range of materials, such as gold, porcelain, plastic, and so forth.

Dental technicians do not engage in direct contact with patients (An Comhairle Fiaclóireachta 2010). However, in some Member States, such as Finland and the United Kingdom, they may have direct contact with the public concerning the repair of dentures. Also, in the United Kingdom, these DCPs are permitted to work with patients alongside a dentist or denturist. The International Federation of Denturists is not content with the fact that dental technicians are restricted from communicating with consumers. In a policy statement, it asserted that their activities depending solely "on the instructions of a go-between is inefficient and frustrating to all concerned and the Patient is often the ultimate loser. It is comparable to an Artist trying to capture someone's portrait on canvas, without meeting the subject personally" (IFD policy statement n.d.).

Dental technicians work usually in dental laboratories in either the public or private sector. In some nations to own a laboratory, this DCP requires additional training. Other possibilities for employment include educational institutions or research structures. Hospitals also provide a workplace for dental technicians that work on maxillofacial products. In this setting, their work takes place in oral surgery, ophthalmic, cancer, and burn units and aiding in the reconstruction of patients' faces impaired by disease and accidents.

Clinical dental technicians or denturists are also known as dental prosthetists, clinical dental technologists, or special dental technicians. They are assigned diverse names in the Member States. In Belgium, they are known as dental prosthetist-denturists; in France, as denturologists; in the Netherlands, as dental prostheticians; and in the United Kingdom, as clinical dental technicians (Education Committee 2016). Their work consists of that of dental technicians and more. These professionals provide independent prosthetic services directly to the patient without the dentist as an intermediary. Their responsibilities are "broadly defined as the practice of construction, supplying and fitting dentures where both chairside and dental laboratory work are performed by one and the same person, specifically qualified and authorized for the purpose" (Benchmark identity of denturists n.d.). In addition, they also screen patients for oral diseases and, if necessary, refer them to an appropriate source.

Such work generally relates to the planning of treatment, as well as the design, construction, fitting, and modification of removable prosthetic devices. The latter include full, partial, flexible, and immediate dentures; implant supported over-dentures; metal frames, substructures, and special attachments; oral protectors; mouth guards and bleaching trays; as well as sleep apnea and anti-snoring units (Benchmark identity of denturists n.d.). All constructed items must meet EU standards. Manufactured mechanisms are now governed by new regulations on medical devices that cancelled existing directives on the topic. The two new documents are Regulation (EU) 2017/745 and Regulation (EU) 2017/746. These new rules that relate to the health and safety of the public will be fully implemented at the end of a transition period that is 3 years after entry into force for the former regulation and 5 years for the latter. Both frameworks entered into force immediately after their passage.

Some clinical dental technicians have mobile denture clinics. Thus, they are able to serve folks restricted to home, those in hospitals and other structures, as well as residents in isolated communities. Generally, denturists work in denture clinics, and their dominant patient group consists of the elderly. However, they also treat the young. For example, in Ireland, these professionals are allowed to treat patients 18 years of age and over, provided the task does not include any action on natural teeth or living tissue. This limitation is not unusual. Scopes of practice for denturists distinguish between adjustment and alteration to natural teeth and tissues of the mouth (Denturism: An overview n.d.).

Relations between the denturist profession and that of dentistry have been, for the most part, quite unfriendly. The historically defined profession and that with an emerging role have not generally had good relations. The two professions have viewed each other as adversaries. Principal squabbles have concerned standards, patient care, and control. Dentists tend to view denturists as professional encroachers, according to denturist literature that contains strong criticism of organized dentistry. It is also noted that dentists are quick to accept referrals from denturists that more than offset any potential loss of revenue from treating fewer denture patients. Studies have confirmed that Finnish dental practitioners did not experience decreased income due to the introduction of denturism. Instead, they were recompensed as a result of denturists' patient referrals (Benchmark identity of denturists n.d.).

An editorial in the newsletter of the International Federation of Denturists was entitled "I have a dream," meaning, hopefully, this conflict will be resolved. It was noted that the dream has been achieved in Denmark, Finland, Ireland, the Netherlands, and the United Kingdom. These are the nations that have formally recognized the denturist profession. Now, Belgium, after an effort that took 41 years, should be included in this list. Also, the editorial asked why other members of the dental squad are not accused of illegal practice for undertaking some of the same treatments as dentists. The response was that these DCPs are responsible for services that enlarge a dentist's revenue, and instead, denturists are viewed as competitors. In encouraging a future role of collaboration between the two professions, denturists note that dentists' care activities relate to natural teeth and diseases of the mouth, whereas denturists' functions focus on dentures (Denturism: An overview n.d.; IFD 2017; Malherbe 2016). There is a difference.

Dentistry, it is claimed, represents the only organized opposition to denturism worldwide (Malherbe 2014). Yet, this profession offers advantages to both the consumer and the dental practitioner. For the former, it is most convenient not to have to deal with a go-between. Also, the patient's area of choice of providers is enlarged. For the latter, as other members of the dental squad, denturists relieve the burden of a dentist. They afford this individual more time to deal with complex problems, especially those that lie only in the realm of this practitioner. Furthermore, with referrals, the name of a practice is spread, and its patient list realizes a contribution.

Staff Health Precautions

Oral healthcare workers may be exposed to and transmit many diseases. Exercising a healthcare profession brings one into contact with the world of pathogens which carries a risk for the practitioner as well as other people. Thus, some Member States undertake health precautions via inoculations for personnel in the dental squad. This activity reduces the possibility that a person will become infected and transmit the pathogens to other individuals, particularly, patients. In fact, in some Member States, certain vaccinations are mandatory for healthcare workers. The most common obligatory one is Hepatitis B. This inoculation is required in some nations that include Belgium, Croatia, the Czech Republic, France, Hungary, Latvia, Malta, the Netherlands, Romania, Slovakia, Slovenia, and the United Kingdom. In addition, in the Czech Republic, DCPs are to be regularly screened for seroconversion. Other inoculations are included in the French requirement. These relate to diphtheria, tetanus, and poliomyelitis (Eaton et al. 2012a; Kravitz et al. 2015).

In some Member States, inoculations are merely recommended. Such occurs in the case of hepatitis B and other vaccinations in Austria, Ireland, Italy, Lithuania, Luxembourg, Poland, Portugal, Spain, and Sweden. The Irish recommendation only applies to general dental practitioners and hospital dentists. The Italian Minister of Health's recommendation concerns the influenza vaccine and that for measles, mumps, rubella, and varicella. In Lithuania, DCPs, in addition to the suggested vaccinations, are to undergo an annual physical examination and to be checked for seroconversion, as well. Hepatitis B is only recommended in Poland, but for dental students, it is obligatory (Kravitz et al. 2014, 2015).

The need for inoculations has been recognized at the European level. The Council in 2009 asserted that a healthcare worker influenza vaccination rate of 75% would be desirable. It was never reached (Betsch 2014). In spite of formal encouragements, promotion campaigns, and the effectiveness of influenza inoculations, the rate of coverage among European healthcare workers has never exceeded 25%. A complete, detailed set of statistics covering the Member States regarding vaccinations of oral healthcare workers or, for that matter, of healthcare workers, in general, does not exist.

Studies indicate that in Germany, the largest number of healthcare workers has decided not to receive an influenza inoculation. The same reaction was found among their Italian colleagues. It appears that, if a vaccine or vaccines are only recommended, the coverage rate is usually assumed to be quite low. In the aforementioned German study of healthcare workers, 70% of the participants claimed that they would accept a vaccination, if it were obligatory. That should open the eyes of policy-makers. Strategies, other than a recommendation, need to be implemented (Alicino et al. 2015; Fortunato et al. 2015; Gilardi et al. 2018; Prato et al. 2010; Wicker and Rabenau 2010).

In most Member States, the influenza inoculation is recommended for healthcare workers. However, unfortunately, exact measurement of its coverage does not automatically happen. It is believed that little or no progress is taking place in healthcare workers' vaccination programs. Coverage, based on what is known, is quite low (European Commission 2014). The EU Commissioner for Health and Food Safety in October 2018 reported that a new study (Larson et al. 2018) has demonstrated that confidence in vaccinations has declined. Four of the ten countries with the lowest vaccine confidence globally are Member States (France, Greece, Italy, and Slovenia), and Poland and Sweden serve as examples of how quickly confidence can decrease. The lowest confidence levels globally are found in Europe. If DCPs are skeptical, the attitude of the general population is not surprising. The EU Commission, earlier in 2018 (April), announced several recommendations to counteract vaccine hesitancy and to enhance inoculation coverage. Prominent among the recommendations were calls for the development of national and/or regional vaccination plans by 2020 and for cooperation and coordination on the matter among the Member States. Also cited in the noted study is the necessity for statistics on the subject, continuous monitoring systems, and the exchange of best practices. Hopefully, such activities will improve the present situation.

Cross-Border Care and Indemnity Insurance

As aforementioned, in these days, societies are becoming more litigious, and more attention is being devoted to patients and their rights. The matter of cross-border health care became a part of EU debate. EU citizens have engaged in seeking health care, as well as oral health care, in Member States other than their own. To ensure access to safe care of superior quality, according to Directive 2011/24/EU, Member States are to guarantee systems of professional liability insurance or a similar arrangement that is equivalent or essentially comparable as regards its purpose and which is appropriate to the nature and the extent of the risk for treatment provided on its territory (Directive 2011/2/EU, Article 4(2)(d)). The requirements of this important provision allow any patient experiencing damage in one form or another from cross-border treatment to seek a remedy.

Prior to the passage of this document, across the Member States, some oral healthcare professionals, but not all, had indemnity insurance to cover them at their place of employment. However, with this directive, all healthcare professionals must have coverage. This has become an EU universal legal requirement that meets the requisites of the cited provision. In the United Kingdom, in order to ensure effectiveness of provision as well as efficiency, coverage has become a requisite of registration for all healthcare professionals. The cited EU legislation also provided for medicinal prescriptions issued in a Member State to be recognized in another one. The same applied to medical devices. This directive represented empowerment for patients.

All Member States were to transpose this cited document into national law by 25 October 2013. However, many did not meet this deadline. Infringement proceedings were initiated against 26 Member States because of late or incomplete notification of transposition (European Commission 2015). Most of these procedures have finally been settled. As a result of this directive, patients' mobility and safety are now ensured. Collaboration on health care, including oral care, across the Member States is promoted, and the responsibility for its organization still lies with the individual Member States.

Direct Access

As noted, team dentistry varies across the EU. In some Member States, such as the Netherlands and Denmark, the concept is well developed and in others, less so, due mainly to the lack of recognition of some auxiliary personnel. Also, as is evident in this discussion, some DCPs in some Member States enjoy a broader scope of practice. Furthermore, patients have free access to some members of the dental squad in several nations, as in Denmark, Finland, the Netherlands, Sweden, and the United Kingdom.

Seven years following the introduction of direct access to dental hygienists in the Netherlands and an enlargement in their scope of practice, a research project focused on perceptions of the policy. It concluded that positive working relationships between dentists and dental hygienists existed within integrated practices and opinions toward independent ones with free access were mixed. There were instances of practices working collaboratively, but unfortunately, relations between the professional associations were found not to be smooth and harmonious. In England, as well, support was found for an integrated model of dentists and hygienists working together (Northcott et al. 2013).

Research concerning the consequences of direct access to treatment by DCPs has been most positive. Patient safety was not found to be endangered, and overall access to dental care, especially for under-served populations, was enhanced. Moreover, patient satisfaction was found to be at a higher level than that for dentists' patients, and dental anxiety was lower. The black mark consisted of the fact that DCPs may over-refer to dentists, but better too many referrals than restraining patient safety and appropriate treatment. Direct access affords DCPs an opportunity to work to their full remit, and thus, it also contributes to job satisfaction (Turner et al. 2012).

Skill Mix and Human Resources Planning

The right number of professionals possessing the right skills must be in the right place to provide the right services at the right time. Thus, planning of the oral healthcare team is of prime importance. Unfortunately, Member States have not received good grades for their planning efforts related to the dental team. Some nations, such as Austria, Bulgaria, Croatia, the Czech Republic, Estonia, Greece, and Portugal, it is claimed, do not have solid planning frameworks in place (Alexa et al. 2015; Džakula et al. 2014; Hofmarcher and Quentin 2013; Katrova and Tzokov 2013; Koletsi-Kounari et al. 2011; Lai et al. 2013; Simões et al. 2017). There is no accord on a definite methodology and technique for oral healthcare planning. The literature points to an integrated approach that combines elements of supply and demand (Lopes et al. 2015).

In addition, there are problems of data availability and performance assessment of the system (Matrix Insight 2012). The EU Commission has established an Expert Group on the latter topic to aid Member States with the identification of appropriate tools and methodologies to assess system performance. In addition, it also sponsors a collaborative project with most Member States, international organizations, and healthcare federations on human resources planning and forecasting. It also confronted workforce planning challenges with its Support for Health Workforce Planning and Forecasting Expert Network established in 2017 and its Joint Action Health Workforce Planning and Forecasting Program created earlier.

Reliable methodologies and standardized data are necessary for favorable human resources planning. Harmonized data collection concerned with all DCPs is a necessity. Some factors to be considered relate to their practice designs, preparation in terms of their formation and continuing education, regulation of their profession, and opinions concerning work conditions (Yamalik et al. 2013, 2014). Also, it must be remembered that providers of services and populations are becoming older. Workforce planning is of the utmost importance.

Teamwork

The Council of European Dentists (2009) in a resolution endorsed the notion of delegation of dental tasks by the dentist to qualified professionals, but not the act of substitution. The dentist is to provide instructions along with the act of delegation, and she/he is to monitor all activity. Also, of importance is that the patient is to be notified that a task has been delegated. Delegation is a significant concept for the simple reason research (Cowpe et al. 2013) has demonstrated that approximately 60% of clinical time is devoted to tasks that could be carried out by dental hygienists and dental therapists. The former professionals can increase daily practice productivity by 33% and the latter by 45%.

The individual fields of dental squad members represent a science and an art. However, being a successful DCP team member requires more than possession of knowledge and skills of a particular profession. It is important to construct positive relationships with patients and all members within the dental team. This means the chemistry of the DCP's squad, like that of any sports team, must be developed. Superior leadership which falls on the dentist's shoulders is required. Each professional involved with a dental patient's treatment must comprehend her/his problem(s), needs, attitudes, values, and expectations. Furthermore, an involved DCP must understand her/his role in the treatment as well as that of other members of the dental team. These should be communicated directly to the patient.

Research has indicated that oral healthcare professionals who studied and trained together have a better comprehension of each other's scope of practice and are better prepared for teamwork. Interprofessional communication among team members and between them and the patient are most significant. It affects the performance of the team as well as the satisfaction of the patient. A team's performance has been linked to its interpersonal relationships, organizational conditions, and the unit's systemic environment (Hamasaki et al. 2017; San Martin-Rodriguez et al. 2005; Wanyonyi et al. 2014).

Unmet Oral Healthcare Needs

All of the EU citizenry, unfortunately, does not enjoy equal access to dental care. This situation is not solely due to low supply measures. To a large extent, these people are elderly and include those with special needs. These folks might have physical limitations, developmental problems, medical complications, or cognitive impairment. Their difficulties are not merely associated with staff shortages and practice closures. They are faced with multiple challenges that include financial worries; communication difficulties related to comprehension due to psychosocial issues, such as sparse oral health literacy, negative dental encounters, and dental anxiety; as well as dental personnel who are not trained to work with these patients (Singh 2017).

In spite of the value of the dental team's approach to dentistry, particularly in reference to quality of care, patient safety, and enlargement of access, in 2016, some 5.6% of the EU's population over age 16 reported unmet dental care needs. The cited percentage was greater than that for unmet medical care necessities. Percentages ranged from 1% of the Austrian population to 15% of Greek inhabitants. In other Member States, such as Bulgaria, Croatia, Latvia, Poland, Romania, and Sweden, those lacking access to oral health care have accounted for over 10% of the population. The dental situation was due principally to financial reasons. The cost of dental care was too expensive for almost two-thirds of all those who reported unmet dental needs. These financial obstructions include user charges and informal or "under-the-table" payments. Transportation problems and long waiting times for appointments were also to blame. Other reported reasons included lack of time, service exclusions, hoped the problem would resolve itself, and no knowledge of a good dentist. Most people experiencing unmet dental needs were middle-aged (45–64 years old) (Cylus and Papanicolas 2015).

It is generally recognized that inequalities in the distribution of professional practitioners serve as a barrier to healthcare services, including those related to dentistry. This maldistribution obstructs equity. It is difficult to imagine, but in Portugal, 30 municipalities or 20% of the total number recently did not claim a registered dentist (Ordem Dos Médicos Dentistas 2014). There are also inequalities across socioeconomic and geographical groups. In Greece and other Member States, there is a noticeable linkage between income and use of dental services. Folks with abundant income have a greater opportunity to utilize dental services (Damaskinos and Economou 2012). On the other hand, in Cyprus, Estonia, and Latvia, the amount of out-of-pocket payments, especially in relation to dental care, impacts greatly on those with lower socioeconomic status (Cylus and Papanicolas 2015; Lai et al. 2013). Large inequities in unmet dental care needs between high- and low-income groups have existed in Belgium, Denmark, Greece, the Netherlands, Portugal, and Spain, as well as in other Member States (Cylus and Papanicolas 2015; Koletsi-Kounari et al. 2011; Murauskiene et al. 2013).

Discrimination also accounts for failure of access to oral health care. For example, people in France earning a low income have had the privilege of a social assistance program that they could use for dental care. A study (Pegon-Machat et al. 2009) of French dentists' relationship with these patients, based on interviews, revealed two categories: good patients and bad patients. The latter featured irregular attendance, and thus, many dentists decided eventually to no longer serve these people. In another study (Lacharpagne et al. 2014), 39% of French dentists refused to treat persons who receive social assistance. This practice is contrary to the rules in some Member States and to many codes of ethics.

The level of one's education is also important in terms of a barrier to dental services. Usually, this relates to socioeconomic status and health literacy, as well. Other personal factors enter into the picture, as in Belgium. Social health inequalities in dental visits are impacted by low level of education, low household income, and being a smoker. Barriers also differ among age groups (Talla et al. 2013). It is noteworthy that, not too long ago, a Spanish research project concluded that there were no social inequalities found in the utilization of healthcare services, excluding dental care (Font-Ribera et al. 2014).

Studies have confirmed that DCPs lack training particularly, in special care dentistry. Students have reported a lack of confidence when treating patients requiring such care and also a lack of hands-on clinical training in the field. Recent literature reveals the same conclusion (Yeaton et al. 2016). Consequently, many institutions that train DCPs have incorporated special care dentistry into their curricula. A multitude of learning outcomes and skills can be transferred across the professional training course (Dougall et al. 2014). Hopefully, such efforts will lead to equal access to dental care for all vulnerable groups.

The Platform for Better Oral Health in Europe has expressed concern with social inequalities and their impact on dental services. This organization is a collaborative venture of the Association for Dental Education in Europe, the Council of European

Chief Dental Officers, the European Association of Dental Public Health, and the European Dental Health Foundation. The structure seeks a harmonized approach to access better oral health care among other things. Its activities reflect its beliefs. It has concluded that financial resources should be congruent with health needs, services should be affordable to all, well-equipped facilities should be within easy reach, an appropriate workforce should be in place, quality medicines and devices should be available at fair prices, services should be accessible to all populations, and people should be able to use them when they are needed (Better Oral Health: European Platform 2015).

The EU has also been involved with the concern related to inequities in access to oral health care. It has noted that within the Member States, financial barriers to access are the major cause of unmet needs. It has also emphasized that policy responses to the problem should reflect its multi-dimensional nature, the significance of intersectoral efforts, as well as the specifics of the particular national and regional contexts (European Commission Expert Panel on Effective Ways of Investing in Health 2015).

Conclusion

As noted, the practice of dentistry has transformed. New materials, instruments, technologies, and professionals have appeared on the treatment scene. The same has occurred with patients' needs and expectations. They have changed as well. Thus, dentists, for all practical purposes, can no longer practice single-handedly. Members of the dental squad have assumed a significance, and the practice of "one size fits all" has been questioned. The introduction of the dental squad into the world of dentistry has stimulated major modifications in its practice with superior results for DCPs, patients, and societies, in spite of the aforementioned concerns. However, its diversity pervades the EU. Chapter 6 will present the dental team's world of work.

References

Albreht, T., Brinovec, R. P., Jošar, D., Poldrugovac, M., Kostnapfel, T., Zaletel, M., et al. (2016). Slovenia: Health system review. *Health Systems in Transition, 18*(3), 1–207.

Alexa, J., Rečka, L., Votápková, J., van Ginneken, E., Spranger, A., & Wittenbecher, F. (2015). Czech Republic: Health system review. *Health Systems in Transition, 17*(1), 1–165.

Alicino, C., Iudici, R., Barberis, I., Paganino, C., Cacciani, R., Zacconi, M., et al. (2015). Influenza vaccination among healthcare workers in Italy. *Human Vaccines & Immunotherapeutics, 11*(1), 95–100.

An Comhairle Fiaclóireachta (Irish Dental Council). (2010, March). Dental technicians information. *Dental Council Newsletter*. http://www.dentalcouncil.ie. Accessed 28 Nov 2016.

Araújo, M. R. (2013). *Dental hygiene around the world*. http://www.dentalcare.com. Accessed 4 Dec 2015.

Azzopardi-Muscat, N., Buttigieg, S., Calleja, N., & Merkur, S. (2017). Malta: Health system review. *Health Systems in Transition, 19*(1), 1–137.

Benchmark identity of denturists in terms of education, scope of practice and redefining relationships within the oral health care team. (n.d.). http://www.international-denturists.org. Accessed 4 Feb 2017.

Betsch, C. (2014). Overcoming healthcare workers' vaccine refusal—Competition between egoism and altruism. *Eurosurveillance, 19*(48). https://doi.org/10.2807/1560-7917.ES2014.19.48.20979.

Better Oral Health: European Platform. (2015). *Best practices in oral health promotion and prevention from across Europe: An overview prepared by the Platform for Better Oral Health in Europe*. http://www.oralhealthplatform.eu. Accessed 16 Oct 2016.

Boyle, S. (2011). United Kingdom (England): Health system review. *Health Systems in Transition, 13*(1), 1–486.

Charalambous, C., & Theodorou, M. (2013). Systems for the provision of oral health care in the Black Sea countries: Part 13: Cyprus. *Oral Health and Dental Management, 12*(1), 3–8.

Charalambous, C., Maniadakis, N., Polyzos, N., Fragoulakis, V., & Theodorou, M. (2013). The efficiency of the public dental services (PDS) in Cyprus and selected determinants. *BMC Health Services Research, 13*, 420. https://doi.org/10.1186/1472-6963-13-420.

Council of European Dentists. (2009). *CED resolution: Delegation yes—Substitution no*. http://www.eudental.eu. Accessed 6 Oct 2015.

Council of European Dentists. (2014). *Annual report 2014: CED in an election year*. http://www.cedentists.eu. Accessed 4 Aug 2018.

Cowpe, J., Barnes, E., & Bullock, A. (2013). Skill-mix in dental teams in Wales. *Vital, 10*(1), 38–43.

Cylus, J., & Papanicolas, I. (2015). An analysis of perceived access to health care in Europe: How universal is universal coverage? *Health Policy, 119*(9), 1133–1144.

Czech Republic. (2018, February). *International Federation of Dental Hygienists eNEWS*. http://www.ifdh.org. Accessed 3 Aug 2018.

Damaskinos, P., & Economou, C. (2012). Systems for the provision of oral health care in the Black Sea., & countries—Part 10: Greece. *Oral Health and Dental Management, 11*(1), 3–10.

Damaskinos, P., Koletsi-Kounari, H., Economou, C., Eaton, K. A., & Widström, E. (2016). The healthcare system and provision of oral healthcare in European Union member states: Part 4: Greece. *British Dental Journal, 220*(5), 253–260.

del Mar García-Calvente, M., Ruiz-Cantero, M. T., del Río-Lozano, M., Borrell, C., & López-Sancho, M. P. (2015). Desigualdades de género en la investigación en salud pública y epidemiología en España (2007–2014) (Gender inequalities in research in public health and epidemiology in Spain (2007–2014)). *Gaceta Sanitaria, 29*(6), 404–411.

Dental nurse boom in Scotland. (2013). *British Dental Journal, 214*(8), 380.

Dental Tribune International. (2017, March 1). *345,000 dentists practise in the European Union. Dental Tribune*. http://www.eu.dental-tribune.com. Accessed 7 Mar 2018.

Denturism: An overview. (n.d.). http://www.international-denturists.org. Accessed 14 Nov 2016.

Dimova, A., Rohova, M., Moutafova, E., Atanasova, E., Koeva, S., Panteli, D., et al. (2012). Bulgaria: Health system review. *Health Systems in Transition, 14*(3), 1–186.

Directive 2011/24/EU of the European Parliament and of the Council of 9 March 2011 on the application of patients' rights in cross-border healthcare.

Domínguez, J. P. (2012). Futuro incierto de la profesión de dentista en España (The uncertain future of the dental profession in Spain). *Gaceta Sanitaria, 26*(6), 495–496.

Dougall, A., Thompson, S. A., Faulks, D., Ting, G., & Nunn, J. (2014). Guidance for the core content of a curriculum in Special Care Dentistry at the undergraduate level. *European Journal of Dental Education, 18*(1), 39–43.

DrBicuspid Staff. (2008, September 10). *A dental clinic in the supermarket?* http://www.drbicuspid.com. Accessed 11 Mar 2017.

Dyer, T. A., Owens, J., & Robinson, P. G. (2013). What matters to patients when their care is delegated to dental therapists? *British Dental Journal, 214*(6), E17. https://doi.org/10.1038/sj.bdj.2013.275.

Džakula, A., Sagan, A., Pavić, N., Lončarek, K., & Sekelj-Kauzlarić, K. (2014). Croatia: Health system review. *Health Systems in Transition, 16*(3), 1–162.

Eaton, K., Garcia, A., Patel, R., & Rincon, V. (2012a). *A practical resource to help in the support of non-UK, EEA qualified dental practitioners practicing in the UK*. http://www.oxforddeanery.nhs.uk. Accessed 17 Jan 2017.

Eaton, K. A., Harris, M., Ross, M. K., & Arevalo, C. (2012b). A survey of dental hygienists in the United Kingdom in 2011: Part 1—Demographics and working patterns as dental hygienists. *British Dental Journal, 213*(10), E18. https://doi.org/10.1038/sj.bdj.2012.1041. Accessed 7 Dec 2016.

EDSA (European Dental Students' Association) press release. (2016, Spring). *EDSA Magazine*, pp. 17–18. http://www.edsaweb.org. Accessed 20 May 2016.

Education and Culture DG (Directorate-General). (2006). *Lifelong Learning Programme (2006–2008): Oral and dental care in Estonia*. http://www.ttk.ee. Accessed 11 Sept 2016.

Education Committee. (2016). http://www.international-denturists.org. Accessed 5 Feb 2017.

ERO (The European Regional Organisation of the Federation Dentaire Internationale) (International Dental Federation). (2012). *Report: Working Group women in dentistry*. http://www.erodental.org. Accessed 30 July 2018.

European Commission. (2014). *Commission staff working document: State of play on implementation of the Council Recommendation of 22 December 2009 on seasonal influenza vaccination (2009/1019/EU). SWD (2014) 8 final.*

European Commission. (2015). *Report from the Commission to the European Parliament and the Council. Commission report on the operation of Directive 2011/24/EU on the application of patients' rights in cross-border healthcare. COM (2015)421 final.*

European Commission. (2016). *Mutual evaluation of regulated professions. Overview of the regulatory framework in the health services sector—Dental hygienists and related professions. Report based on information transmitted by Member States and discussion in the meeting of 20 April 2015*. GROW/ES- 29 April 2016.

European Commission Expert Panel on Effective Ways of Investing in Health. (2015). *Access to health services in the European Union*. http://www.ec.europa.eu. Accessed 14 Mar 2018.

European Dental Hygienists Federation. (2016). *EDHF (European Dental Hygienists Federation) Resolution: Professional profile and competences of dental hygienists in Europe*. http://www.edhf.eu. Accessed 31 Oct 2017.

Font-Ribera, L., García-Continente, X., Davó-Blanes, M. C., Ariza, C., Díez, E., del Mar García Calvente, M., et al. (2014). El estudio de las desigualdades sociales en la salud infantil y adolescente en España (Study of social inequalities in child and adolescent health in Spain). *Gaceta Sanitaria, 28*(4), 316–325.

Fortunato, F., Tafuri, S., Cozza, V., Martinelli, D., & Prato, R. (2015). Low vaccination coverage among Italian healthcare workers in 2013. *Human Vaccines & Immunotherapeutics, 11*(1), 133–139.

Furtinger, V. B., Alyeva, R., & Maximevskoya, L. N. (2013). Is European dentistry becoming a female profession? *Acta Stomatologica Croatica, 47*(1), 51–57.

Gilardi, F., Gattinara, G. C., Vinci, M. R., Degli Atti, M. C., Santilli, V., Brugaletta, R., et al. (2018). Seasonal influenza vaccination in health care workers: A pre-post intervention study in an Italian paediatric hospital. *International Journal of Environmental Research and Public Health, 15*(5), Article 841.

Global migrants: Which are the most wanted professions? (2013, March 26). *BBC News*. http://www.bbc.com/news/business-21938085. Accessed 9 Nov 2015.

Goldacre, M., Lee, P., Stear, S., Sidebottom, E., & Richards, R. (2000). Views of academic dentists about careers in academic dentistry in the United Kingdom. *British Dental Journal, 188*(3), 154–159.

Gross, D., & Schäfer, G. (2011). "Feminization" in German dentistry: Career paths and opportunities—A gender comparison. *Women's Studies International Forum, 34*(2), 130–139.

Hach, M., Aaberg, K. B., Lempert, S. M., & Danielsen, B. (2017). Work assignments, delegation of tasks and job satisfaction among Danish dental hygienists. *International Journal of Dental Hygiene, 15*(3), 229–235.

Hamasaki, T., Kato, H., Kumagai, T., & Hagihara, A. (2017). Association between dentist-dental hygienist communication and dental treatment outcomes. *Health Communication, 32*(3), 288–297.

Healthcare personnel statistics—Dentists, pharmacists and physiotherapists. (2016). http://www.ec.europa.eu. Accessed 12 Mar 2017.

Hofmarcher, M., & Quentin, W. (2013). Austria: Health system review. *Health Systems in Transition, 15*(7), 1–291.

IFD (International Federation of Denturists). (2017). Working for denturists worldwide: News from around the world. *IFD Newsletter*, Edition 3, 6–9.

IFD (International Federation of Denturists) IFD policy statement. (n.d.). http://www.internationaldenturists.org. Accessed 22 June 2019.

International Federation of Dental Hygienists. (2019). *Social responsibility action plan*. http://www.ifdh.org. Accessed 2 Nov 2019.

International Labour Organization. (2012). *Updating the standard classifications of occupations ISCO Draft ISCO-08 group definitions: Occupations in health*. http://www.ilo.org. Accessed 13 Apr 2018.

International Labour Organization. (ESCO 08 Code 2261). (2008). *International standard classification of occupations*. http://www.ilo.org. Accessed 19 July 2019.

Janulyte, V., Aleksejuniene, J., Puriene, A., Peciuliene, V., & Benzian, H. (2014). Current employment characteristics and career intentions of Lithuanian dentists. *Human Resources for Health, 12*(1), 74. https://doi.org/10.1186/1478-4491-12-74.

Jongbloed-Zoet, C., Bol-van den Hil, E. M., La Rivière-Ilsen, J., & van der Sanden-Stoelinga, M. S. E. (2012). Dental hygienists in the Netherlands: The past, present and future. *International Journal of Dental Hygiene, 10*(3), 148–154.

Katrova, L., & Tzokov, K. (2013). Demography and market impacts on dental practices' development in Bulgaria during the period of transition: 1990–2010. *Acta Medica Academica, 42*(2), 229–237.

Koletsi-Kounari, H., Papaioannou, W., & Stefaniotis, T. (2011). Greece's high dentist to population ratio: Comparisons, causes and effects. *Journal of Dental Education, 75*(11), 1507–1515.

Koppelman, J., Vitzthum, K., & Simon, L. (2016). Expanding where dental therapists can practice could increase Americans' access to cost efficient care. *Health Affairs, 35*(12), 2200–2206.

Kravitz, A. S., & Treasure, E. T. (2007). Utilisation of dental auxiliaries—Attitudinal review from six developed countries. *International Dental Journal, 57*(4), 267–273.

Kravitz, A. S., Bullock, A., Cowpe, J., & Barnes, E. (2014). *Council of European Dentists manual of dental practice 2014* (5th ed.). n.p.: Council of European Dentists.

Kravitz, A. S., Bullock, A., Cowpe, J., & Barnes, E. (2015). *Council of European Dentists: EU manual of dental practice 2015* (5.1 ed.). Brussels: Council of European Dentists.

Lacharpagne, L., Lévesque, M. C., & Bedos, C. (2014). Discrimination and access to dental care: What can the dental profession do? *Journal of the Canadian Dental Association, 80*, e52. http://www.jcda.ca/article/e52. Accessed 9 Nov 2015.

Lai, T., Habicht, T., Kahur, K., Reinap, M., Kiivet, R., & van Ginneken, E. (2013). Estonia: Health system review. *Health Systems in Transition, 15*(6), 1–196.

Langelier, M., Continelli, T., Moore, J., Baker, B., & Surdu, S. (2016). Expanded scopes of practice for dental hygienists associated with improved oral health outcomes for adults. *Health Affairs, 35*(12), 2207–2215.

Larson, H., de Figueiredo, A., Karafillakis, E., & Rawal, M. (2018). *State of vaccine confidence in the EU 2018*. Luxembourg: Publications Office of the European Union.

Lopes, M. A., Almeida, Á. S., & Almada-Lobo, B. (2015). Handling healthcare workforce planning with care. Where do we stand? *Human Resources for Health, 13*, 38. https://doi.org/10.1186/s12960-015-0028-0.

Macey, R., Glenny, A., Walsh, T., Tickle, M., Worthington, H., Ashley, J., et al. (2015). The efficacy of screening for common dental diseases by hygiene-therapists: A diagnostic test accuracy study. *Journal of Dental Research, 34*(3 suppl), 70S–78S.

Malherbe, D. (2014). Editorial—Branding of the denturism profession. *IFD (International Federation of Denturists) Newsletter, 1*(1), 3–4.

Malherbe, D. (2016, February). Editorial—I have a dream! *IFD (International Federation of Denturists) Newsletter, 2*(1), 2–3.

Malkiewicz, K., Malkiewicz, E., Eaton, K. A., & Widström, E. (2016). The health care system and the provision of oral healthcare in European Union Member States. Part 6: Poland. *British Dental Journal, 221*(8), 501–507.

Matrix Insight. (2012). *EU level collaboration on forecasting health workforce needs, workforce planning and health workforce trends—A feasibility study.* http://www.ec.europa.eu. Accessed 18 Feb 2015.

Minford Chartered Accountants. (2016, May 12). *Women in dentistry: A gender for change.* http://www.smile-onnews.com. Accessed 30 Aug 2016.

Mitenbergs, U., Taube, M., Misins, J., Mikitis, E., Martinsons, A., Rurane, A., et al. (2012). Latvia: Health system review. *Health Systems in Transition, 14*(8), 1–191.

Murauskiene, L., Janoniene, R., Veniute, M., van Ginneken, E., & Karanikolos, M. (2013). Lithuania: Health system review. *Health Systems in Transition, 15*(2), 1–150.

Nash, D. A., Friedman, J. W., & Mathu-Muju, K. R. (2012). *A review of the global literature on dental therapists in the context of the movement to add dental therapists to the oral health workforce in the United States.* http://www.depts.washington.edu. Accessed 11 Sept 2016.

NHS (National Health Service), National Patient Safety Agency, & National Clinical Assessment Service. (2011). *Factors influencing dental practitioner performance: A literature review.* http://www.ncas.nhs.uk. Accessed 12 Feb 2017.

Northcott, A., Brocklehurst, K., Jerković-Ćosić, J. J. R., McDermott, I., & Tickle, M. (2013). Direct access: Lessons learnt from the Netherlands. *British Dental Journal, 215*(12), 607–610.

O'Hehir, T. E. (n.d.). *The value of a hygienist.* http://www.dentaleconomics.com. Accessed 16 Jan 2017.

Oancea, R., Amariei, C., Eaton, K. A., & Widström, E. (2016). The healthcare system and the provision of oral healthcare in European Union member states: Part 5: Romania. *British Dental Journal, 220*(7), 361–366.

Ordem Dos Médicos Dentistas (Portuguese Dental Association). (2014). *The numbers of the Portuguese Dental Association: Statistics 2014.* http://www.omd.pt. Accessed 1 Nov 2016.

Panda, A., Garg, I., & Bhobe, A. P. (2014). Children's perspective on the dentist's attire. *International Journal of Paediatric Dentistry, 24*(2), 98–103.

Parkash, H., Mathur, V. P., Duggal, R., & Jhuraney, B. (2006). Dental workforce issues: A global concern. *Journal of Dental Education, 70*(11 suppl), 22–26.

Pegon-Machat, E., Tubert-Jeannin, S., Loignon, C., Landry, A., & Bedos, C. (2009). Dentists' experience with low-income patients benefiting from a public insurance program. *European Journal of Oral Sciences, 117*(4), 398–406.

Prato, R., Tafuri, S., Fortunato, F., & Martinelli, D. (2010). Vaccination in healthcare workers: An Italian perspective. *Expert Review of Vaccines, 9*(3), 277–283.

Puriene, A., Balciuniene, I., & Drobnys, P. (2008). Who is thought to be a "reliable dentist"? Lithuanian dentists' opinion. *Stomatologija, Baltic Dental and Maxillofacial Journal, 210*(3), 83–88.

Regulation *(EU) 2017/745 of the European Parliament and of the Council of 5 April 2017 on medical devices, amending Directive 2001/83/EC, Regulation (EC) No. 178/2002 and Regulation (EC) No. 1223/2009 and repealing Council Directives 90/385/EEC and 93/42/EEC.*

Regulation (EU) *2017/746 of the European Parliament and of the Council of 5 April 2017 on in vitro diagnostic medical devices and repealing Directive 98/79/EC and Commission Decision 2010/227/EU.*

Reinders, J. J., Krijnen, W. P., Onclin, P., van der Schans, C. P., & Stegenga, B. (2017). Attitudes among dentists and dental hygienists towards extended scope and independent practice of dental hygienists. *International Dental Journal, 67*(1), 46–58.

Riley, J. L., 3rd, Gordan, W., Hudak-Boss, S. E., Fellows, J. L., Rindal, D. B., Gilbert, G. H., et al. (2014). Concordance between patient satisfaction and the dentist's view: Findings from the National Dental Practice-Based Research Network. *Journal of the American Dental Association, 145*(4), 355–362.

Rooney, C., Dhaliwal, H., & Hodge, T. (2016). Orthodontic therapists—Has their introduction affected outcomes? *British Dental Journal, 221*(7), 421–424.

Rowbotham, J. S., Godson, J. H., Williams, S. A., Csikar, J. I., & Bradley, S. (2009). Dental therapy in the United Kingdom: Part 1. Developments in therapists' training and role. *British Dental Journal, 207*(8), 355–359.

San Martin-Rodriguez, L., Beaulieu, M.-D., D'Amour, D., & Ferrada-Videla, M. (2005). The determinants of successful collaboration: A review of theoretical and empirical studies. *Journal of Interprofessional Care, 19*(sup 1), 132–147.

Simões, J., Augusto, G. F., Fronteira, I., & Hernández-Quevedo, C. (2017). Portugal: Health system review. *Health Systems in Transition, 19*(2), 1–184.

Singh, S. (2017, December 6). *Dental care for patients with special needs.* http://www.dentistry.co.uk. Accessed 7 Apr 2018.

Slot, D. E. (2013). *Dental hygiene in the Netherlands.* http://www.dentistryiq.com. Accessed 30 Jan 2017.

Smith, M. K., & Dundes, L. (2008). The implications of gender stereotypes for the dentist-patient relationship. *Journal of Dental Education, 72*(5), 562–570.

Swami, V., McClelland, A., Bedi, R., & Furnham, A. (2011). The influence of practitioner nationality, experience, and sex in shaping patient preferences for dentists. *International Dental Journal, 61*(4), 193–198.

Talla, P. K., Gagnon, M.-P., Dramaix, M., & Leveque, A. (2013). Barriers to dental visits in Belgium: A secondary analysis of the 2004 National Health Interview Survey. *Journal of Public Health Dentistry, 73*(1), 32–40.

Turner, S., Tripathee, S., & MacGillivray, S. (2012). *Benefits and risks of direct access to treatment by dental care professionals: A rapid evidence review. Final report to the General Dental Council.* http://www.gdc-uk.org. Accessed 30 Jan 2017.

van Dam, B. A., den Boer, J. C., & Bruers, J. J. (2009). Recently graduated dentists: Working situation and future plans. *Ned Tijdschrift Tandheelkunde, 116*(9), 499–506.

Virtanen, J. I., Tseveenjav, B., Wang, N. J., & Widström, E. (2011). Nordic dental hygienists' willingness to perform new treatment measures: Barriers and facilitators they encounter. *Scandinavian Journal of Caring Sciences, 25*(2), 311–316.

Virtanen, J. I., Pellikka, E., Singh, S., & Widström, E. (2016). The professional role of a dental hygienist in Finland—Educators' views. *International Journal of Dental Hygiene, 14*(3), 231–238.

Visser, A., Deccache, A., & Bensing, J. (2001). Patient education in Europe: United differences. *Patient Education and Counseling, 44*(1), 1–5.

Vrangbaek, K. (2016). The Danish health care system, 2015. In E. Mossialos, M. Wenzl, R. Osborn, & D. Sornak (Eds.), *2015 international profiles of health care systems* (pp. 39–47). New York: The Commonwealth Fund.

Wanyonyi, K. L., Radford, D. R., & Gallagher, J. E. (2014). Dental skill mix: A cross-sectional analysis of delegation practices between dental and dental hygiene-therapy students involved in team training in the South of England. *Human Resources for Health, 12*, Article Number 65.

Wanyonyi, K. L., Radford, D. R., Harper, P. R., & Gallagher, J. E. (2015). Alternative scenarios: Harnessing mid-level providers and evidence-based practice in primary dental care in England through operational research. *Human Resources for Health, 13*, 18. Article Number 78.

Whelton, H., & Wardman, M. J. (2015). The landscape for women leaders in dental education, research, and practice. *Journal of Dental Education, 79*(5 Suppl), S7–12.

Wicker, S., & Rabenau, H. F. (2010). A patient safety issue: Mandatory influenza vaccination for health care workers. *Procedia in Vaccinology, 2*(1), 101–105.

Widström, E., Väisänen, A., & Barenthin, I. (2009). Justification for a public dental service: Finnish, Norwegian and Swedish experiences. *Oral Health and Dental Management, 8*(1), 17–24.

Yamalik, N., Ensaldo-Carrasco, E., & Bourgeois, D. (2013). Oral health workforce planning. Part I: Data available in a sample of FDI (International Dental Federation) countries. *International Dental Journal, 63*(6), 298–305.

Yamalik, N., Ensaldo-Carrasco, E., Cavalle, E., & Kell, K. (2014). Oral health workforce planning. Part 2: Figures, determinants and trends in a sample of World Dental Federation member countries. *International Dental Journal, 64*(3), 117–126.

Yeaton, S., Moorthy, A., Rice, J., Coghlan, D., O'Dwyer, L., Green, E., et al. (2016). Special care dentistry: How prepared are we? *European Journal of Dental Education, 20*(1), 9–13.

Yusuf, Y. H., Tsakos, G., Ntouve, A., Murphy, M., Porter, J., Newton, T., et al. (2015). Differences by age and sex in general dental practitioners' knowledge, attitudes and behaviours in delivering prevention. *British Dental Journal, 219*(6), E7. https://doi.org/10.1038/sj.bdj.2015.711.

Ziller, S., Eaton, K. E., & Widström, E. (2015). The health care system and the provision of oral health care in the European Union member states. Part 1: Germany. *British Dental Journal, 218*(4), 239–244.

Chapter 6
The Workplace

Advertising, Consumers' Rights, and Electronic Commerce

The available services and staff of a dental office have to be made known to the public. This could be accomplished through publicity in the press and telephone directories, or on the radio and television, or with the use of websites, mailings, and distribution of leaflets. Again, diversity is reflected in the regulations governing advertising of dental care professionals' (DCPs') services across the European Union (EU). Not all of these elements may be utilized in every Member State. For example, in the Czech Republic, such publicity is prohibited on the radio and television (The Czech Republic n.d.). And, in some Member States, dental practices are not allowed to advertise. These nations include Belgium, France, Greece, Luxembourg, Malta, Portugal, Romania, and Slovakia. Such advertising operates under restrictions in several countries. For example, in Ireland, publicity of a price list has been prohibited and new practices have been limited to a maximum of six newspaper advertisements in their first year of existence. Such or similar restrictions exist across the EU (The Competition Authority 2007; Kravitz et al. 2014, 2015). It has been affirmed that empirical evidence and economic theory suggest that restrictions on advertising, such as the noted ones, result in an augment of prices, small or no impact on the quality of service delivered, and enlarged consumer search costs (Conrad and Emerson 1981).

The EU became involved in issuing laws concerning the regulation of such advertising, due to the lack of harmonization of regulations on the subject and inadequate levels of consumer protection across the Member States. Thus, Council Directive 84/450/EEC of 10 September 1984 relating to the approximation of the laws, regulations, and administrative provisions of the Member States concerning misleading advertising became law. It criticized misleading publicity and the diversity in Member States' rules on the matter mainly because consumers and non-misleading advertisers suffered severe damages. According to the European

S. Z. Koff, *The Dental Team in the European Union*,
https://doi.org/10.1007/978-3-030-72232-6_6

Advertising Standards Alliance, misleading publicity has been the most complained about subject by European consumers (Ford 1993).

The same type of EU legislation focused on commercial practices that influence consumers' transactional decisions. Directive 2005/29/EC of the European Parliament and of the Council of 11 May 2005 aimed to protect "consumer economic interests from unfair business-to-consumer commercial practices" (Directive 2005/29/EC, Recital 8). Member States were to adopt "effective, proportionate, and dissuasive" (Directive 2005/29/EC, Article 13) penalties for infringements of national regulations. More recently, Directive 2006/114/EC concerning misleading and comparative advertising set forth the basic traits of these types. All Member States were to ensure that people or organizations through either a judicial or administrative organ could seek relief from unlawful publicity.

The so-called e-Commerce Directive, Directive 2000/31/EC, designed the basic legal framework for online services. An objective was to eliminate barriers to the development of cross-border services in the EU which professionals might offer on the Internet (Directive 2000/31/EC, Recital 32). Member States were obliged to remove legal obstacles to using electronic contracts (Directive 2000/31/EC, Recital 37). Also, there was encouragement to develop codes of conduct and paths for dispute settlement as well by the Member States (Articles 16–18).

In September 2017, Jean-Claude Juncker, former President of the EU Commission, in his State of the Union speech announced a program entitled The New Deal for Consumers. Its purpose was to make the application of EU consumer law stronger within an increasing threat of violations across the Member States. In general, the program when fully developed, it is hoped, will update and improve application of EU consumer regulations, given market developments and the enhanced role of the digital economy (The history of the European Union-2017 2017).

So that European consumers fully enjoy their benefits under EU law, the announced program is to eventually augment online consumer rights and the methods used to enforce these rights and receive compensation, establish effective sanctions for EU consumer law infringements, tackle the dual quality of consumer products, and improve conditions for businesses. All affected by the program, it is believed, will eventually recognize the injection of more flexibility in consumer-business undertakings.

Work Time

Significant areas of work conditions have been covered by EU law. Provisions have related to working hours, information to employees, consultation of workers, occupational health and safety at work, and employee types, meaning full-time, part-time, and temporary agency workers. A significant document exercising guidance over the workplace is Directive 2003/88/EC. The purpose of the law was to create "minimum safety and health requirements for the organisation of working time" (Directive 2003/88/EC, Article 1(1)). It is applicable to workers in the public and private sectors of activity. Maximum weekly working hours are established at an average of 48 hours for 7 days including overtime over a reference period of up to 4 months (Directive 2003/88/EC, Articles 6, 16). This limit, according to the CJEU, is to include all on-call time at the workplace.

Furthermore, the Directive provides for three types of minimum rest periods to enhance workers' safety and health. These include rest breaks when one works longer than 6 hours, a minimum daily rest of 11 consecutive hours, and a weekly continuous rest for a minimum of 35 h (Directive 2003/88/EC, Articles 3, 4, 5). The length of the first-mentioned rest break is to be determined by the individual Member States. The most common amount of time allotted has been a half hour (European Commission 2017a).

According to the Directive, every employee is entitled to 4 weeks of paid annual leave. It is only possible to replace this benefit with a financial payment, if the worker's contract has expired before she/he has taken all of the annual leave (Directive 2003/88/EC, Article 7). It is noteworthy that in several Member States, the amount of this leave is extended as the employee ages or as her/his period of employment increases. Moreover, the CJEU held that an employee on sick leave who has not been able to benefit from the annual paid leave may carry it over to the next year (European Commission 2017a). Obviously, this notion of annual leave sharply contrasts with that in the United States which is the only country with an advanced economy that does not feature paid annual leave of this nature for workers.

Certain individuals, including management executives and other persons with autonomous decision-making authority, can be declared exempt from specific provisions of the Directive (Directive 2003/88/EC, Article 17). In addition, Member States are to issue a report every 5 years on the operation of the Directive (Directive 2003/88/EC, Article 24) which also contains special references to night workers and those that are employed in sea fishing and urban passenger transportation (Directive 2003/88/EC, Articles 20, 21, 25, 26).

The Commission is currently reviewing this document and undertaking an impact assessment. So far, an agreement on change has not been achieved. Employers' associations have been of the opinion that the Directive meets its purpose of protecting the health and safety of workers. However, they have believed that flexibility is lacking in making working time arrangements congruent with the needs of both employers and employees. The Member States thought that the Directive contributed to making national law simpler and more effective. They also were of the opinion that it extended legal protection to those persons previously excluded as well as augmented the level of protection for workers and their work-private life balance. However, some were not happy that on-call time was included in the calculation of working time. Also, they noted the problem of complying with the Directive's provisions and, particularly, the CJEU's decision related to on-call time and its impact on health care and other 24-h services (European Commission 2010).

This Directive is extremely significant in that the balance between working time and private life, or work-life balance, is related not only to employees' health and well-being but also to job satisfaction. An unsatisfactory relationship between these elements can cause a worker to select early retirement, and, in addition, it can damage the performance of an undertaking.

Equality, Non-discrimination, and Pay

Work life and working conditions are an important subject in EU law, and an EU objective of significance is the promotion of equality between females and males. In fact, the notion of equal pay for equal work was provided for in the aforementioned Treaty of Rome. Since their birth, EU institutions have regularly noted the doctrine reaffirming it as a major principle of the organization. Unfortunately, the doctrine has not been fully realized in practice.

Equal treatment for females and males has provided more subject matter for EU legislation. Known as the so-called Recast Directive, Directive 2006/54/EC's purpose was to simplify and blend existing legislation with this focus as it relates to employment and occupation. This law discusses equal treatment as linked to entry to employment, promotion, vocational training, wages, and social security programs. In short, the document presents a general framework for equal treatment in employment and occupation in which direct and indirect discrimination are prohibited. The prohibitions apply to the public and private sectors. As stated many times, Member States are to provide processes and sanctions for infringement as well as to engage in social dialogue and dialogue with non-governmental organizations on the matter (Directive 2006/54/EC, Articles 13, 14, 17). Earlier Council Directive 2000/78/EC prohibited both types of discrimination founded on religion, beliefs, disability, age, or sexual orientation (Council Directive 2000/78/EC, Recital 12), and Council Directive 2000/43/EC outlawed discrimination on the basis of race and ethnic origin. These documents provided a boost to EU equality law which for decades merely focused on discrimination based on gender. Applicability to diverse concepts and terms took place along with an expansion of the basis for discrimination (Waddington and Bell 2001).

In spite of multiple statements and EU legal documents pertaining to the realization of gender equality, multiple inequalities still exist for females across the EU. Some of these have been noted. A gap in stipend between men and women is still noticeable and notable. The same holds true for pensions on retirement. In fact, the gender pay gap for work of equal value is and has been a formidable challenge. On the average, males across the EU earn over 16.2% more than females (Eurofound 2018; European Commission 2017b).

A recent step by the Commission was the adoption of an Action Plan to confront this gender pay gap. This project is dedicated to improving the practical use of the equal pay principle; combating segregation of employees in occupations and sectors; assigning more value to females' skills, efforts, and responsibilities; combating reliance on stereotypes; releasing information about differences in stipends between genders; and collaborating with others to confront the gender pay gap (European Commission 2017b). To date, progress in this sector has been quite slow.

In a positive vein, let's hope that this recent Action Plan produces incontestable results in fast fashion.

The subject of severance pay or the payment to an employee who has been involuntarily released from employment lies with the Member States. The matter is not legally regulated in all of them. For example, Finland and Sweden fail to regulate this subject. Generally, the employer is responsible for this payment. However, in some cases, other organizations are involved, as in Cyprus. In this Member State, employers contribute 1.2% of their payroll up to a maximum amount to a national fund that provides severance payments to dismissed employees. The amount of severance pay, for the most part, depends on length of time at the place of employment and the level of one's stipend. Obviously, females, as with wages and pensions, tend to receive a lower severance payment. Also, often to receive such a payment, certain requisites have to be met (Eurofound n.d.).

These efforts and statements on the part of the EU in reference to inequality are pleasing to the reader, and the EU's shift from focusing primarily on gender inequalities to multiple inequalities is heartening. However, Verloo (2006) notes that a "one-size-fits-all" approach to remedy inequalities overlooks their differentiated nature and basic dynamics. Moreover, it also ignores the political facet of the problem. The conclusion is that a more comprehensive method to erase multiple inequalities is necessary. Also, it has been asserted that specific national norms and culture dictate the meaning assigned to terms and the structure and authority of equality bodies in the Member States. These can serve as barriers to the accomplishment of equality goals (Bell 2008; Verloo 2006).

Social Rights

The Commission, reacting to the impact of the economic crisis on the social objectives of the EU, exhibited a focus on social rights with its presentation of the European Pillar of Social Rights on 26 April 2017. This project was primarily conceived for the Member States of the euro area, and it remains open to all Member States that wish to participate in it (European Commission 2017c, d). It is to deliver new and, hopefully, more effective rights for EU citizens via its three facets that concern equal opportunities and access to the labor market, fair working conditions, and social protection and inclusion.

The project enunciated 20 significant principles and rights to support these foci, the responsibility for which is assigned to EU units, the Member States, and various stakeholders. The first facet consists of the right to education, training, and lifelong learning, gender equality, equal opportunities, and active support to employment. The second sector is concerned with the right to secure an adaptable employment, adequate and fair wages, information about employment conditions and protection in case of dismissal, social dialogue and involvement of workers, work-life balance, and a healthy, safe, and well-adapted work environment and data protection. The third group is comprised of rights regarding child care and support to children, social protection, unemployment benefits, minimum income, old age income and pensions, health care, inclusion of people with disabilities, long-term care, housing and assistance for the homeless, and access to essential services (European Commission 2017d). At this time, social rights, some of which concern employment, are at the center of the EU stage with launched ideas for achievement. Now, they need to be completely implemented.

One legal scholar acknowledges that:

> *all three [categories of proposals] have the potential to address pressing issues of social justice and protection facing European workers and labour markets today. As such, it can be concluded that if it [the EU] manages to deliver on these three key initiatives, the Pillar will resuscitate...Social Europe significantly improving the social situation of EU citizens, and the social output of the EU overall.* (Garben 2018, pp. 226–227)

And Dhéret (2018) warns that the costs of a non-social Europe could be tremendous and cannot be ignored along with the political backlash that could result.

Most recently, in March 2018, the Commission presented its Social Fairness Package which is concerned with monitoring the implementation of the European Pillar of Social Rights, the creation of the European Labour Authority, and access to social protection for employees and the self-employed, among other matters. Guidance is offered on the implementation of and available EU funding for the noted Pillar project.

The function of the new agency, the European Labour Authority, which was to begin operation sometime in 2019 and is to be fully operational by 2023, features a support role, an operational role, and a mandatory role. It is to aid individuals, firms, and national administrations in the taking of full advantage of available free movement and to guarantee that workers have a level playing field to do so. Also, it is to facilitate workers' and employers' access to information regarding their rights and obligations, to enhance cooperation between Member States in reference to the cross-border enforcement of EU law, and to help pave the way to solutions to cross-border disputes or labor market disruptions. In addition, it is to undertake analyses and risk assessments on matters related to cross-border worker mobility.

The Right to Information and Consultation

In the workplace, employees have the right to receive information from employers and to be consulted by them as provided for in Directive 2002/14/EC which presents a general framework for informing and consulting employees throughout the Member States. The document applies to undertakings in the public and private sectors that employ at least 50 persons in any Member State or to those that have at least 20 employees in any Member State (Directive 2002/1/EC, Directive 2002/14/EC, Recital 19). It is left to the Member States to select how the right to information and consultation shall be operationalized (Directive 2002/14/EC, Articles 2(a),

3(1a), 3(1b), 4(1)). The EU legislation only establishes minimum requirements for the stated rights (Directive 2002/14/EC, Recital 18).

Topics for both procedures are set forth in the legislation. They include the structure's activities, development, and economic situation, its employment scene, and modifications likely to have a significant impact on work organization or the nature of contracts (Directive 2002/14/EC, Article 4). Ground rules for consultations are presented with the objective of obtaining "an agreement on decisions within the scope of the employer's powers" (Directive 2002/14/EC, Article 4(e)).

Work-Life Balance

Whether or not EU citizens are able to enjoy a positive work-life balance, to a certain extent, depends on the nature of social and health and safety policies featured by the EU and the Member States. Council Directive 92/85/EEC offered safety and health provisions for pregnant workers and those who have recently given birth or those who are breastfeeding. It provides for an assessment of the chemical, biological, and physical elements in the workplace that are considered hazardous to these groups of people, and it also relates to movements and postures, mental and physical fatigue, as well as other stress factors linked with the work performed by these individuals. If need be, it is the employer's responsibility to determine the measures to be taken, due to a revealed risk. If movement to another position is not feasible, the person is to be placed on leave (Council Directive 992/85/EEC, Articles 3, 4, 5). It is generally acknowledged that work requisites influence individuals' views of the work-life balance (Guillén 2011).

The document also provides for a maternity leave of at least 14 weeks, two of which must take place prior to delivery. During this leave period, dismissal of employees is possible only under exceptional circumstances, and workers are able to maintain their wages or entitlement to an adequate allowance (Council Directive 92/85/EEC, Articles 8, 10, 11). In the majority of Member States, employees receive 100% of their stipend during the entire leave or, if not, 80% to 90% of it. Exceptions to this trend are provided by Cyprus (72%), the Czech Republic (70%), Hungary (70%), and Slovakia (65%). In Austria, France, Germany, and Spain, those on leave receive 100% of their pay for 14 weeks, and then the rate decreases (Fabris 2016).

In 2008, the Commission proposed Procedure 2008/0193/COD to increase the maternity leave to 18 weeks. The EP favored 20 weeks plus a minimum of 2 weeks of non-transferable paternity leave. The Council was unable to agree. The official proposal remained deadlocked in the EU legislative system for 7 years until the Commission, in desperation, withdrew it in 2015 with a promise to issue another suggestion. It is noteworthy that paternity and maternity leaves as practiced throughout the EU are not uniform. The time allowed and the allotted payments are very diverse.

The principal elements of the new proposal, announced in April 2017, refer to paternity, parental, and carers' leaves. The paternity leave is to consist of at least 10 working days with a minimum compensation equal to sick pay. Most Member States have regulations on the subject of paternity leave. However, Austria, Croatia, Cyprus, the Czech Republic, Germany, Luxembourg, and Slovakia do not. There is also a suggested non-transferable parental leave of 4 months per parent that can be taken full-time or part-time after delivery or adoption until the child reaches age 12. The amount of compensation relates to sick pay. The hope is to encourage more fathers to take time off and assume a larger share of caring responsibilities.

Unique is the suggestion of a carers' leave which would entitle the worker to 5 days per year to take care of a gravely sick or dependent relative with compensation equal to sick pay. This proposal is significant in that policies related to the work-life balance have been primarily focused on families with children. These other dependents have been overlooked (Guillén 2011). Lastly, the proposal would allow workers with a child under age 12 and carers as well to seek flexible and reduced working time. The proposal is currently under negotiation. Changes in existing practices were announced as an important part of the aforementioned European Pillar of Social Rights.

The importance of paternity leave and parental leave for fathers has been demonstrated. Fathers become more involved in the child's future care as an infant and during childhood. Such activity also aids children's cognitive development and helps close the caring gap between females and males. Research has concluded that more fathers are participating in paternity and parental leaves, but such progress has taken place at a slow pace (Aumayr-Pintar 2018).

Parental leave is also significant due to its important relationship with the economy. With its availability, it is more likely that both heads of family, when their child is born or they complete an adoption, will remain employed. Moreover, unemployment, absenteeism, and turnover in the work squad are tempered. In addition, productivity, in general, and participation of females in the labor market are enhanced. In terms of reductions in costs, these apply to structures in relation to recruiting and to parents concerning childcare. And then there are positive advantages related to the quality of life and people's health (Fabris 2016; Ray et al. 2010).

DCPs' Occupational Health Hazards and Disorders

In exercising their profession, all DCPs are confronted by a multitude of hazards of a biological, chemical, physical, and psychological nature. More specifically, they are predisposed to a galaxy of infectious diseases, musculoskeletal maladies, as well as eye, hearing, respiratory, and psychosocial problems, among others.

Some of DCPs' risks relate to biological agents nurtured in patients' blood and saliva. Through treatment procedures and/or injuries from instruments or needles that are not blunt, they come into contact with these substances. In addition, exposure to infectious respiratory diseases takes place via air and droplet transmissions, as well as splatters from body fluids and projectiles caused by the use of high-speed equipment. It is noteworthy that it has been demonstrated that during the work day the average air bacterial load augments more than three times (Szymańska 1999).

Chemical hazards include medicines, diverse materials used for dental treatments, and those adopted for disinfection and cleaning efforts related to patient care. Protective devices, such as latex gloves, may involve chemical risks as well. These elements are the source of allergies and skin diseases. Physical hazards are related to dental treatments that involve exposure to laser beams; ionizing radiation when doing X-rays; punctures from sharps instruments, including needles; hazards affiliated with tripping, slipping, and falling; ergonomic risks due to awkward postures over long periods of time and repetitious actions; as well as those resulting from computer use or workplace design.

. Psychological hazards are also well-known in the work world of DCPs. These arise from excessive workplace stressors, often resulting in substance abuse, burnout, depression, anxiety, and sleep and other disorders. Stress can also be related to an individual's work-life balance and abuse by patients, co-workers, or members of the public. Hazards concerning medical emergencies, threats of or actual violence in the workplace, use of new technologies, the influence of aging in a profession, workload and working hours, exposure to noise levels, poor air quality, and artificial lighting often induce stress along with hearing loss and eye difficulties. In fact, dental professionals believe their work is more stressful than that of other professions (Ayatollahi et al. 2012). As noted, the abovementioned hazards or risks of DCPs may be classified in biological, chemical, physical, and psychosocial categories. This classification, however, is not stationary because more modern technologies, new equipment and materials for dental procedures, sterilization, and disinfection, appear along with socioeconomic and political changes (Şoaita 2014). DCPs must be flexible and react appropriately to such transformations.

Dentistry, regardless of one's role in it, is physically and psychosocially demanding. Members of the dental team report a high prevalence of work-related ailments. Musculoskeletal, dermatological, ophthalmologic, audiological, and neurological disorders are prevalent (Vodanovic et al. 2016).

The most frequently reported work-related problem is complex and multifactorial. It consists of musculoskeletal disorders. These affect a high percentage of members of the dental squad and are well-documented. In fact, the healthcare sector holds second place in terms of occurrence of these maladies. The construction industry ranks number one. For this disorder, complaints concern pain in the back, elbows, arms, shoulders, wrists, hands, fingers, legs, and feet. The physical workload of a practitioner has been related to this difficulty, along with the assumption of precision work in awkward and flexed postures (Zarra and Lambrianidis 2014), use of non-ergonomic instruments, time pressures (FDI 2007), job strain, low coworker support (Pensola et al. 2016), long work schedules without breaks (Guignon 2015), and the emotional climate of the workplace (Lindfors et al. 2006). These are some causes of problems in the musculoskeletal system and of the peripheral nervous system which, in turn, change the manner in which the respiratory, cardiovascular, and alimentary systems function (Szymańska 1999).

Across the EU, musculoskeletal difficulties are the most common cause for long-term pain and disability. The healthcare and social costs of this condition are great. It even causes some practitioners to leave their profession. Furthermore, economic losses are generated due to absences from the workplace and decreased productivity. Also, one's private life is significantly affected. It is known that these difficulties increase with age, obesity, and lack of physical exercise. Studies of dentists in the Czech Republic and Poland revealed that 96.9% and 92%, respectively, of participants claimed musculoskeletal problems. The percentages are startling. These difficulties plague all members of the dental team and students as well (FDI 2007; Hayes et al. 2010; Musculoskeletal health in Europe Report v5,0 2013; Vodanovic et al. 2016).

A study of final year dental students' knowledge and practice of ergonomic requisites was undertaken a while ago (Garbin et al. 2011). Among the participants, 65.7% provided correct written responses to test questions. However, pictures taken of these people delivering oral health care to patients indicated a different situation. Only 35% of the student participants clinically applied ergonomic requisites.

The Dutch several years ago developed an ergonomic intervention program to decrease these disorders in dental clinics. Half (50%) of the attendees undertook the recommendations completely or nearly so, and 40% practically implemented them. It was found to be difficult to develop new routines, and the financial aspects also served as barriers. However, the recommended ergonomic measures worked. Musculoskeletal disorders were relieved in many cases. These difficulties are preventable, but continuity in such efforts is a significant challenge and a necessity (Droeze and Jonsson 2005; FDI 2007).

Denturists, in addition to musculoskeletal problems, have also experienced others. These include chronic fatigue syndrome, irritation, itching, and rashes on the hands, restlessness and aggression, and eye difficulties, resulting from watery and itchy eyes. Again, work organization has been related to occupational health (Garus-Pakowska et al. 2016). For dental technicians, some occupational health problems are somewhat different, and many are the same. Job responsibilities account for several hazards. Ergonomics and stress are responsible for musculoskeletal and neurological reactions. Chemical pollution, grinding dust, and the nature of the indoor environment contribute to dermatological, respiratory, and systemic problems (Jacobsen et al. 1996).

Dentists experience many of these same ailments. They claim hearing impairment, due mainly to exposure to high-speed hand pieces and other noise-intensive instruments, vision problems, as well as neurological and dermal disorders. Skin diseases rank right behind musculoskeletal difficulties on the list of most common occupational maladies. They occupy second place. Dentists in their work utilize diverse chemicals, drugs, and other irritants. All of these diverse health difficulties could cause members of the dental squad to take early retirement (Vodanovic et al. 2016; Willershausen et al. 2014).

Students of dental care professions are no exception. They are subject to all of these disorders as well. Although any dental care professional is subject to these ailments, education on occupational health is not usually integrated into DCPs' curricula. Research on students' erudition of the clinical application of ergonomic postural principles demonstrated their very limited practice of them and restricted knowledge. Thus, pleas have been made for inclusion of this subject matter in clinical studies (Garbin et al. 2011; Katrova et al. 2012; Matos et al. 2016).

Safety and Health at Work

Health and safety in the workplace is a topic of significance on the EU agenda. Council Directive 89/391/EEC of 12 June 1989 on the introduction of measures to encourage improvements in the safety and health of workers at work is known as the Framework Directive on this subject. Its objective was the introduction "of measures to encourage improvements in the safety and health of workers at work" (Council Directive 89/391/EEC, Article 1(1)). Moreover, its provisions were broad in scope. They apply to the private, public, industrial, agricultural, commercial, administrative, service, educational, cultural, leisure, etc. sectors (Council Directive 89/391/EEC, Article 2(1)).

The Directive states that the employer is responsible for ensuring the safety and health of the worker in every aspect linked to the job. It then sets forth the employers' responsibilities (Council Directive 89/391/EEC, Article 6), such as those related to protective measures and giving appropriate instructions to employees. Serious and imminent dangers are provided for related to first aid, firefighting, and evacuation of workers.

Information to workers is assigned significance, and the employer is responsible for seeing that employees and/or their representatives receive materials related to the firm or job (Article 10). Consultation and participation of workers are provided for in any measures which may amply impact on their safety and health (Council Directive 89/391/EEC, Article 11 (2a)). Training of workers is discussed as well.

The workers or employees, like the employers, also have obligations. In the first place, the worker is responsible for her/his own safety and health and those of her/his colleagues in terms of her/his activities. Other obligations are set forth (Council Directive 89/391/EEC, Section III, Article 13). It is also provided that risk groups who happen to be particularly sensitive must be protected against hazards that affect them (Council Directive 89/391/EEC, Article 15). They should also enjoy safety and health at work.

Other documents deal with specific aspects of safety and health at the workplace, such as equipment, signs, exposure to biological and chemical agents and physical hazards, personal protective equipment, and explicit groups of workers and specific workplaces. Directive 2009/104/EC presents minimum requisites for the use of work equipment. It is the employer's responsibility to ensure the appropriateness and safety of the utilized equipment which must meet certain requirements (Directive 2009/104/EC, Article 1, Annex 1). Proper installation, maintenance, periodic inspections of the instruments involved, and training of workers in their operation, as well as instructions concerning ergonomic principles and potential abnormal occurrences, are obligations of the employer (Directive 2009/104/EC, Articles 4, 5, 7, 8, 9).

Anybody that has been to a dentist's office will have noted that various members of the dental squad wear diverse types of personal protective equipment, such as face masks, jackets, body gowns, protective eye wear, and gloves. These items the oral healthcare provider wears to protect oneself from many of the aforementioned hazards evident in the practice of oral health care. In the interest of safety at the workplace, the EU passed a regulation (Regulation (EU) 2016/425) that assures certain health and safety standards for this type of equipment placed on the market. These measures relate to the design and manufacture of the item, and the EU declaration of conformity with the enunciated standards is a mandatory CE marking (abbreviation for Conformité Européenne, meaning European Conformity) that indicates the item has been certified by an accredited authority. Exempt from the Regulation are the personal protective equipment for sporting activities and that utilized by the armed forces. The Regulation discusses not only the obligations of manufacturers but also those of importers and distributors. Many of these firms are also concerned about the quality of the goods with which they work. For example, Malaysia, the world's largest exporter of medical gloves, also has a quality certification program (Malaysian Rubber Export Promotion Council 2016). Barrier protection elements with inferior quality could expose both the patient and providers of service to critical agents.

Council Directive 2013/59/EURATOM presents guidelines for protection from ionizing radiation. Also, the European Commission has presented the same along with suggestions for the training of healthcare professionals across the Member States on the subject matter. In addition, radiation is also regulated in the Member States. For example, it is accomplished in Ireland via licensure where a license must be obtained from the Environmental Protection Agency for radioactive substances and irradiating apparatus including dental X-ray units which are regularly inspected. The results of these inspections are published.

Many Member States that regulate ionizing radiation require that DCPs fulfill mandatory continuing professional development (CPD) on the matter every so often. The period for this study is usually every 5 years, more or less, and the number of hours is specified. Cyprus, Denmark, Greece, Ireland, Malta, the Netherlands, Portugal, Romania, Spain, and Sweden do not feature such a requirement (Kravitz et al. 2015).

In the presentation of DCPs' occupational hazards, injuries from sharps, including needles, were cited. A sharps injury is defined as "a penetrating stab wound from a needle, scalpel. or other sharp object that may result in exposure to blood, or other body fluids" (Yaneva-Deliverska 2012. p. 357). The topic became a priority for the EU because these injuries can cause infections from 30 potentially dangerous blood-borne pathogens and healthcare-associated infections. The latter include hepatitis B, hepatitis C, and HIV. Moreover, psychological imbalances can result from these injuries which are costly to individuals, employers, and civil society (Mphil n.d.). It is estimated that over one million needlestick injuries take place annually throughout the Member States. This author found that the number occurring among DCPs or within their individual professions were, in general, unavailable. For workers in the European healthcare sector, these injuries are among the most frequent and most severe. A survey by the British Association of Dental Nurses found that 51.2% of the participants had experienced needlesticks and 60% of those reporting more than one (Allen 2015). Forty-one percent of those surveyed reported their injury took place after use and before disposal of the needle. Fortunately, 97.4% of those who had a mishap knew what measures to take (Over half of dental nurses have had a needlestick injury 2014; Survey says dental nurses are at high risk of sharps injury 2014). Preventive efforts were deemed necessary. A response to the hazard was needed.

The outcome of the EU's and others' efforts was Council Directive 2010/32/EU of 10 May 2010 implementing the Framework Agreement on prevention from sharp injuries in the hospital and healthcare sector concluded by the European Hospital and Healthcare Employers' Association and the European Federation of Public Service Unions. This document incorporates the Framework Agreement (Council Directive 2010/32/EU, Annex) recognized by the Commission and approved by these European social partners. The directive is of significance because it is the first one concerned with occupational health and safety resulting from dialogue between social partners (Bruton 2014). The purpose of the accord was the betterment of working conditions (Council Directive 2010/32/EU, Recital 8) and the achievement of the best possible work environment in which all sharps injuries are prevented (Council Directive 2010/32/EU, Annex, Clause 3).

It is stated that the employer's responsibility is to protect the safety and health of employees and to draw up necessary policies in consultation with them and their representatives. Risk assessments are to be conducted when deemed necessary, and guidelines are provided for the procedure (Council Directive 2010/32/EU, Annex, Clauses 4, 5, 6) as well as actions to be undertaken to reduce the risk of exposure and appropriately protect workers' safety and health.

The accord also refers to information and awareness-raising as related to the use of work equipment, risks involved, existing relevant legislation, the reporting of accidents, and the availability of support programs. More than awareness-raising via the provision of information is involved. Actual training of personnel is an affirmed requisite, and the topics to be covered are specified (Council Directive 2010/32/EU, Annex, Clauses 7, 8). It is also provided that all injuries are to be reported and data systems should be revised so as to include local, national, and European-wide information. Moreover, the agreement also affirms the response and follow-up actions to be taken after a sharps injury has occurred (Council Directive 2010/32/EU, Clauses 9, 10).

This Directive and Framework Agreement possess a significance in that the health and safety of employees in the healthcare sector is related to the patients' health. Furthermore, all activities focused on the workers' health and safety of health care reflect on the nature of the services delivered and also decrease the potential for negative results caused by these services (Council Directive 2010/32/EU, Annex, Preamble; Yaneva-Deliverska 2012).

Three years after the Directive's implementation date of May 2013, the European Biosafety Network and the European Agency for Safety and Health at Work undertook a survey of the Framework Agreement's provisions related to awareness, training, and implementation of improved sharps policies. The questionnaire was distributed in all Member States to persons active in the prevention of sharps injuries. The results for dental practices were not heartening. Hospitals and clinics scored high levels of awareness and observance of the accord. Dentistry practices were labeled "a cause for concern." The rate of changeover to safer sharps mechanisms placed the profession at the bottom of the continuum. Levels of awareness of the Agreement were found to be relatively high, but 20% of the participants affirmed that risk assessments and training were not taking place, and sharps injuries were not being reported. Reporting is very important. It leads to a more accurate understanding of any matter. Also, it was found that more than a third of the injection mechanisms and other sharps were still of the older type. They had not been changed. It is noteworthy that the Spanish Nurses Association exhibited the importance of having personnel that use the instruments participate in their selection (European Biosafety Network n.d.).

Some Member States, such as Belgium, France, Germany, Ireland, the Netherlands, those in Scandinavia, and the United Kingdom, have turned to safer sharps, and thus, awareness of the legislation and compliance, as well, are greater. On the other hand, other Member States, including Cyprus, Estonia, Greece, Hungary, Poland, and Slovenia, are less aware, and, as a result, compliance is also less (EBN sharps survey 2016 results n.d.). These results demonstrate that more has to be accomplished, especially on the part of dentistry.

Water for Use in Dental Practices

Dental chair units have systems that supply instruments and services needed for a large number of dental treatments. Water, obtained through a dental unit waterline system, is utilized to irrigate and cool instruments, such as dental handpieces, triple spray syringes, turbines, and scalers, as well as on the oral cavity of the patient. In addition, this water is used for filling a patient's cup and cleaning the spittoon with the bowl-rinse outlet. It has been acknowledged that, in general, these systems are associated with a risk for both DCPs and patients. Contamination results from the nature of the water that often contains microorganisms, especially bacteria. If untreated, the bacteria can augment, attach to the surfaces in the complex waterline network, and create biofilm or slime on the equipment's tubes. Once formed, biofilm can detach and transfer to the dental output water (Berck n.d.; Coleman et al. 2009; Health Protection Scotland and National Services Scotland 2018; Lai 2016; Walker et al. n.d.). This creates problems for both patients and DCPs. Contaminated water produces aerosols capable of causing infection (Kumar et al. 2010).

An early research project (Kamma et al. 2006) involving dental unit water systems and dentists' attitudes toward the microbial contamination linked to them focused on the United Kingdom, Denmark, Germany, the Netherlands, Greece, Spain, and Ireland. It was found that practitioners in these Member States at that time did not clean, disinfect, or give thought to the microbial load of their systems. However, they were wholeheartedly open to regular audits, advice on system maintenance, as well as the creation of guidelines on the subject.

Moreover, an Irish study (Burke et al. 2005), undertaken a year earlier, revealed similar results. Likewise, a majority of practitioners failed to treat their systems, but yet they demonstrated concern about water quality. All were unaware of national and international guidelines for microbial contamination of dental unit water systems. Like other practitioners, they would welcome regular water testing and advice on the cleansing of their units. Opinions of these EU professionals appear similar. In a more recent survey of practices in France, an analysis of the microbiological quality of the dentistry waterline was performed in only 2.6% of the practices indicating that improved training was needed by DCPs (Baudet et al. 2019).

Strangely, there is no EU standard regarding the quality of dental units' output water, and some Member States, such as France, have not regulated dental unit waterlines (Offner et al. 2016). National regulations and recommendations, once again, are diverse. The EU, however, several years ago, approved a law (Council Directive 98/83/EC) on the quality of water intended for human consumption. It establishes quality standards; monitoring, remedial actions, and limitations on usage, if parametric values are not met; as well as the availability of information to the public and reports to be issued by the Member States triannually on the quality of water for human consumption in their territory.

For more than 30 years, the EU has had a potable water policy. The potable water directive has been in effect for over 20 years and was under revision, even though the Regulatory Fitness and Performance program's evaluation declared it fit for purpose, but with the necessary updates. As a response to the European Citizens' Initiative Right2Water and as an effort to meet the objectives of the Sustainable Development Goals, on 1 February 2018, the Commission released a recast of the directive presently governing water for human consumption.

Water quality standards were brought up-to-date because the noted evaluation stated that criteria did not reflect scientific developments. Also, safety standards became congruent with those of the World Health Organization. Authorities were empowered to meet the challenges of polluters and risks to the water supply. A risk-based approach was added to the monitoring of the water process. The information oriented toward consumers was streamlined and improved. In addition, the standards for elements in contact with potable water were harmonized, and obligations to upgrade everyone's access to water were highlighted. Of importance is the fact that the recast contributes to the notion of a circular economy and that it is in line with the aforementioned European Pillar of Social Rights (Baudet, et al. 2019; Laaninen 2018).

After the publication of the proposal, online consultation with the citizenry took place until the end of March 2018. After this, the proposal was to be submitted to both the EP and the Council so negotiations could begin. Hopefully, in the near future, a similar directive on the subject matter of dental unit water systems will be born so that patient safety will be enhanced in the same manner.

Infections and Infection Control

In terms of patient safety, cross-infections are an ultra-important issue. These occur when damaging microorganisms, commonly, bacteria and viruses, are transmitted between individuals and dental instruments or within the body. Also, there are many transmission channels within the clinical environment: unsterilized tools, coughing and sneezing, and contact with humans, different species of plants and animals, or contaminated objects. The hazard is greater when undergoing oral healthcare treatment.

Transmission of cross-infection takes place between patients and, as noted, between patients and DCPs, whose risk of infection is dependent on the exact nature of their professional chores and work zones. There are a galaxy of infectious diseases that can be transmitted. This is especially true within the clinical dentistry setting. The oral cavity contains over 300 species of microbial flora, and then one must not forget the environment, dentistry devices, and installations difficult to sterilize (Barlean and Danila 2003; Shah and Wyne 2010).

Closely related to the subjects of infection and medicinal products is that of antimicrobial resistance (AMR). One finds, as noted, that the EU agenda is oriented toward patients as well as toward healthcare workers. Presently, the EU is dealing with this problem which occurs when microorganisms resist antimicrobial treatments. The extravagant and incorrect use of antimicrobials, especially antibiotics, has caused an increase in multi-resistant bacteria. As time passes, antimicrobials do not work as well, and eventually, they become unproductive. Thus, AMR is a major threat to public health and a critical challenge across the Member States and even the world. Each year in the EU and EEA, more than 33,000 deaths occur, and globally, at least 700,000 deaths are caused by infections with antibiotic-resistant bacteria, and if the current trend continues, ten million deaths annually are foreseen until 2050 (Council of the European Union 2014; European Commission n.d.-a; Sweeney 2019). AMR has a negative impact on humans, animals, the environment, agriculture, and national economies.

The situation is costly from many perspectives. Firstly, it is costly in terms of expenses for medicines utilized for multidrug-resistant bacterial infections which nearly doubled in Europe in the 2010–2014 period (Council of the European Union 2014; European Commission n.d.-a). There are also extra healthcare costs. Productivity decreases as well, and specific losses related to trade and agriculture take place. The AMR problem affects not only humans but also animals. In fact, many antimicrobials are taken by animals. In 2015, following reports that *Escherichia coli* or *E. coli* was found in chicken meat, Norwegian chicken sales slumped 20% for many distributors. Globally, infection control programs are to be found in less than 40% of the nations (European Commission n.d.-a).

The EU has dedicated its efforts to this serious problem for almost two decades. It has undertaken activities singly and in collaboration with international forums and with multilateral associations, such as the World Health Organization, the World Organisation for Animal Health, and the Food and Agriculture Organization of the

United Nations. In fact, the World Health Organization's Global Action Plan on AMR has been labeled a "global blue print for AMR activities" by the European Commission (n.d.-b, p. 18).

EU activities are based on its "One Health" approach which is collaborative, interdisciplinary, and multisectoral. Furthermore, it acknowledges that people, animals, plants, and their various environments are interrelated. The EU Action Plan against AMR (European Commission 2020) has three pillars at its foundation: (1) making the EU a best practice region; (2) promoting research, development, and innovation; and (3) shaping the global agenda. International cooperation is at the center of the EU program whose major objective is maintenance of effectual treatment of infections in both animals and humans. In addition, the Council has stated that collaboration between the human and veterinary health sectors should be enhanced along with research and innovation activities on AMR (Council of the European Union 2014).

Also, a part of the EU program is the EU AMR One-Health Network, chaired by the European Commission. Members include government experts from the Member States on human and animal health and the environment, plus Commission experts, and representatives from the EU scientific agencies. The Network formally meets regularly to discuss policies and policy options.

At a meeting of the One-Health Network in October 2018, there was a presentation of the EP's report on the EU's One Health Action Plan against AMR (Royston 2018). The EP recommended that the One-Health Network and the EU Joint Action on AMR and the Healthcare Associated Infections Organization involve other important stakeholders in addition to the Member States. It noted that the EU to conquer the AMR challenge needs standardized data and it should provide for its development.

It also called for closer collaboration between EU agencies and EU projects. It promoted "health literacy" as an aid to public awareness. It was of the belief that quality standards should be integrated into EU-wide curricula for DCPs so as to promote interdisciplinary curricula and the same should be done for CPD. In addition, a call was issued to restrict the sale of antibiotics. Furthermore, pollution by antibiotic residues was highlighted as a problem that needs to be tackled because the environment suffers. The release of pharmaceuticals into the environment via wastewater was noted as a challenge leading to the emergence of AMR that requires attention as well. Calls for a review of environmental risk assessments and adhesion to manufacturing procedures and the distribution of pharmaceuticals should be given attention. Animal husbandry and animal welfare were noted as subjects on which the Commission could suggest a new EU strategy.

The Commission was also urged to increase funding for interdisciplinary research related to AMR. Moreover, it was encouraged to advocate EU standards for solving AMR problems in its trade accords. Lastly, it was hoped that the Commission would continue its fight against AMR in its collaborative spirit (Royston 2018). It is evident that the EP demonstrated specificity in its review of the AMR project which in all its facets is concerned with the lives of patients across the EU and in the world.

In November 2018, after 4 years of negotiations, an agreement regarding new regulations related to the challenge of AMR took place. The preventive use of antibiotics in groups of animals was prohibited, and limitations were placed on the use of antimicrobials as treatment to prevent the spread of infection. Furthermore, it became possible to restrict specific antimicrobials for human use only. Member States became responsible for collecting data on the sale and utilization of antimicrobials. Other provisions, for example, cover veterinary medicinal products that are exported from non-EU Member States, medicated animal food, etc. In relation to AMR, the new legislation definitely promotes the appropriate use of antimicrobials. In announcing the agreement, which will be fully operationalized by 2021, the EU Commissioner for Health and Food Safety stated that the EU was a world leader against AMR and has contributed to advancement in this important sector (EU Action on Antimicrobial Resistance, n.d.).

Most recently, in recognition of the risks that the release of medicinal products poses to the environment, the Commission presented the Strategic Approach to Pharmaceuticals in the Environment. As aforementioned, across Europe, the surface and groundwater used for irrigation and drinking contain pharmaceuticals. The purpose of the recent release was to acquaint the public with the hazard and to identify areas for confrontation of the problem (European Commission Press Release 2019).

A notable and ambitious EU document on the subjects of patient safety and healthcare-associated infections is Council Recommendation of 9 June 2009. One of its purposes was "to stimulate policy development and future action in and between Member States to address the key patient safety issues confronting the EU" (Council Recommendation of 9 June 2009, Recital 8). Basically, it recommended the same should be done in the preventive and control sectors of healthcare-associated infections (Council Recommendation of 9 June 2009, Recital 14). The Council document noted gaps in policies related to both subject areas. Thus, it set forth efforts to be undertaken by the Member States.

In the area of general patient safety, national policies were to be developed and implemented, citizens and patients were to be empowered and informed, blame-free reporting systems on adverse incidents were to be established or re-energized, and the education of healthcare personnel was to include the subject matter of public safety. Also, it was provided that patient safety should be measured at the EU level via collaboration between the Member States and the Commission. Experiences were to be shared in the same manner with the same partners, plus relevant international and European structures. Lastly, on the topic of patient safety, research was to be encouraged and developed (Council Recommendation of 9 June 2009, 1(1)-1(7)).

As noted, the Council Recommendation also set forth measures regarding prevention and control of healthcare-associated infections. Member States were to establish and implement appropriate policies on the matter to which all healthcare structures would be subject. In addition, they were to develop or reinforce active surveillance systems at the national or regional level as well as at the level of healthcare structures. Promotion of the education of healthcare personnel was to take place at all levels, information given to patients by providers of services was to be upgraded, and research in various related sectors was to be advocated (Council

Recommendation of 9 June 2009, II (8)). Lastly, the Council Recommendation was to be distributed to healthcare structures, professional entities, and educational institutions (Council Recommendation of 9 June 2009, III (10)). Many of the Council's recommended measures have been implemented, but across the Member States, implementation varies (European Patients Forum 2016). Diversity once again describes the scene. The Council document and the aforementioned Directive 2011/24/EU concerned with cross-border health care have been at the base of many EU activities.

Given the aforementioned circumstances related to AMR and other possibilities for infection, infection control becomes of prime importance. The Council of European Dentists (2014) in a resolution that was unanimously adopted affirmed that all dental treatment should be offered in a manner so as to decrease as much as possible the risk of healthcare-associated infections. Moreover, dentists, as leaders of the dental team, are responsible for protecting patients from infection. According to the resolution, as part of CPD, these professionals should acquire more knowledge of infection control. However, it is noteworthy that the impact of CPD on patient safety has not been demonstrated in that the topic has not been a common one for research. Moreover, practitioners are to follow relevant guidelines on the subject and to encourage national dentistry associations to produce guidance publications on the matter that would also be available online. Furthermore, dentists across the EU should be informed of national policies on infection control related to oral health care. It was noted that the organization would appreciate the creation of unambiguous regulations concerning the reprocessing of single-use devices.

Elements of routine infection control relate to instrument sterilization, surface and device disinfection, as well as appropriate disposal of sharps and other waste. All of these infection control activities involve compliance with strict rules of clinical behavior (Barlean and Danila 2003; Shah and Wyne 2010). A highlighted issue in infection control has been cross-infection via contaminated instruments. A while ago, it was demonstrated that the sterilization procedure may not be totally effective (Hogg and Morrison 2005). Single-use devices are now utilized. They are of two types: optional and obligatory. Included in the first group are certain mirrors, metallic bands, and impression trays. The problem has been somewhat alleviated.

A while back, a study was undertaken in Lithuania of attitudes related to infection control (Rimkuvienė 2011). The majority of DCPs acknowledged its significance and affirmed that in their workplaces, they take care of the process themselves. A difference was found in attitude toward infection control and engagement in procedures used. The dividing line was between those who worked in larger cities and private structures and had been in practice for less time and those who were employed in other regions, worked in the public sector, and had a longer professional experience. The first cited group garnered more correct attitudes toward infection control and displayed more appropriate procedures.

It was found that in the public sector, DCPs had insufficient access to personal protective items. The lack of knowledge concerning infection control on the part of those who had more practice experience may be a result of the era in which they were trained. The EU was not in existence with its training laws. Moreover, it was found that few were vaccinated against hepatitis B. However, more of those with less professional experience provided an exception.

The results of this project provide the rationale for the aforementioned Council resolution and also confirm that for the formation in 2009 of the Association for European Safety & Infection Control in Dentistry. One of its objectives is the harmonization of legislation on infection control and dental hygiene. Another important goal is the sharing of knowledge across Europe. The founders realized that in the European context, diversity penetrated infection control practices. Infection control has been judged substandard in terms of the attention it receives in dental education. It tends to be overlooked in all European nations. The result is that both students' and faculties' knowledge of the subject is viewed as minimal. This seems strange because inadequate infection control and oral hygiene cause severe health hazards (Adriaanse 2012). The aforementioned association believes it is important to develop a curriculum for all DCPs containing minimal requisites for knowledge of infection control. Let's hope the organization is successful in its mission.

Dental technicians of one type or another, even though they do not always work with the dental squad, in their workplaces, experience a high risk of infection. Fortunately, many, but not all, undertake procedures to control the transfer of infections. It is interesting that in one research project (Bârlean et al. 2011), 90.2% of the participants in a survey asserted that it was necessary to disinfect prosthetic items on arrival from the dental practice. Protective equipment was used by 49.1% of the subjects. Most used safety glasses (45.9%) and the fewest (18%) full equipment. A majority (59.1%) of the laboratories used air ventilation, and surfaces were regularly disinfected in 85.2% of the workplaces. It so happens that some of the technicians disinfected the products they produced. For example, 62.1% disinfected the impressions they made, and 26.1% did the same for final prostheses. These results were not considered satisfactory. It was concluded that dental technicians should participate in educational programs to increase their awareness of appropriate decontamination measures. The Council of European Dentists in its aforementioned 2014 resolution also championed this conclusion for the entire dental squad. Further investment is required.

Waste Management

The topic of waste management is also related to patient and staff safety, infections, and infection control as well, in that some waste from dental practices, as noted, is contaminated. If not disposed of properly, providers of service, patients, janitorial staff, garbage collectors, and many others, as well as the environment, are at risk. Dental waste, in this day and age, has become a critical environmental problem (Muhamedagic et al. 2009). The EU over the years has displayed an interest in waste management policy. A goal for many stakeholders is Zero Waste. However, a literature review has revealed that there is no consensus about the definition of the concept (Pietzsch et al. 2017).

Activities in this sector across the EU once again are diverse. There has been an improvement in waste management recently, but still more than 25% of municipal waste is landfilled, and less than 50% is recycled or composted. Thus, based on the notion of a circular economy, most recently a new law (Directive (EU) 2018/851) was approved on the topic of waste. In a circular economy, "economic activity builds and rebuilds overall system health. The concept recognises the importance of the economy needing to work effectively…for large and small businesses, for organisations and individuals, globally and locally" (Ellen MacArthur Foundation 2017). Transition to the circular approach involves the separation of economic activity from the usage of finite resources and the elimination of waste from the system (Ellen MacArthur Foundation 2017).

The objective of the recent legislation was to decrease the amount of waste throughout the Member States. These units were assigned the task of stimulating the development of products fit for multiple use. They also became responsible for the prevention of waste, improving resource use, participation in electronic registries of hazardous waste, the reinforcement of record-keeping on hazardous waste, and ensuring that waste undergoes preparation for reuse and that unhealthy waste is separated and recycled at its source or collected separately. Also, recycling requisites were changed. Future goals were set. Member States will now have to recycle at least 55% of their municipal waste by 2025, 5% more by 2030, and an additional 5% by 2035. A 10% limit on landfill is required by the latter date.

Prior to the approval of the recent legislation, the Commission's Joint Research Center issued a report on the topic of best practices in waste management. Those that led to a superior overall performance were construction of a waste management strategy, promotion of waste prevention, effective waste collection, and efforts to stimulate waste and product reuse and recycling (Dri et al. 2018). The recent legislation contains all these elements.

Improving waste management and resources use via the circular economy approach can be a win-win situation for all: the environment, the climate, patient and staff health and safety, as well as the EU's population, economy, and competitiveness. To one and all, it has the potential for long-term resilience, to perpetuate economic and business opportunities, and to provide environmental and societal advantages at the same time (Ellen MacArthur Foundation 2017; European Commission 2015a).

The Council of European Dentists unanimously adopted the Commission's proposal for the recent waste management directive (CED 2016). It welcomed the project to lead Europe in the direction of a circular economy and to advocate the recycling and reuse of waste materials. It acknowledged that waste management, especially its influence on the environment, has always been worrisome for dentistry. Although the document questioned the clarity of some of the proposal's provisions, the Council of European Dentists offered its support. In reference to the creation of an electronic registry on hazardous waste, it acquiesced, provided more red tape is not created for dentists. It did not do so in reference to the development of electronic records for other waste streams (CED 2016).

The challenge of waste management requires the collaboration of policy-makers, researchers, educators, providers of oral health care, patients, and other stakeholders (Public Health England, Centre for Sustainable Healthcare 2018).

Liability for Defective Products

Also related to safety concerns is the so-called Product Liability Directive, Council Directive 85/374/EEC, which was approved after some 10 years of debate and which, according to formal evaluation, is still considered appropriate. A purpose was to make sure individuals were protected against damage to health or property by defective items. Another objective was to quell the diversity in the Member States' laws on the matter. The legislation, which applies to products, not services, assigns the responsibility for issuing strict product liability laws to the Member States, and these entities are to cast the same on persons who produce defective products. The defective nature of an item is not to be determined by its fitness for use, but by its inadequate safety. It was and still is believed that the public has the right to expect product safety. The law refers to two groups of harm: (1) personal injury or death and (2) property damage.

The producer of a defective item must assume the burden of damage to health or property caused by the defect. The injured person must prove the damage suffered, the defect of the product, and the relationship between the two elements. The individual requesting compensation faces a time limitation period of 3 years. Also, there is a financial liability restriction as well (Delaney and van de Zande 2001). The Directive also provides that special liability systems in effect at its time of approval are not affected by its enforcement. Germany featured such a structure related to medicinal products (Dodds-Smith 2017).

Computer-aided design and computer-aided manufacturing have become common in dental practices and laboratories. They are used in relation to inlays, fixed partial dentures, full-mouth reconstruction, orthodontics, onlays, veneers, and crowns, as well as other restorations. The technology is used to secure the strength of the restoration, to design one that seems natural, to decrease the time and effort needed, and to augment its accuracy. The Council of European Dentists in a statement unanimously adopted at a general meeting on 16 November 2018, in reference to a medical device regulation (Regulation (EU) 2017/745), declared that the adoption of computer-aided design and computer-aided manufacturing does not make members of the dentistry profession manufacturers or producers. They merely utilize a product already on the market and adjust it to the needs of specific patients (CED 2018; Davidowitz and Kotick 2011).

Although the Product Liability Directive was put into effect many years ago, as noted, its provisions are still considered useful. Its appropriateness was questioned, particularly, in this day and age of sophisticated technological crescendos. The

Commission conducted a formal study of the Directive's performance in terms of its coherence, relevance, effectiveness, efficiency, and EU-added values. It received a passing score, and thus, as aforementioned, it is considered appropriate for the contemporary climate (Council of the European Union 2014).

Medical Devices

The EU medical device regulatory scene has been developing since the early 1990s. There have been several directives on the subject that recently have been replaced by a new regulatory framework, deemed necessary because of the lack of clarity revealed in the directives' requisites that led to scandals as well as their diverse implementation throughout the Member States. Thus, it was deemed that in the interest of patient safety, the rules needed upgrading. The documents are to be replaced by Regulation (EU) 2017/745 and Regulation (EU) 2017/746 after transition periods. The new Regulations consolidate the role of the EU on the matter and integrate recent technological and scientific developments into the laws. Furthermore, they provide for stricter control of high-risk devices, the establishment of an EU database on medical artifices, the inclusion of new devices under their jurisdiction, a new risk classification system, more forceful post-market control mechanisms, and diverse procedures for coordination between the Member States. Also, given previous experience in the sector, the Medical Device Coordination Group was created. It is to consist of experts from the various Member States and is to advise the EU and the Member States on the subject and specifically on the implementation of both Regulations.

The new rules also include an enlarged definition of the products governed by them. For example, certain aesthetic elements are now included. Thus, any products existing at the time of their passage are to be recertified. The enlarged definition of a medical device now refers to some non-medical and cosmetic units, including specific device cleaning products. This enlarged definition means that many firms that were formerly unregulated now become regulated. In terms of thc tracking and control devices, units will now exhibit a Unique Device Identification which relates to the European Database on Medical Devices.

Furthermore, manufacturers have to report within a time limit to this EU portal incidents related to medical devices so that patients now have access to more appropriate information. Moreover, market and post-market surveillance have been broadened, and manufacturers must have an authority among their employees responsible for the application of regulations. In addition, manufacturers are to be audited at least once every 5 years. Control is definitely greater than in the past, and more pertinent information and personal safety will be available to patients when the regulations come into full application by 26 May 2020 (Duhs 2018; Edwards 2018).

Cosmetic Products

Strange as it might seem, some oral care products are termed cosmetics. They are governed by EU law with the objective of consumer or patient safety. Originally, the sector was ruled by Council Directive 76/768/EEC that established requisites concerning the composition, labeling, and packaging of cosmetics and market surveillance. It also prohibited the testing of such products or their ingredients on animals as well as the marketing of those that had been tested on animals. If a cosmetic was found to be harmful to human health, the Member State was to notify the others and the Commission. Otherwise, free movement applied. The Directive also listed prohibited materials as well as those with restricted use in the manufacture of cosmetic products.

Again, diversity prevailed in terms of the Directive's implementation. Given the nature of this sector, the role of ingredients in its products, plus the multitude of scientific innovations, the noted Directive was reevaluated and replaced by Regulation (EC) No 1223/2009. This document became the governance framework for finished cosmetic products in the EU. Basically, it was a recast of the noted Directive with several new provisions. When a Member State transposes a directive, it can add superior requisites. Thus, the 1976 Directive's national legal frameworks for the Member States numbered 27. All were different and 3500 pages of legal text resulted. Such cannot happen with a regulation (Struessmann 2010). The 2009 effort, enacted on 11 July 2013, was to garner streamlined harmonization as opposed to the existing diversity in implementation of the Directive and to regulate all stages in the development of cosmetic products so that their safety would be strengthened (Struessmann 2010).

The regulation discussed ingredient selection, the process to evaluate cosmetics for safety, product presentation, replacement of animal tests with non-animal approaches, placement of a product on the market, advertising, product labeling, distributors' responsibilities, and the cosmetovigilance and market surveillance systems. The figure of a "responsible person" with specific responsibilities was introduced in the Regulation. Each product must have one before it can be put on the market. Moreover, all products being placed on the market must be listed in the EU Cosmetic Products Notification Portal. The information is then passed on to competent authorities and poison control centers or care centers in the Member States.

In addition, the manufacturing of cosmetic products is also regulated by the good manufacturing practices set forth in ISO 22716:2007. This international standard relates to the quality of a product and was reviewed in 2017, after being in effect for 10 years. It was reconfirmed. It consists of guidelines for product control, storage, and shipment of cosmetic products. Personnel, equipment, production stages, utilization of raw materials, packaging, and quality control are among its topics.

More stress has been placed on product safety since Regulation 1223/2009/EC came into effect. Several cosmetics have been recalled as posing a risk to consumers, according to RAPEX, the EU's rapid alert system for signaling dangerous non-food products that could cause damage to consumers. Included in the recalled elements related to dentistry were products that contained heavy metals, including mercury, and a tooth whitening product containing hydrogen peroxide. The latter subject will be discussed in a later chapter.

In this sector, the EU's involvement has primarily emphasized product safety and harmonization of rules in an effort to avoid the situation existing when Council Directive 76/768/EEC was in effect. In fact, in its proposal for the Regulation now offering the governing framework for cosmetic products, the Commission stated that the most significant element would be the "introduction of clear minimum requirements for the cosmetics' safety assessment" (Commission of the European Communities 2008, p. 4).

Medicinal Products

The EU has had a role in the handling of medicinal products for about a half a century. The incident that triggered its activities in this sector would seem like ancient history to many folks. It was the births that took place in the latter part of the 1950s. A multitude of babies were born with deformed arms and legs due to the medicine their pregnant mothers consumed. These incidents illustrated that medicinal products should not be placed on the market without prior authorization. Since then, in the EU, much activity in this sector has taken place.

Prominent in medicinal products operations is the European Medicines Agency, a part of the EU structure. Founded in 1995, it works in the areas of human and veterinary medicines and was established to ensure superior utilization of scientific resources across the Member States. The agency also prepares guidelines for medicine developers that are globally available, and it offers advice to firms that create medicines. In addition, it supervises the medicinal sector in the EU, carries out scientific analyses of products, and surveils their safety. In addition, it is "responsible for coordinating the existing scientific resources put at its disposal by Member States for the evaluation, supervision and pharmacovigilance of medicinal products" (Regulation (EC) No 726/2004, Article 55).

Regulation (EU) No 536/2014 provides the structural frame for carrying out clinical trials on medicinal products for human use in the EU. Basically, the document simplifies and increases transparency and harmonization of the rules related to clinical trials. These trials are undertaken to analyze the effectiveness and safety of medications by surveilling their impact on people. The cited legal framework was to guarantee the rights, safety, and well-being of the participants and that the resultant data would be noteworthy and ethical in nature. Such trials are usually carried out by government health agencies, healthcare institutions, university healthcare faculty, independent researchers, and industry.

Very often, authorization of a new medicinal product is significantly determined by the nature and outcome of a clinical trial. Clinical trial results may be positive, meaning the new medicine is superior to others, or they may be labeled non-inferior indicating the evaluated medicinal product is equivalent to standard ones. Results might also be inconclusive in nature, demonstrating that the evaluated medication was not superior or inferior to others. Lastly, the outcome of a clinical trial may be negative, meaning that the medicine tested was not equivalent to standard treatment. It was inferior.

Inspections of the trials were regulated as well by Commission Implementing Regulation (EU) 2017/556 and in the last-mentioned Regulation. These inspections may be conducted in nations outside the EU, if the clinical trial is related to an authorization application submitted to the EU. Member States were charged with establishing inspection systems. In carrying out inspections, they were urged to have recourse to sanctions.

Commission Implementing Regulation (EU) 2017/556 discusses the inspection of clinical trials in relation to good manufacturing and clinical practices. It establishes a time frame for inspections (Commission Implementing Regulation (EU) 2017/556, Article 2), as well as requisites related to the qualifications, training, and experience of inspectors, their conflicts of interest and impartiality, their rights, and inspection procedures. Records and reports of all clinical trial inspections are to be submitted via the EU data portal (Commission Implementing Regulation (EU) 2017/556, Chapter III, Articles 10, 13). Unfortunately, information technology problems have arisen concerning the EU Portal and Database. These mechanisms were to be the foundation of the new EU policy for clinical trials. The initiation of these instruments has been postponed from 2018, as originally stated, to 2020. Until the problem concerning information technology is solved, the Clinical Trials Directive (Directive 2001/20/EC) will remain in effect. Solution will close the transitory period, and Regulation (EU) No 536/2014 will reign. The form of legislation in this case followed the pattern for cosmetic products: directive to regulation.

Nowadays, in the EU, medicinal products for human use are authorized by a few pathways. The purpose of market authorization is to verify the quality of the product, its safety, and its efficacy. One route is termed the centralized procedure. It takes place at the European level. It was established by Regulation (EC) No. 726/2004. The applicant applies to the European Medicines Agency for authorization. The agency then conducts an evaluation of the application that must be completed within a specified time limit. When completed, the Commission forwards the decision to the Member States for their perusal. They too have a restricted time period to respond with their opinion. If a positive consensus is reached, authorization is granted by the Commission, and it is valid initially in all Member States for 5 years. If renewed, an authorization is valid for an unlimited period. Not all seekers of medicinal authorization can take advantage of the centralized procedure which is obligatory for most innovative medicinal products, including "orphan drugs" or those for rare diseases (European Medicines Agency 2016; Regulation 726/2004, Article 14; Scholz 2015).

Most medicines follow a decentralized authorization process involving national authorities of a Member State or Member States. In this decentralized procedure which was set forth in Directive 2004/27/EC, an application for authorization is usually submitted simultaneously to several Member States, one of which becomes the Reference Member State and leads the pathway of the application. If a Member State disagrees with the opinion of the others involved, the issue falls into the hands of a coordination group, in this case, the Coordination Group for Mutual Recognition and Decentralised Procedures, in the hope of reaching a consensual decision within, once again, a fixed time period. If one is not forthcoming, the issue is then turned over to the European Medicines Agency for its assessment which is then forwarded to the Commission for its action. Authorization, if granted, is valid in the Member States concerned.

A third pathway to authorization is labeled the mutual-recognition procedure. This process applies to medicinal products that have already obtained authorization in one Member State and wish to be recognized in others. It is decentralized as well. In addition, there are regulations specifically related to pediatric (European Commission 2017e; Regulation (EC) No 1907/2006), geriatric (Directive 2004/27/EC), advanced therapy (Regulation (EC) No 1394/2007), herbal (Directive 2004/24/EC), homeopathic, and non-prescription drugs (Directive 2001/83/EC).

The outcome of every application for authorization is reviewed by the European Medicines Agency and, whether positive or negative, is recorded and is available in a European Public Assessment Report. Transparency is a significant characteristic of the EU's medicinal regulatory system (European Medicines Agency 2016).

Once a market authorization has been awarded, regardless of the process utilized, price and reimbursement rates are set at the level of the Member State. An aid in this step is EURIPID, a non-profit structure with EU financial support, involving 26 European nations. It has constructed a database, available to national competent authorities, containing information on the prices of medicines in several countries. Moreover, the original objective of the cooperative effort, initiated in 2010, was to augment the transparency of the partners' pricing of medicinal products by using information in common with one another and reinforcing collaboration between pricing and reimbursement authorities. It was believed that such action would afford citizens wider access to medicines. In some countries, at least in Norway, re-evaluation of a large percentage of the medicinal market takes place on an annual basis.

Not all Member States adopt the same pathway in establishing prices of medicines. In Sweden, a price is suggested by the manufacturer and then it is negotiated. In Austria, the Ministry of Health names the cost, and then reimbursement is decided in meetings between social insurance authorities and manufacturers. Price in the Netherlands is determined by the Ministry of Health, Welfare, and Sport and in Poland, by the Ministry of Health. On the other hand, the so-called free-pricing Member States in which the manufacturers primarily set the cost include Denmark, Germany, and the United Kingdom. These nations comprise a minority (Panteli et al. 2016).

In some Member States, the VAT for goods and services is reduced for medicinal products. Again, diverse practices apply. Standard rates are applicable to medicines only in Denmark and Germany. In France, the tax amount depends on whether the medicine is reimbursable or not. In Sweden and the United Kingdom, the only medicines that are tax-free are those that require a prescription. For over-the-counter medicines, the practice is diverse. Usually the individual is expected to pay the full cost. The highest tax rates for over-the-counter drugs are found in Denmark and Sweden where the standard rates for 2018 stood at 25%. Ireland ranked second at 23%. Luxembourg and Malta were at the bottom of the continuum with the former Member State having a rate of 3% and Malta 0% for over-the-counter drugs (Panteli et al. 2016).

A leaflet is to be included in all packages of medicines. It should present information on the product including its name, manufacturer, therapeutic indications, dosage, shelf life, possible adverse reactions, as well as other specifics. A black symbol (black triangle) signals that additional monitoring is required. Also, it serves to urge healthcare professionals and consumers to report adverse reactions immediately to competent authorities. Furthermore, data on leaflets should be presented in the official language(s) of the country concerned and in a manner to be comprehended by persons of all ages and literary capacities (Directive 2012/26/EU; European Commission: Health and Food Safety Directorate-General 2017).

After a medicine has been authorized for the market, its safety, quality, and efficacy are still of significance. It is continually observed for the duration of its life span via pharmacovigilance duties carried out by competent authorities or reviews of the benefit-risk balance so as to permit rapid market withdrawal of drugs not affording superior advantages. Pharmacovigilance has been defined as "the science and activities relating to the detection, assessment, understanding and prevention of adverse effects or any other drug-related problem" (WHO n.d.). Regulation (EC) No 726/2004 and Directive 2001/83 establish the legal justification of pharmacovigilance functions for EU-marketed medicines.

Multi-faceted groups take part in these activities. They include the consumers of medicinal products, healthcare professionals, regulatory and national authorities, pharmaceutical firms, the EU Commission, and the European Medicines Agency. The latter organization has the task of coordinating the pharmacovigilance operations of the Member States. In terms of good manufacturing, laboratory, and clinical practices, it is the Commission's responsibility to make sure they are observed (Regulation (EC) No 726/2004, Recitals 29, 30, 31).

Given pharmacovigilance incidents, the necessity of having harmonized rules throughout the Member States for these functions was recognized. The result was Directive 2012/26/EU. After all, globalization and state interdependence stimulate the setting for harmonization (Wiktorowicz et al. 2018).

The EU also protects individuals from falsified medicines, the amount of which alarmingly augmented (Directive 2011/62/EU, Recital 2). These products are often claimed to be genuine, when they feature falsities related to history, source, and identity as well as other factors. Such a situation poses a serious risk to one's health and maybe even to the person's life, when unbeknown use is suggested by a provider of service.

The so-called Falsified Medicines Directive (Directive 2011/62/EU) manifested a belief that harmonization of the safety features of medicinal products was critical to the elimination of falsified medicines. Thus, controls concerning medicinal commerce were reinforced. Specific obligatory safety features were also set forth in

Commission Delegated Regulation (EU) 2016/161which supplements the aforementioned Directive and was to be fully implemented in 2019. In addition, the supplement identifies how the genuine nature of medications should be identified and by whom.

The specified safety features include certain items to be evident on each package, such as a tamper-proof security seal and a barcode, manifesting a serialized number, to be checked in a database prior to dispensing the product on the basis of a prescription. All prescription medicines require a barcode. There are only a few exceptions. Moreover, all legal online pharmacies to demonstrate their legality must display a common EU-wide logo on each page of their website, and the Member State location should be evident as well. Also, rules concerning control and inspections of medicinal products and their producers were strengthened. In addition, the wholesale distribution of medicines became more controlled along with the import of pharmaceutical ingredients. Record-keeping for wholesale distributors was enhanced. Furthermore, when these legal requisites do not reach the intended goal, the noted Directive, as in other cases, requires the Member States to have "effective, proportionate, and dissuasive" (Directive 2011/62/EU, Article 118a) sanctions (Commission Delegated Regulation (EU) 2016/161; Directive 2011/62/EU; Robinson 2016).

In terms of medicinal products, EU legislation has focused a great deal on their quality and safety, ranging from their market authorization, manufacturing, and distribution practices, and accessibility. Surveillance and control continue on many facets of the medicinal product throughout its life span. The EU has not only been concerned with its own territory. It has collaborated with many other entities located elsewhere on the globe and has acted in the interest of dentistry professionals and their patients.

Conclusion

EU efforts at the workplace have focused on the personal safety and health of patients as well as those of DCPs. As defined by the Council, this "means freedom, for a patient, from unnecessary harm or potential harm associated with healthcare" (Council Recommendation of 9 June 2009, Recital 19). The same freedom can be applied to DCPs as well. For the European Patients Forum, safety is both a goal and a practice. It definitely has a very broad meaning and significance. Moreover, it is an important segment of the quality of health care in general for both oral healthcare providers and their patients. The construction of a safety culture is an arduous task. At its forefront is the acknowledgement that error is possible and that practice must promote continuous learning and feature improvement procedures and strong leadership. It is noteworthy that the Council advocates an interprofessional safety culture (Council of the European Union 2014; European Patients Forum 2016).

The EU has exhibited a great interest in the workplace as is evident from its activities in various sectors noted in this chapter. Its efforts demonstrate that it hoped to simplify the rules applicable to work activities and the items utilized and that it desired to harmonize them. Such was shown by using Regulations to replace Directives in some instances impacting the nature of work operations. Moreover, there have been efforts articulated in EU rules to educate the citizenry by circulating information on specific problems, such as healthcare-associated infections, and to encourage dialogue and discussion. It has been concluded that EU activities have added benefits to Member State's health policies, especially those concerning the regulation of medicinal products and medical devices (Lomba 2019).

Still, the EU has assumed more should be accomplished. In addition, in a press release, the Commission (2014) noted that much remains to be done in terms of patient empowerment and the education and training of healthcare personnel. It asserted the latter rarely includes patient safety. Thus, the EU felt the need to undertake efforts related to two interrelated themes: patient safety and quality of care. In addition, in the EU Occupational Safety and Health Strategic Framework, it proposed to further consolidate national health and safety strategies via further efforts of coordination, to simplify existing legal documents by ridding them of unnecessary administrative obligations, to improve data collection and its monitoring, and to strengthen collaboration with other international associations. With these activities, the EU hoped to better implement health and safety practices, to improve prevention of diseases and hazards associated with oral healthcare work, and to provide for the aging of the workforce (European Commission, Directorate-General for Employment, Social Affairs & Inclusion n.d.).

The quality of oral health care and the health of all its providers with a focus on patient safety has occupied center stage in the EU. An instrument on which the Commission can rely is the Expert Panel on Effective Ways of Investing in Health. This organ is composed of 16 scientists appointed for a 3-year term. Each member has more than 10 years of professional and multidisciplinary experience in the health sector. The Commission requests health-related opinions from the group. The panel was asked to provide an EU agenda related to the quality of health care with a special focus on patient safety. It cited five dimensions of quality for all healthcare services. They must produce desired and superior results. They must be safe, appropriate, and congruent with contemporary professional knowledge and meet approved standards. They must be patient-centered in nature and engage patients in care procedures. Lastly, they should be efficient and equitable and lead to equal access to available quality care. The panel also developed a set of indicators useful for measuring and evaluating EU healthcare structures from a quality/safety and comparative view. In addition, it suggested a Health System Performance Analysis Framework that would allow for comparisons of healthcare policies and their impact. Furthermore, it proposed a health technology assessment network to examine impact on healthcare delivery systems. The Panel believed that these actions and others would help to enhance the quality of services as well as their safety (Expert Panel on Effective Ways of Investing in Health 2014). Care that is not penetrated with safety immediately damages patients' health and well-being and is accompanied with economic consequences. Furthermore, it can also negatively affect patients' confidence and trust in a healthcare delivery system.

Of significance is the fact that in a flash Eurobarometer survey of working conditions, a majority of participants signaled approval of them (European Commission 2015b). Such illustrates that EU rules governing the workplace have appeal. They have contributed to its safety and, in the case of DCPs specifically, to their effectiveness and the quality of their care. In short, the oral healthcare system with the EU governance framework has become more transparent, resilient, effective, and efficient. Patients have benefited from an enhanced role and safety in many sectors as well as recognition of their basic rights. However, there are certain issues, in addition to the ones already mentioned, that have created discussion in the sector. Some of these will be presented in Chap. 7.

References

Adriaanse, B. (2012, March 28). Interview: Infection control is continually neglected in dental education. *Dental Tribune Netherlands*. https://eu.dental-tribune.com/. Accessed 4 Dec 2018.

Allen, R. (2015, March 27). Needlestick safety for the whole dental team. *British Dental Journal Team*, 13–14.

Aumayr-Pintar, C. (2018, October). *Progress in paternity and parental leave for fathers–Are baby steps enough?* http://eurofound.europa.eu. Accessed 10 Nov 2018.

Ayatollahi, J., Ayatollahi, F., Ardekani, A. M., Bahrololoomi, R., Ayatollahi, J., Ayatollahi, A., et al. (2012). Occupational hazards to dental staff. *Dental Research Journal (Isfahan), 9*(1), 2–7.

Barlean, L., & Danila, I. (2003). Infection control in dentistry–Present requirements. *Oral Health and Dental Management, 2*(2), 13–17.

Bârlean, L., Dănilă, I., & Săveanu, I. (2011). Prevention of infection transmission in dental laboratories. *Revista medico-chirurgicăla a Societătii de Medici şi Naturalişti din laşi, 115*(2), 548–553.

Baudet, A., Lizon, T., Martrehe, J. M., Camelot, F., Florentin, A., & Clement, C. (2019). Dental unit waterlines: A survey of practices in eastern France. *International Journal of Environmental Research and Public Health, 16*(21), E4242.

Bell, M. (2008). The implementation of European anti-discrimination directives: Converging towards a common model? *The Political Quarterly, 79*(1), 36–44.

Berck, J. (n.d.). *White paper*. http://www.judyb.com. Accessed 29 Oct 2015.

Bruton, R. (2014). *Statutory injuries in the healthcare sector regulations 2014*. Dublin: Stationary Office.

Burke, F. M., O'Mullane, D., & O'Sullivan, M. (2005). Attitudes of European dentists to water quality of dental unit water systems. *Journal of the Irish Dental Association, 51*(3), 119–125.

CED (Council of European Dentists). (2016, December). *CED position: Commission's proposal amending directive on waste*. http://www.cedentists.eu. Accessed 20 Jan 2018.

CED (Council of European Dentists). (2018, November). *CED statement: Medical devices regulation and chairside CAD/CAM (computer-aided design/computer-aided manufacturing) procedures: Right of dentists not to be defined as manufacturers*. http://www.cedentists.eu. Accessed 28 Nov 2018.

Coleman, D. C., O'Donnell, M. J., Shore, A. C., & Russell, R. J. (2009). Biofilm problems in dental unit water systems and its practical control. *Journal of Applied Microbiology, 106*(5), 1424–1437.

Commission Delegated Regulation (EU). 2016/161 of 2 October 2015 supplementing Directive 2001/83/EC of the European Parliament and of the Council by laying down detailed rules for the safety features appearing on the packaging of medicinal products for human use.

Commission Implementing Regulation (EU) 2017/556 of 24 March 2017 on the detailed arrangements for the good clinical practice inspection procedures pursuant to Regulation (EU) No 536/2014 of the European Parliament and of the Council.

Commission of the European Communities. (2008). *Proposal for a Regulation of the European Parliament and of the Council on cosmetic products. COM(2008) 49 final.*

Conrad, D. A., & Emerson, M. L. (1981). State dental practice acts: Implications for competition. *Journal of Health Politics, Policy and Law, 5*(4), 610–630.

Council Directive 2000/43/EC of 29 June 2000 implementing the principle of equal treatment between persons irrespective of racial or ethnic origin.

Council Directive 2000/78/EC of 27 November 2000 establishing a general framework for equal treatment in employment and occupation.

Council Directive 2010/32/EU of 10 May 2010 implementing the Framework Agreement on prevention from sharp injuries in the hospital and healthcare sector concluded by HOSPEEM (European Hospital and Healthcare Employers' Association) and EPSU (European Federation of Public Service Unions) (Text with EEA relevance).

Council Directive 2013/59/EURATOM of 5 December 2013 laying down basic safety standards for protection against the dangers arising from exposure to ionizing radiation, and repealing Directives 89/618, Euratom, 90/641/Euratom, 96/29/Euratom, 97/43/Euratom and 2003/122/Euratom.

Council Directive 76/768/EEC of 27 July 1976 on the approximation of the laws of the Member States relating to cosmetic products (Cosmetics Directive).

Council Directive 84/450/EEC of 10 September 1984 relating to the approximation of the laws, regulations and administrative provisions of the Member States concerning misleading advertising.

Council Directive 85/374/EEC of 25 July 1985 on the approximation of the laws, regulations and administrative provisions of the Member States concerning liability for defective products.

Council Directive 89/391/EEC of 12 June 1989 on the introduction of measures to encourage improvements in the safety and health of workers at work.

Council Directive 92/85/EEC of 19 October 1992 on the introduction of measures to encourage improvements in the safety and health at work of pregnant workers and workers who have recently given birth or are breastfeeding (tenth individual Directive within the meaning of Article 16(1) of Directive 89/391/EEC).

Council Directive 98/83/EC of 3 November 1998 on the quality of water intended for human consumption.

Council of European Dentists. (2014). *CED resolution: Infection control and waste management in dentistry*. http://www.eudental.eu. Accessed 16 Oct 2015.

Council of the European Union. (2014). *Council conclusions on patient safety and quality of care, including the prevention and control of healthcare associated infections and antimicrobial resistance*. http://www.consilium.europa.eu. Accessed 28 Nov 2018.

Council Recommendation of 9 June 2009 on patient safety, including the prevention and control of healthcare associated infections, (2009/C 151/01).

Davidowitz, G., & Kotick, P. G. (2011). The use of CAD/CAM (computer-aided design/computer-aided manufacturing) in dentistry. *Dental Clinics, 55*(3), 559–570.

Delaney, H., & van de Zande, R. (2001). *A guide to the EU directive concerning liability for defective products (product liability directive)*. Gaithersburg: U.S. Department of Commerce, National Institute of Standards and Technology.

Dhéret, C. (2018). *European Pillar of Social Rights: Member States must shoulder the responsibility of delivery*. http://www.epc.eu. Accessed 24 Sept 2018.

Directive 2000/31/EC of the European Parliament and of the Council of 8 June 2000 on certain legal aspects of information society services, in particular electronic commerce, in the Internal Market (Directive on electronic commerce).

Directive 2001/20/EC of the European Parliament and of the Council of 4 April 2001 on the approximation of the laws, regulations and administrative provisions of the Member States relating to the implementation of good clinical practice in the conduct of clinical trials of medicinal products for human use.

Directive 2002/14/EC of the European Parliament and of the Council of 11 March 2002 establishing a general framework for informing and consulting employees of the European Community--Joint declaration of the European Parliament, the Council and the Commission on employee representation.

Directive 2003/88/EC of the European Parliament and of the Council of 4 November 2003 concerning certain aspects of the organization of working time.

Directive 2004/24/EC of the European Parliament and of the Council of 31 March 2004 amending. as regards traditional herbal medicinal products, Directive 2001/83/EC on the Community code relating to medicinal products for human use.

Directive 2001/83/EC of the European Parliament and of the Council of 6 November 2001 on the Community code relating to medicinal products for human use.

Directive (EU) 2018/851 of the European Parliament and of the Council of 30 May 2018 amending Directive 2008/98/EC on waste.

Directive 2004/27/EC of the European Parliament and of the Council of 31 March 2004 amending Directive 2001/83/EC on the Community code relating to medicinal products for human use.

Directive 2005/29/EC of the European Parliament and of the Council of 11 May 2005 concerning unfair business-to- consumer commercial practices in the internal market and amending Council Directive 84/450/EEC, Directive 97/7/EC, 98/27/EC and 2002/65/EC of the European Parliament and of the Council and Regulation (EC) No 2006/2004 of the European Parliament and of the Council ('Unfair Commercial Practices Directive').

Directive 2006/114/EC of the European Parliament and of the Council of 12 December 2006 concerning misleading and comparative advertising (codified version).

Directive 2006/54/EC of the European Parliament and the Council of 5 July 2006 on the implementation of the principle of equal opportunities and equal treatment of men and women in matters of employment and occupation (recast).

Directive 2009/104/EC of the European Parliament and of the Council of 16 September 2009 concerning the minimum safety and health requirements for the use of work equipment by workers at work (second individual Directive within the meaning of Article 16(1) of Directive 89/391/EEC).

Directive 2011/24/EU of the European Parliament and of the Council of 9 March 2011 on the application of patients' rights in cross-border healthcare.

Directive 2011/62/EU of the European Parliament and of the Council of 8 June 2011 amending Directive 2001/83/EC on the Community code relating to medicinal products for human use, as regards the prevention of the entry into the legal supply chain of falsified medicinal products.

Directive 2012/26/EU of the European Parliament and of the Council of 25 October 2012 amending Directive 2001/83/EC as regards pharmacovigilance.

Dodds-Smith, I. (2017, May 21). *Recent developments in European product liability*. http://www.arnoldporter.com. Accessed 5 Dec 2018.

Dri, M., Canfora, P., Antonopoulos, I., & Gaudillat, P. (2018). *Best environmental management practices for the waste management sector*. Luxembourg: Publications Office of the European Union.

Droeze, E. H., & Jonsson, H. (2005). Evaluation of ergonomic interventions to reduce musculoskeletal disorders of dentists in the Netherlands. *Work, 25*(3), 211–220.

Duhs, G. (2018, April). A new landscape for medical devices. *Pharma Times*. http://www.pharmatimes.com. Accessed 7 Dec 2018.

EBN (European Biosafety Network) sharps survey 2016 results. (n.d.). http://www.europeanbiosafetynetwork. Accessed 20 Nov 2018.

Edwards, C. (2018). *Explainer: What's changing with EU's medical device regulation?* http://www.medicaldevice-network.com. Accessed 8 Dec 2018.

Ellen MacArthur Foundation. (2017). *What is a circular economy?* http://www.ellenmacarthurfoundation.org. Accessed 25 Nov 2018.

EU Action on Antimicrobial Resistance. (n.d.). http://www.ec.europa.eu. Accessed 21 Oct 2019.

Eurofound (European Foundation for the Improvement of Living and Working Conditions). (n.d.). Statutory regulations on severance pay in Europe. http://www.eurofound.europa.eu. Accessed 23 Mar. 2019.

Eurofound. (European Foundation for the Improvement of Living and Working Conditions). (2018, November 2). *Pay is just one aspect of disadvantage for women on the labour market*. http://www.eurofound.europa.eu. Accessed 10 Nov 2018.

European Biosafety Network. (n.d.). *Prevention of sharps injuries in the hospital and healthcare sector: Implementation guidance for the EU Framework Agreement, Council Directive and associated national legislation*. http://www.europeanbiosafetynetwork.eu. Accessed 21 Nov 2018.

European Commission (2010). Report from the Commission to the European Parliament, the Council, the European Economic and Social Committee and the Committee of the Regions on implementation by Member States of Directive 2003/88/EC ('The Working Time Directive') (SEC(2010) 1611 final).

European Commission (2015a). Communication from the Commission to the European Parliament, the Council, the European Economic and Social Committee and the Committee of the Regions-Closing the loop-An EU plan for the Circular Economy. COM(2015)614 final.

European Commission. (2015b). Flash Eurobarometer 398: Working Conditions.

European Commission. (2017a). Commission Staff Working Document. Detailed report on the implementation by Member States of Directive 2003/88/EC concerning certain aspects of the organization of working time. Accompanying the document Report from the Commission to the European Parliament, the Council and the European Economic and Social Committee, Report on the implementation by Member States of Directive 2003/88/EC concerning certain aspects of the organisation of working time (COM(2017) 254 final).

European Commission. (2017b, November 20). Communication from the Commission to the European Parliament, the Council and the European Economic and Social Committee; EU Action Plan 2017–2019: Tackling the gender pay gap (COM(2017)678 final).

European Commission. (2017c). Communication from the Commission to the European Parliament, the Council, the European Economic and Social Committee and the Committee of the Regions on Establishing a European Pillar of Social Rights (COM(2017) 250 final.

European Commission. (2017d). The European pillar of social rights in 20 principles.

European Commission. (2017e). State of paediatricines in the EU: 10 years of the EU paediatric regulation; Report from the Commission to the European Parliament and the Council. COM (2017)626.

European Commission. (2020, January). A European One Health Action Plan against Antimicrobial Resistance.

European Commission. (n.d.-a). AMR (Antimicrobial Resistance): A major European and global challenge.

European Commission. (n.d.-b). A European One Health action plan against antimicrobial resistance (AMR).

European Commission Directorate-General for Employment, Social Affairs & Inclusion. (n.d.). *EU Occupational Safety and Health (OSH) Strategic Framework 2014–2020*. http://www.ec.europa.eu. Accessed 3 Apr 2018.

European Commission Press Release. (2014, June 19). *Patient safety: Progress made, more needed*. http://www.ec.europa.eu. Accessed 27 Nov 2018.

European Commission Press Release. (2019, March 11). *Strategic Approach to pharmaceuticals in the environment*. http://www.ec.europa.eu. Accessed 3 June 2019.

European Commission: Health and Food Safety Directorate-General. (2017, March 22). *Commission report recommends improvements to package leaflets*. E-News.

European Medicines Agency. (2016). *The European regulatory system for medicines and the European medicines agency: A consistent approach to medicines regulation across the European Union*. London: Author.

European Patients Forum. (2016, May). *Briefing paper on patient safety*. http://www.eu-patient.eu. Accessed 27 Oct 2018.

Expert Panel on Effective Ways of Investing in Health. (2014, October 9). *Final report on future EU agenda on quality of health care with a special emphasis on patient safety.* http://www.ec.europa.eu. Accessed 29 Nov 2018.

Fabris, B. L. (2016). *Maternity, paternity and parental leave in the European Union*. http://www.secondowelfare.it. Accessed 9 Nov 2018.

FDI (Federation Dentaire Internationale-International Dental Federation). (2007, October 26). *FDI policy statement: Musculoskeletal disorders and dental practice*. http://www.fdiworlddental.org. Accessed 20 June 2016.

Ford, G. T. (1993). Regulation of advertising in the European Community: An overview. *European Advances in Consumer Research, 1*, 559–564.

Garben, S. (2018). The European pillar of social rights: Effectively addressing displacement? *European Constitutional Law Review, 14*(1), 210–230.

Garbin, A. J. I., Garbin, C. A. S., Diniz, D. G., & Yarid, S. D. (2011). Dental students' knowledge of ergonomic postural requirements and their application during clinical care. *European Journal of Dental Education, 15*(1), 31–35.

Garus-Pakowska, A., Leśniewska, A., Gaszyńska, E., & Szatko, F. (2016). Occupational exposure and health problems among polish denturists: A population-based study in Lódź province. *International Dental Journal, 66*(4), 237–246.

Guignon, A. N. (2015). "We're not invincible": Dental hygienists need time to allow the body to repair itself. *RDH Magazine, 35*(12). http://www.rdhmag.com. Accessed 10 Jan 2016.

Guillén, A. M. (2011). Concluding thoughts on tensions between work and private life and policy responses. In S. Drobnic & A. M. Guillén (Eds.), *Work-life balance in Europe: The role of job quality* (pp. 253–259). Houndmills/Basingstoke/New York: Palgrave Macmillan.

Hayes, M. J., Smith, D. R., & Cockrell, D. (2010). An international review of musculoskeletal disorders in the dental hygiene profession. *International Dental Journal, 60*(5), 343–352.

Health Protection Scotland and National Services Scotland. (2018, March). *Literature review and recommendations: Management of dental unit waterlines*. http://www.hps.scot.nhs.uk. Accessed 7 Dec 2018.

Hogg, N. J. V., & Morrison, A. D. (2005). Resterilization of instruments used in a hospital-based oral and maxillofacial surgery clinic. *Journal of the Canadian Dental Association, 71*(3), 179–182.

ISO (International Organization for Standardization) 22716:2007. Cosmetics--Good manufacturing practices (GMP)–Guidelines on good manufacturing practices.

Jacobsen, N., Derand, T., & Hensten-Pettersen, A. (1996). Profile of work-related health complaints among Swedish dental laboratory technicians. *Community Dentistry and Oral Epidemiology, 24*(2), 138–144.

Kamma, J. J., Bradshaw, D. J., Fulford, M. R., Marsh, P. D., Frandsen, E., Ostergaard, E., et al. (2006). Attitudes of general dental practitioners in Europe to the microbial risk associated with dental unit water systems. *International Dental Journal, 56*(4), 187–195.

Katrova, L. G., Ivanov, I., Ivanov, M., & Pejcheva, K. (2012). 'Ergonomization' of the working environment and building up of healthy working posture of dental students. *Journal of IMAB, 18*(4), 243–250.

Kravitz, A. S., Bullock, A., & Cowpe, J., with Barnes, E. (2014). *Council of European* Dentists *manual of dental practice 2014* (5th edn.). n.p,: Council of European Dentists.

Kravitz, A.S., Bullock, A., & Cowpe, J., with Barnes, E. (2015). *Council of European dentists: EU manual of dental practice 2015* (5.1 edn.). Brussels, Council of European Dentists.

Kumar, S., Atray, D., Paiwal, D., Balasubramanyarn, G., Duraiswamy, P., & Kulkami, S. (2010). Dental unit waterlines: Source of contamination and cross-infection. *Journal of Hospital Infection, 74*(2), 99–111.

Laaninen, T. (2018, October). *Revision of the drinking water directive*. http://www.europarl.europa.eu. Accessed 9 Dec 2018.

Lai, S. (2016). *Investigating contamination of dental unit waterline systems and microbial biofilm ecology*. A thesis submitted in partial fulfilment of the requirements for the degree of Doctor of Philosophy at the University of Central Lancashire. http://www.uclan.ac.uk. Accessed 27 Oct 2018.

Lindfors, P., von Thiele, U., & Lundberg, U. (2006). Work characteristics and upper extremity disorders in female dental health workers. *Journal of Occupational Health, 48*(3), 192–197.

Lomba, N. (2019). *The benefit of EU action in health policy: The record to date*. Brussels: European Union.

Malaysian Rubber Export Promotion Council. (2016, June). Barrier protection critical with dental gloves. *Dental Tribune U.S. Edition*, p. A6. http://www.dental-tribune.com. Accessed 11 June 2016.

Matoš, K., Jurec, Z., Galic, I., & Vodanovic, M. (2016). Education on occupational health and health related habits among dental students in Croatia. *Acta Stomatologica Croatica, 50*(1), 49–57.

Mphil, P. D. R. (n.d.). *Healthcare worker safety after the EU Sharps Directive*. http://www.efnweb.be. Accessed 20 Nov 2018.

Muhamedagic, B., Muhamedagic, L., & Masic, I. (2009). Dental office waste- public health and ecological risk. *Materia Sociomedica, 21*(1), 35–38.

Musculoskeletal health in Europe: Report v5.0. (2013). http://www.eumusc.net. Accessed 29 Oct 2016.

Offner, D., Fioretti, F., & Musset, A.-M. (2016). Contamination of dental unit waterlines: Assessment of three continuous water disinfection systems. *British Dental Journal Open, 2*, Article Number 16007. https://doi.org/10.1038/bdjopen.2016.7.

Over half of dental nurses have had a needlestick injury. (2014). *British Dental Journal, 217*(9), 490.

Panteli, D., Arickx, F., Cleemput, I., Dedet, G., Eckhardt, H., Fogarty, E., et al. (2016). Pharmaceutical regulation in 15 European countries: Review. *Health Systems in Transition, 18*(5), 1–118.

Pensola, T., Haukka, E., Kaila-Kangas, L., Neupane, S., & Leino-Arjas, P. (2016). Good work ability despite multisite musculoskeletal pain? A study among occupationally active Finns. *Scandinavian Journal of Public Health, 44*(3), 300–310.

Pietzsch, N., Ribeiro, J. L. D., & de Medeiros, J. F. (2017). Benefits, challenges and critical factors of success for zero waste: A systematic literature review. *Waste Management, 67*(1), 324–353.

Procedure 2008/0193/COD. Proposal for a Directive of the European Parliament and of the Council amending Council Directive 92/85/EEC on the introduction of measures to encourage improvements in the health and safety at work of workers who are pregnant, and workers who have recently given birth or are breastfeeding.

Public Health England, Centre for Sustainable Healthcare. (2018). *Carbon modelling within dentistry rewards a sustainable future*. London: PHS Publications.

Ray, R., Gornick, J. C., & Schmitt, J. (2010). Who cares? Assessing generosity and gender equality in parental leave policy designs in 21 countries. *Journal of European Social Policy, 20*(3), 196–216.

Regulation (EC) No 1223/2009 of the European Parliament and of the Council of 30 November 2009 on cosmetic products.

Regulation (EC) No 1394/2007 of the European Parliament and of the Council of 13 November 2007 on advanced therapy medicinal products and amending Directive 2001/83/EC and Regulation (EC) No 726/2004.

Regulation (EC) No 1907/2006 of the European Parliament and of the Council of 18 December 2006 concerning the registration, evaluation, authorization and restriction of chemicals (REACH), establishing a European Chemicals Agency, amending Directive 1999/45/EC and repealing Council Regulation (EEC) No 793/93 and Commission Regulation (EC) No 1488/94 as well as Council Directive 76/769/EEC and Commission Directives 91/155 EEC, 93/105/EC and 2000/21/EC.

Regulation (EC) No 726/2004 of the European Parliament and of the Council of 31 March 2004 laying down Community procedures for the authorisation and supervision of medicinal products for human and veterinary use and establishing a European Medicines Agency.

Regulation (EU) 2016/425 of the European Parliament and of the Council of 9 March 2016 on personal protective equipment and repealing Council Directive 89/686/EEC.

Regulation (EU) 2017/745 of the European Parliament and of the Council of 5 April 2017 on medical devices, amending Directive 2001/83/EC, Regulation (EC) No. 178/2002 and Regulation (EC) No. 1223/2009 and repealing Council Directives 90/385/EEC and 93/42/EEC.

Regulation (EU) 2017/746 of the European Parliament and of the Council of 5 April 2017 on in vitro diagnostic medical devices and repealing Directive 98/79/EC and Commission Decision 2010/227/EU.

Regulation (EU) No 536/2014 of the European Parliament and of the Council of 16 April 2014 on clinical trials on medicinal products for human use, and repealing Directive 2001/20/EC.

Rimkuvienė, D. J. (2011). *Attitudes towards infection control among dental health care professionals*. Unpublished doctoral dissertation biomedical sciences. Vilnius University, Vilnius, Lithuania. http://www.yourscribe.com. Accessed 20 Jan 2017.

Robinson, J. (2016, October). What is the falsified medicines directive? *The Pharmaceutical Journal, 297*(7894). https://doi.org/10.1211/PJ.2016.20201820.

Royston, V. (2018). *Presentation of the European parliament report: A European one health action plan against antimicrobial resistance*. http://www.ec.europa.eu. Accessed 22 Nov 2018.

Scholz, N. (2015). *Medicinal products in the European Union: The legal framework for medicines for human use*. n.p.: European Parliamentary Research Service.

Shah, A. H., & Wyne, A. H. (2010). Cross-infection control in dentistry: A review (report). *Pakistan Oral and Dental Journal, 30*(1), 168–174.

Şoaita, C. (2014). Identifying occupational risks in dentistry. *Procedia Technology, 12*, 558–565.

Struessmann, A. (2010, January 12). *EU regulatory update: Recast of the Cosmetics Directive published*. http://www.cosmeticsandtoiletries.com. Accessed 10 Dec 2018.

Survey says dental nurses are at high risk of sharps injury. (2014, October 31). *BDJ Team*. Article number 1410.

Sweeney, C. (2019, March 12). Can vaccines help fight the rise of drug-resistant microbes? *Harvard T. H. Chan School of Public Health News*. http://www.hsph.harvard.edu/news. Accessed 15 Mar 2019.

Szymańska, J. (1999). Occupational hazards of dentistry. *Annals of Agricultural and Environmental Medicine, 6*(1), 13–19.

The Competition Authority. (2007). *Competition in professional services: Dentists*. n. p.: Author.

The Czech Republic. (n.d.). http://www.dent.cz. Accessed 1 Sept 2016.

The History of the European Union-2017. (2017). http://www.europa.eu. Accessed 29 July 2018.

Verloo, M. (2006). Multiple inequalities, intersectionality and the European Union. *European Journal of Women's Studies, 13*(3), 211–228.

Vodanovic, M., Sovic, S., & Galic, I. (2016). Occupational health problems among dentists in Croatia. *Acta Stomatologica Croatica, 50*(4), 310–320.

Waddington, L., & Bell, M. (2001). More equal than others: Distinguishing European Union equality directives. *Common Market Law Review, 38*(3), 587–611.

Walker, J. T., Frandsen, E., ten Cate, B., Kamma, J. J., O'Mullane, D., & Stoesser, L., et al. (n.d.). *Microbial risk assessment of dental unit water systems (DUWS) in General Dental Practice (GDP)*. http://www.ec.europa.eu. Accessed 29 Oct 2015.

Wiktorowicz, M., Moscou, K., & Lexchin, J. (2018). Transnational pharmacogovernance: Emergent patterns in the jazz of pharmaceutical policy convergence. *Globalization and Health, 14*(1), 86. https://doi.org/10.1186/1746-160x-10-1.

Willershausen, B., Callaway, A., Wolf, T. G., Ehlers, V., Scholz, L., Wolf, D., et al. (2014). Hearing assessment in dental practitioners and other academic professionals from an urban setting. *Head and Face Medicine, 10*, 1. https://doi.org/10.1186/1746-160x-10-1.

World Health Organization. (n.d.). *Pharmacovigilance*. https://www.who.int/teams/regulation-prequalification/pharmacovigilance. Accessed 24 Jan 2021.

Yaneva-Deliverska, M. (2012). European Union regulation on prevention from sharps injuries in hospital[s] and [the] healthcare sector. *Journal of International Medical Association Bulgaria, 18*(3), 357–359.

Zarra, T., & Lambrianidis, T. (2014). Musculoskeletal disorders amongst Greek endodontists: A national questionnaire survey. *International Endodontic Journal, 47*(8), 791–801.

Chapter 7
Subjects for Discussion in the Professions

Teeth Whitening

In this day and age, cosmetic embellishment has become fashionable, and a facet of it, teeth whitening, has become popular. This procedure has become a topic of debate. Discussion has focused on who is capable of performing it and what products may be utilized in the process. The European Union (EU) has become involved in the polemic. The Scientific Committee on Consumer Products, after an assessment of the process and the materials used in it, issued a decision stating that there was a risk in adopting tooth whitening or bleaching products that contained more than 0.1% and up to 6% present or released hydrogen peroxide (Council Directive 2011/84/EU, Recital 2; Scientific Committee on Consumer Products 2007).

Moreover, it was noted that the hazard augments with higher concentrations of hydrogen peroxide and habitual use. Thus, it was recommended that sales to consumers of tooth whitening products be restricted to those containing at most 0.1% present or released hydrogen peroxide. Higher percentages of this substance were deemed unsafe for consumer use. Elements of the Committee's assessment were incorporated into Council Directive 2011/84/EU. This document was eventually repealed by Regulation (EC) No 1223/2009(recast) that also updated, according to scientific developments, Council Directive 76/768/EEC focused on cosmetic products. Previously, such materials were classified as medical devices and, thus, were governed by the EU documents related to these mechanisms. Now, they became classified as cosmetic products.

As it stands, the sale of bleaching products to consumers is permissible, if the concentration manifests a limit of 0.1% of present or released hydrogen peroxide. Only dentists may obtain materials containing more than 0.1% and up to 6% present or released hydrogen peroxide. Products composed of hydrogen peroxide levels superior to 6% are prohibited for use. They are banned, although it has been reported that they are utilized (Dental Tribune 2011; Nouvelles du rendez-vous de midi 2011).

S. Z. Koff, *The Dental Team in the European Union*,
https://doi.org/10.1007/978-3-030-72232-6_7

Rules on the use of tooth whitening materials allow the use of hydrogen peroxide as noted, as well as other solutions that release this substance. These include carbamide peroxide and zinc peroxide. These products, however, release less hydrogen peroxide. For example, a compound consisting of 10% carbamide peroxide releases at most 3.6% hydrogen peroxide. Thus, products commonly utilized containing 16% carbamide peroxide are not banned because they release less than the 6% limit of hydrogen peroxide.

Use of materials over 0.1% hydrogen peroxide present or released is subject to regulation. The first use of each cycle of the product is to be carried out by a dentist after the performance of a clinical examination. If a suitable level of safety is available, an appropriately trained dental care professional (DCP) may carry out the procedure under the dentist's direct supervision. After the cycle has been started, the patient is given the materials to complete it on her/his own. In the United Kingdom, if safety is ensured, and if considered competent, dental hygienists and therapists perform the procedure under a dentist's prescription.

The Council of European Dentists was most satisfied with the assessment of tooth whitening products issued by the Scientific Committee on Consumer Products. Thus, the regulation of these compounds presented up to this point was considered satisfactory. It was believed that patient safety was assured and that clarity was evident as to how, by whom, and in what places tooth whitening was to be carried out (Dental Tribune 2011). However, the one rule that did not sit well with the representatives of the dental profession was that which prohibits the use of tooth whitening products of any kind on people under 18 years of age.

In April 2017, the Council of European Dentists, in an effort to abolish the prohibition of tooth whitening on persons under 18, requested a review by the Commission of the assessment issued years earlier by the Scientific Committee on Consumer Products. Obviously, the noted restriction has limited dentists' options in the treatment of children. The association asserted that "tooth whitening is the most conservative means of managing teeth which are discoloured as a consequence of traumas or due to developmental or genetic causes" (Council of European Dentists 2017). In the appeal, it was claimed that tooth whitening is performed on children without any harm in vast parts of the globe. Thus, a treatment that contravenes the United Nations Convention on the Rights of a Child and the Constitution of the World Health Organization should not be prohibited and substituted with inferior restorative management (Council of European Dentists 2017). Other associations and professionals were consulted on this matter by the dental council, and significant support was received. The Council of European Dentists, however, was not convincing. The prohibition still exists and consensus does not. Many dentists in the EU are confronted with an ethical dilemma: should they act as they see fit or follow the restriction?

Use of whitening lamps has provided another concern to the dental profession in the Member States. Utilization of these mechanisms was on the increase. Asserting that the scientific literature did not offer support to their use, the Council of European Dentists has advised professionals not to use them because they do not have an advantageous effect on the bleaching process and, potentially, they could produce adverse results (Council of European Dentists 2015).

Dental Amalgam

As in the case of tooth whitening, dental materials have been an issue for other procedures as well. Dental amalgam and alternatives to it, such as glass ionomer cements, resin-based composites, ceramics, and gold alloys, have provided a subject for discussion in reference to treatment of dental cavities. Dental amalgam is an alloy of mercury and other metals, such as silver, copper, tin, and additional trace metals. It has caused concern because of its mercury content which amounts to 50% in its elemental form and the silver only arrives at 35%. The toxicity of mercury has long been acknowledged.

Dental amalgam was introduced early in the nineteenth century, and it immediately became controversial as a dental material (BIO Intelligence Service 2012). It is known that the substance is particularly toxic during early brain development, even before birth, and it impacts other matters related to health. Not only is mercury a hazard to health, but it is the same to the environment. National borders have no meaning once mercury enters the environment. Up to 80% of the substance found in the EU Member States travels from non-EU nations. Mercury in the environment is an international concern. It accumulates in fish, seafood, the food chain, as well as the atmosphere, the soil, vegetation, and water.

Dental amalgam was used freely for years. Its positive elements include it being inexpensive, durable, reliable, effective, and very hard. On the other hand, it is silver in color, and thus, it is always apparent. Moreover, the dentist using amalgam must drill a large cavity and also remove healthy substance from the tooth in order to secure the dental amalgam. This product fails to adhere to remaining tooth tissues, and it must be contained in the tooth mechanically (European Commission 2015a; Nicholson 2017; Taut 2013). It appears that the alternatives to amalgam, even if they are more expensive, are becoming more common. It might be due to the fact that they tend to blend with tooth enamel and also fit in with the aforementioned fashionable cosmetic embellishment (European Commission 2015a).

The EU has been involved in this discussion concerning the safety of mercury products for a long while. In 2005, it announced its Mercury Strategy that contained 20 actions to temper use of the product and to protect the environment (Commission of the European Communities 2005). When preparing policies, the Commission often requests opinions from independent Scientific Committees. It did so in reference to the effects of mercury in dental amalgam on the environment and human health. Both structures consulted, the Committee for Environmental and Health Risk and the Committee for Emerging and Newly Identified Health Risks issued inconclusive reports because the available scientific data was not appropriate for firm answers. The latter unit affirmed that "current evidence does not preclude the use of either amalgam or alternative materials in dental restorative treatment" (Scientific Committee on Emerging and Newly Identified Health Risks 2015). It was asserted that the practitioner should select the treatment material based on characteristics of the patient. However, the Committee recommended that alternative materials be utilized when treating children and pregnant females. The Commission seconded the recommendation based on the potential for amalgam fillings to poison genetically susceptible persons.

On the other hand, the International Academy of Oral Medicine and Toxicology issued a contrasting opinion. Objectives of the association were to terminate the use of amalgam fillings, to assist DCPs and their patients in comprehending the role of mercury in amalgam and its potential effects, and to educate all concerned about the benefits of alternatives to amalgam and the safe removal of such fillings. A good part of its report was devoted to potential harms of the mercury in amalgam and especially to people with specific ailments (International Academy of Oral Medicine and Toxicology 2016). These contrasting opinions represent the stage for debate on the matter.

The Minamata Convention (2013) is named after a Japanese city that experienced in 1956 a huge tragedy caused by mercury pollution. Discussions related to this international treaty were initiated by the United Nations Environment Programme, and the accord was agreed to in 2013. It was accepted by a multitude of nations as well as by the EU. The objective of the global treaty was to protect human health and the environment from the negative impacts of mercury. In the words of the Convention, its purpose was "to protect the human health and the environment from anthropogenic emissions and releases of mercury and mercury compounds" (Minamata Convention, Article 1). The Convention relates to the complete life cycle of mercury commencing with its mining and ending with its waste disposal. Several of the Convention's affirmations were inspirations received from the EU (European Commission 2017). It is noteworthy that the Council of European Dentists immediately acknowledged the significance of the Minamata Convention and, particularly, its flexible approach to the mercury problem and its "good balance" between using amalgam and its alternatives.

Immediately after the Minamata Convention was agreed to, the EU sought to align its practices with the global treaty. This was accomplished in Regulation (EU) 2017/852 that notes that the largest use of mercury in the EU is represented by dental amalgam. Thus, it is affirmed that its use should be phased down in accordance with the Convention. Moreover, a phase out on its use, preferably by 2030, should be considered. In addition, it was stated that protective standards should be established for children and pregnant or breastfeeding females (Regulation (EU) 2017/852, Recital 21). Another item pertaining to amalgam asserts that only predosed encapsulated forms should be used and bulk forms should be banned. Furthermore, amalgam separators should be required in any space which contains the substance, and a minimum level of retention efficiency should be established. In addition, waste management should be appropriate so that nothing is allowed to enter the environment (Regulation (EU) 2017/852, Recital 22). It was also recommended that dental students and practitioners be trained to use materials alternative to dental amalgam. In addition, it was recommended that they be stimulated to undertake research projects and develop new solutions to the mercury problem in order to further decrease its use (Regulation (EU) 2017/852, Recital 23).

Article 10 of the Regulation is devoted solely to dental amalgam. It enforces much of what is stated in the noted Recitals and what is reported above. It affirms that beginning 1 July 2018, dental amalgam is not to be used in the treatment of deciduous teeth of children under 15 years of age and of pregnant or breastfeeding females unless the dentist determines that the patient's medical condition absolutely dictates a reversal of the provision. This so-called phase down could have been the first step of a phase out. The Regulation also declares that as of 1 January 2019, dental amalgam may only be used in pre-dosed encapsulated form so as not to expose the patient and the provider of service to mercury. And by 1 July 2019, Member States were required to have posted online a program with the objective of adopting less dental amalgam.

As of the start of 2019 (January 1), all dental practices using or removing amalgam in procedures must be equipped with amalgam separators maintaining a retention level of 95%. Moreover, amalgam waste must be collected only by authorized firms. This equipment is not new. It was used by the Swedish in the 1980s. It is utilized to eliminate very fine waste amalgam from the rinse water in the vacuum line before it arrives in the sewer. Also, it has the capacity of eliminating up to 99% of the mercurial content from the waste water before it departs from the dental practice. Utilization of a separator greatly decreases the amount of waste placed in the environment. Unfortunately, it has been claimed that the efficiency of this equipment has not been properly controlled by individual dental practices (Muhamedagic et al. 2009; Report on laws and recommendations on dental mercury management in the EU 2018).

Surveys demonstrate that dental waste is occasionally treated as medical or municipal waste when at all times it should be considered hazardous waste requiring diverse treatment. It is also noteworthy that amalgam separators are mandated where dental mercury exists in some form in a dental practice. However, it is estimated that only 75% of dental facilities have this equipment. On the other hand, there are Member States in which dentists' practice centers are fully equipped at 100%. Such has occurred in Austria, the Czech Republic, Denmark, Finland, Germany, Latvia, Malta, Portugal, and Sweden. In several Member States, legal requirements have to be met before the installation of amalgam separators (Report on laws and recommendations on dental mercury management in the EU 2018).

Member States are assigned the responsibility of creating sanctions for violation of the Regulation's provisions. They are to be, as usual, "effective, proportionate, and dissuasive" (Regulation (EU) 2017/852, Article 16). The Commission is to be notified of these penalties and any amendment to them. The noted provisions denote the major ones contained in the Regulation that affect the practice of dentistry.

The EU has been involved with the subject of mercury for an extended period of time and from a variety of perspectives. It has dealt with mercury supply and trade, its storage, its industrial emissions, its content in products, mercury and the manufacturing process, its impact on the environment, mercury and electronic equipment, mercury and toys, mercury and artisanal and small-scale gold mining, and mercury waste management. The list is long and could be even longer. And a most recent problem that of a dental material containing mercury has arisen and remains to be totally solved. At least the stage has been set with the Minamata Convention and the most recent EU Regulation on the subject.

Domestic Violence, Maltreatment, Child Abuse, and Neglect

Domestic violence, violence against children and adolescents, plus child abuse and neglect are weighty global public health issues causing significant harm to victims that is sometimes irreparable. This violence, a threat to physical and mental well-being, is of several types: physical, sexual, emotional, economic, or psychological in nature. In the Netherlands, annually, a minimum of 200,000 persons become victims, and 83% of the affronters are male (van Dam et al. 2015; Vesna 2016). DCPs are in a unique position to detect maltreatment of many sorts and aid its victims.

Several Member States have laws on the subject. Most of their requisites require the matter to be referred to authorities, such as the social services and/or the police. In fact, the law in Sweden and those in some other Member States as well affirm that a suspicion of maltreatment merits a referral. A diagnosis is not required (Vesna 2016).

Studies have been undertaken on the role of DCPs concerning situations of maltreatment. Dental care participants in surveys have related claims of suspected abuse of their patients, but often have failed to report it to authorities. In one survey carried out in the United Kingdom, 67% of the participants suspected abuse or neglect of a patient, but only 29% ever made a referral (Harris et al. 2009). In the Netherlands, in a web survey, 24% of participating dentists reported suspected domestic violence in recent patients. Eighty-one percent of these professionals noted the suspicion in patients' files, and 54% of the remainder undertook actions in a different manner. However, there were no referrals (van Dam et al. 2015). In Croatia, 26.27% of dentists responding to a questionnaire suspected child abuse and neglect in patients, but only 5.1% reported their suspicion (Cukovic-Bagic et al. 2014).

In Norway, a national survey administered to dentists and dental hygienists in the public dental health services demonstrated that the majority (60%) had made referrals of child maltreatment to authorities. On the other hand, 32.6% of the participants had suspected child maltreatment and did not report it. The percentage of referrals to authorities in this survey are much higher in this EEA associate than in many EU Member States. Analysis of responses to this survey demonstrated that the probability of referral was stimulated by the professional's age, work experience, number of patients treated, and size of her/his city and its geographic region (Brattabø et al. 2016).

Looking at the percentages of reports or referrals, the question becomes why are some professionals so hesitant to make referrals of diagnosed or suspected maltreatment? The barriers are several. There is the thought of more violence being aimed at the patient suspected of being subject to or diagnosed with maltreatment after referral. Then, often, the professional is not confident of her/his knowledge of the symptoms of abuse and domestic violence that include bite marks, perioral and intraoral injuries, infections, caries in early childhood, and maladies indicating abuse and neglect. The same outcome was evident in a French regional study. Then many dentists affirm that they do not have enough knowledge about what steps to take to make a referral. They need more information (van Dam et al. 2015; Drigeard et al. 2012; Nuzzolese et al. 2009).

A survey was undertaken at the University of Zagreb in Croatia of all students enrolled in its 6-year dentistry program. The objective of the project was to determine students' knowledge of child physical and sexual abuse. The conclusion was that these future professionals had sparse knowledge of the subject matter. Those further along in the program were more knowledgeable, but the researchers concluded that the students should be better prepared on the subject (Jordan et al. 2012).

An information campaign is definitely necessary (Improved child protection training needed 2009; Uldum et al. 2017). Symptoms of domestic violence and maltreatment and how to deal with suspicion or diagnosis should be incorporated in all DCP curricula. This is also an important topic for continuing professional development (CPD). In most of the surveys cited, a large percentage of the participants, if not a majority, expressed a favorable attitude toward acquiring more knowledge on the subject of maltreatment. They should be positive in attitude because, after all, they have a legal and ethical obligation to aid victims of such damaging behavior.

Abuse, violence, and maltreatment have primarily been the responsibility of the Member States because the EU does not have general responsibility for protecting children and others from violence. In recent years, thanks to the Lisbon Treaty, the EU has become active in promoting protection of children's rights. Obviously, its activities in this sector impact on those of the Member States.

In 2006, the EU presented its Strategy on the Rights of the Child (Commission of the European Communities 2006a), and 5 years later, it announced the EU Agenda for the Rights of the Child (European Commission 2011) that set forth some recommendations for the complete implementation of the United Nations Convention on the Rights of the Child and the most possible mainstreaming of children's rights. Moreover, at the base of the agenda were the notions that these rights should be a constituent of the EU's fundamental rights policy, that future policies should be developed on the basis of sound data, and that collaboration with stakeholders should take place via the European Forum on the Rights of the Child, an annual conference created by the EU and organized by the Commission. It involves the Member States and the nations included in the EEA (Dimitrova-Stull 2014).

There are also legal documents that demonstrate the EU's seriousness of purpose in promoting children's rights. In addition, the EU developed a strategy to eliminate trafficking of human beings (European Commission 2012). Directive 2011/36/EU relates to preventing and combating such trafficking in human beings. Basically, it contains recommendations related to this maltreatment, and also, it contains a focus on its young victims.

Directive 2011/92/EU is concerned with forms of sexual abuse of children. It offers definitions of the diverse types and creates augmented levels of penalties for infringements of the laws on the topic. Moreover, the legislation also provides assistance and support measures for child victims. The EU is of the belief that crime victims should be protected and should be able to take advantage of some minimum standards. Directive 2012/29/EU spoke to the creation of standards on victims' of crime and their rights, support, and protection. Children are part of the audience on this standardization process.

And then there is the EU Daphne Programme that is focused on prevention of all forms of violence in the public and private sectors and especially against children, youth, and women. In its fight against violence, it offers grants for preventive projects and assistance to programs that support victims. Applications for grants are accepted from local and regional authorities; schools; trade union federations; development, non-governmental, non-profit, and international organizations; and universities. The program serves the Member States, candidate nations, the EEA, and the Balkans. Even though the EU does not possess a formal general responsibility in reference to maltreatment, it has entered the field of violence, abuse, and maltreatment in a unique manner and made itself heard.

Lifestyle

Dental and other maladies often arise because of the individual's lack of a healthy lifestyle. Such, in many cases, has been attributed to poor dietary behavior, smoking, alcohol, and obesity or overweight measures, among other factors that impinge on both one's systemic and oral health. Unhealthy dietary behaviors, featuring a great deal of fastfood and sugary soft and energy drinks, have been associated with the nutrition of overweight or obese children, youth, and adults of all ages (Nihtila et al. 2016).

Obesity or being overweight are severe problems throughout the EU. They have been particularly harsh in Cyprus, the Netherlands, Sweden, Denmark, and Portugal. In the United Kingdom, Scotland has had the most prevalence of obese and overweight children, doubling that in the Netherlands. In Great Britain, one-fifth of the children that enter elementary school have one or the other of these conditions, and by the time they finish this level of education, the figure augments to one-third. Unfortunately, often, these weight problems are identified with social and economic inequalities, and, having doubled over the past two decades, they have become the most common medical condition of childhood (Kantovitz et al. 2006; Lazarou and Soteriades 2010; Levine 2012).

Research has been undertaken on the relationship between oral health status and weight problems. An oral inflammatory disease, periodontitis, was found more often in obese persons. It is a destructive dental malady "involving the supporting tissues of the teeth due to microorganisms which results in a progressive destruction of supporting structures of the periodontium" (Deshpande and Amrutiya 2017, p. 229). The presence of this inflammatory malady in persons with weight problems, as opposed to those that did not have them, led a research team to conclude that there is a stringent correlation between the two elements. Others have arrived at the same conclusion (Palle et al. 2013; Saito et al. 2001).

Studies have also focused on the association between oral health status and body mass index of older folks. Body mass index is a method to determine if an individual is obese or overweight. It relates a person's weight to height. Metric units are used. It is calculated by dividing the individual's weight in kilograms by the square of her/his height in meters. If the result is 30 or more, the person is 30 pounds overweight and obese. Classification as overweight requires a result of 27.3 or more for females and 27.8 or more for males. It has been found that British elderly with more than 20 teeth were more likely to have a normal body mass index, whereas individuals with fewer teeth were, on the average, more than three times more likely to be obese (Sheiham et al. 2002).

The direct association between obesity and dental caries has also been explored. Outcomes or the conclusions reached have been quite diverse. Some studies claimed not to have uncovered a correlation between dental decay and obesity (Paisi et al. 2018; Silva et al. 2013; Tripathi et al. 2010; Vallogini et al. 2017).

One conclusion affirmed that caries and obesity coexist in children of low socioeconomic status. Thus, dietary education and access to appropriate meals would decrease the hazard of both maladies (Marshall et al. 2007). Other authors propose a different and broader solution. Rather than solely suggesting a reversal of unhealthy behaviors, given the deprivation of many persons, they indicate the necessity of supportive environments, education, employment, and appropriate housing (Paisi et al. 2018).

Other researchers (Hayden et al. 2012) have formed a diverse opinion. They concluded that, on the whole, in manuscripts prepared between 1980 and 2010, there exists a significant association between dental caries and obesity, particularly in childhood. The relationship between the two diseases was especially significant in children with permanent dentitions. Moreover, an investigation of obesity and dental caries among adolescents aged 15 to 18 concluded that a positive longitudinal association exists (Li et al. 2017). As sometimes, there is a category for inconclusive opinions or conclusions. These contend further research utilizing certain factors is necessary (Hooley et al. 2012; Kantovitz et al. 2006).

As in the case of domestic violence, maltreatment, and child abuse and neglect, most DCPs are in a unique position to deal with weight problems in patients. A survey was carried out of dentists and their thoughts on the issue (Curran et al. 2010). Results indicated that 4.8% of the participants already offered counseling on the matter and 50.5% claimed an interest in the same. However, lack of appropriate staff presented a problem for 46.3% of these professionals. Interestingly enough, 53.8% were afraid that patients might be insulted.

Such a service could be helpful to some persons and risky or harmful to others. It could help people lose weight and garner a healthier lifestyle. On the other hand, it could also cause anxiety, stigmatization, and other negative consequences and, thus, produce an increase in weight (Vallgårda 2016). This could be why 82% of dentists participating in the survey claimed they would be more inclined to offer the service, if weight problems were definitively related to oral maladies. They have been related to some as noted, but yet not all.

Diet is important to the prevention of oral maladies. Sugars have been acknowledged as the principal dietary element related to dental caries in both children and the elderly. Moreover, researchers (Sheiham and James 2015) assert that the sole cause of caries is dietary sugar. In addition, research (Peres et al. 2016) has confirmed that greater consumption of sugar leads to more dental caries. Thus, utilization of sugars should be controlled, and unfortunately, it does not always happen, even though children are consuming three times the recommended quantity. It is also noteworthy that in Great Britain more children have been admitted to hospitals for tooth decay than for any other condition. And over a 4-year period, the number of children experiencing tooth extractions performed in hospitals has augmented 10% (British Dental Association 2016). A reduction of the frequency and amount of sugar consumption is definitely a necessity (Council of European Dentists 2016; Gupta et al. 2013; Moynihan 2005).

Member States have taken action to confront caries and obesity. France initiated the notion of a tax on drinks with added sugars. It was thought that the tax would affect the quantity consumed and it did. Consumption decreased. Other Member States followed suit. Some form of a sugar tax exists in 11 of the Member States. These nations include Belgium, Bulgaria, Denmark, Estonia, Finland, France, Hungary, Ireland, Portugal, and the United Kingdom. In Spain, the tax is making its way through the court system, but the Spanish Autonomous Community of Catalonia has implemented a levy. These taxes are not uniform. Some systems also include artificial sweeteners and other items, such as unhealthy food, as in Bulgaria. In some places, behind the tax, there was a push for the reformulation of beverages to reduce the sugar content as well as the portion size by 2020 (An Roinn Sláinte 2016; Baker 2018; Harvard T. H. Chan School of Public Health 2016). The levy on drinks with added sugars is only one of a number of measures implemented to tackle caries and obesity.

School-based techniques for changing behavior have received good grades (Wechsler et al. 2000). Several Member States have utilized these institutions in relation to food policies. For example, artificial sweeteners are banned in schools in Greece, Hungary, Latvia, Malta, Northern Ireland, Spain, and Wales. The prohibition has different dimensions, according to Member State. In Greece, it applies to middle and high schools, whereas, in Hungary, it is applicable to students under 6 years of age. On the other hand, there is a general prohibition at all scholastic levels in Malta, Spain, and Wales. In Latvia, lunch is eliminated from the ban. In Northern Ireland, artificial sweeteners are permitted only when serving combination drinks. As the old saying goes, "different strokes for different folks."

Most Member States have food programs in scholastic institutions whose major objectives are to have students learn healthy habits, to improve nutrition, to reduce or prevent obesity, and to improve school attendance. The first noted goal has been considered the most important. It is surprising to discover that in Spain, in 2012, 23.2% of male students aged 9 were classified as obese and 51.1% were said to be overweight; 16.2% of their female colleagues of the same age were noted as obese and 43.6% as overweight. Given similar problems, an objective of the Irish tax on sugar-sweetened drinks and other efforts in its obesity policies is to reduce in the Irish population the average person's weight by 5% (An Roinn Sláinte 2016).

Obviously, given the nature of the school day in all Member States, most scholastic food programs revolve around lunch and snacks. In several programs, as aforementioned, drinks have been limited to specific types. Also, in most schools in the Member States, sweet treats have been restricted, but not in Luxembourg, the Netherlands, Belgium (Flanders), Malta, and Portugal. As for vending machines, they have suffered severe restrictions across the Member States. In fact, in several, they do not exist or have been prohibited.

In Finland, the National Board of Education and the National Institute for Health and Welfare recommended that the schools in the upper levels of education should not sell sweets. The recommendation was accepted, and scholastic environments were improved with the addition of oral health protecting items. Thus, schools became oral health promoters (Anttila et al. 2015).

Numerous diverse programs with many facets, only a few of which have been presented here, to transform unhealthy behaviors and to combat weight gain and dental caries have been established throughout the Member States and have realized success. Moreover, many received the avid support of organizations representing DCPs and others. The EU has also been involved. Coordination of activities between the Member States is offered by the High Level Group on Nutrition and Physical Activity, a unit, led by the Commission, consisting of EU government representatives and those from the European Free Trade Association. It is the responsibility of the EU Platform for Action, on Diet, Physical Activity and Health, a forum for European-level associations, to garner supporters for healthy nutrition and exercise.

The EU has also initiated valuable efforts in this sector. In particular, it has tended to advocate joint initiatives related to the reduction of sugars, fats, and salt in food products, aggressive advertising aimed at children, and improvement of food labels. In addition, it secured an agreement with food manufacturers to reformulate the aforementioned ingredients of food products and to monitor their actions. Furthermore, it has worked collaboratively with schools and developed a methodology so that they could obtain better food catering contracts and carried out a study on the marketing of foods that require reformulation (European Commission 2015b).

The Commission's efforts have also been concerned with the organization of workshops and conferences related to food taxes and reformulation (Roadmap for action on food product improvement 2016). To create awareness of the child obesity problem and to stop its spread, an action plan on the matter was designed and circulated across the Member States. Many valuable and noteworthy projects related to health and nutrition behaviors have been financed by the EU either solely or in conjunction with others. They have been aimed at general and vulnerable populations (European Commission 2018b).

Physical Activity

Physical activity for all ages is important for one's health status and lifestyle. Its benefits are several. It aids in decreasing the hazards of noncommunicable maladies and often leads to lower levels of obesity, overweight, stress, anxiety, and depression (Breda et al. 2018). In spite of the fact that its advantages have been generally acknowledged, 46% of Europeans never undertake exercise or play a sport. This figure has augmented and is part of a general trend commenced in 2009. Moreover, 44% fail to engage in another form of physical activity, such as cycling, dancing, or gardening, at least once a week (European Commission 2018c). This situation presents a problem.

There is preoccupation with youth, in particular, because exercise tends to decrease a great deal during adolescence, especially among girls. This relates to weight management as well as systemic and oral health. Among adults, males exercise, play sports, or engage in other physical activities more than females, and among the elderly, participation is relatively meager. Engagement in physical activity among the population within the EU is highest in the Nordic Member States: Finland (69%), Sweden (67%), and Denmark (63%). At the bottom of the ladder, one finds Bulgaria, Greece, and Portugal in each one of which 68% of the people never play a sport or exercise. It is noteworthy that physical activity is lower among individuals having less education and among those suffering financially. The principal explanation given in a Eurobarometer survey (European Commission 2018c) for failure to engage in physical activity was a lack of time. Other reasons offered were a lack of interest or motivation and having a disability or illness.

Member States have promoted physical activity. Prime structures for undertaking this promotion have been primary and secondary schools. Physical education has been integrated into the curriculum in all Member States in diverse manners. In all programs, participation, unfortunately, is not obligatory. In some, it is entirely or partly optional. In primary schools in 79% of the Member States (22 countries), physical education programs are compulsory in nature. The percentage is less in reference to secondary structures. It stands at 20 countries or 71% of the Member States (European Commission and World Health Organization 2018). Exercise activities before and after school, during school vacations, and for recesses also exist. In the academic environment, physical activity benefits concentration as well as cognitive and academic performance.

Obviously, sports clubs are also prime structures for the promotion of physical activity in relation to lifestyle and health. However, it is noteworthy that access is narrow for those of a lower socioeconomic background and these are the persons who undertake less physical activity. In addition, workplaces often feature exercise programs to encourage improved physical activity on the part of employees. Undertaking such efforts can enhance productivity. Also, many areas have featured public information campaigns on the subject of physical activity and its rewards. Some of these efforts have been aimed at the population in general and others have focused on diverse groups, such as the elderly or adolescents. The efforts on the part of the Member States have enhanced public awareness of the importance of physical activity in one form or another. It is definitely a significant facet of a healthy lifestyle.

The Member States have principal responsibility for promoting health-enhancing physical activity, and the Commission supports, coordinates, and complements their efforts on the matter. As in other sectors, the Commission has developed institutional partnerships, and it collaborates with the World Health Organization. Also, it has undertaken research projects related to a particular subject and supported conferences and other gatherings to bring together diverse stakeholders for the exchange of ideas. The EU Sport Forum, an annual encounter between those identified with sport as stakeholders, the Member States, and EU units, has been created. Sponsored by the EU, there is also the #BeActive Campaign identified with the European Week of Sport and several other activities and the #BeInclusive EU Sport Award that is given to organizations that use sport to enhance social inclusion for disadvantaged folks.

An EU effort, the seminar on Healthy Lifestyle, held in Tartu in 2017, finished with the Tartu Call for Healthy Lifestyle. Its basic objective, revealed in its name, was to promote a healthy lifestyle. The Call produced a list of significant activities in various fields, such as sport, nutrition, and health, to challenge sedentary behavior and promote healthy activities, especially among children. Mentioned were increased funding for programs advocating the promotion of sport and innovative procedures for creating awareness of the advantages of a healthy lifestyle via the EU's innovation and technology networks. The Call also foresaw making use of EU initiatives and funding.

An inter-service group on the promotion of healthy lifestyles was established within the Directorate-General for Education and Culture as a reaction to the Tartu Call. Its purpose is to coordinate activities to stimulate healthy lifestyle and related funding. It also is to strengthen collaboration among pertinent Commission services. It met for the first time in January 2019.

The EU has also launched the EU Physical Activity Guidelines, and it has recommended a cross-sectoral approach to stimulate and develop physical activity. In a Council Recommendation (2013), this body recognized the need to reinforce collaboration between the Commission and the Member States on the subject matter of physical activity. Even though the Member States have major responsibility for its promotion, the EU has been quite active in the sector and accomplished positive achievements.

Climate Change

Climate change has taken place. According to the United Nations Convention on Climate Change, it results "from direct or indirect human activities that lead to alteration in the composition of [the] global atmosphere and this, in turn, leads to the changes observed in the environment" (Kemoli 2019). Many of its facets, such as higher temperatures, forest destruction, and flooding of coastal areas, among others, must be recognized. It has many and complex consequences. For example, it encourages hazards to human health, ecosystems, social and cultural systems, as well as economic development and production not only in the EU Member States but in other parts of the globe as well. Globally, the number of extreme weather events has almost quadrupled since the 1960s. These often destroy homes, shelters, healthcare facilities, and those of other essential services. At the same time, climate change presents opportunities. Reactions to the phenomenon should include attempts to assess and mitigate its hazards and to take advantage of any evident opportunities (Scheraga et al. 2003).

Climate change has an influence on a multitude of sectors, such as agriculture, forestry, water resources (their quality and quantity), air quality, transportation, ecosystems and biodiversity, human settlements, cultural resources, and the economy, all of which affect oral health. Above all, climate change impacts human health and, specifically, oral health (Bosello et al. 2005; Sandhu 2017).

It has been stated that we are what we eat. As aforementioned, diet is significant for oral health. Many foods and livestock production face challenges and are at risk due to changed precipitation, higher temperatures, and total climate change, in general. It is noteworthy that animal farming increases greenhouse gas production and contributes to climate change. Often, due to climate change, food insecurity results in many parts of the globe. Also, some peoples' healing practices rely on herbal medicines. These drugs and food are sometimes threatened because of climate change (EA Editors n.d.; Green 2019; Khanna 2010b).

Malnutrition is sometimes experienced by the vulnerable population, consisting, to a large extent, of the poor, the elderly, children, coastal populations, and ethnic groups exposed to high risks. Local oral hygiene practices contribute to several diseases. Genetic abnormalities, such as sickle cell anemia and Down syndrome, often thrive and increase the burden of disabilities. Infectious diseases flourish and frequently are affiliated with hearing impairment. In addition, there are skeletal and dental fluorosis related to the quality of surface water and groundwater. Fluoride in water is essential for protection against dental caries, but it also can have a negative impact on one's oral health. Fluoride poisoning accounts for tooth discoloration and damage, opaque white lesions on teeth, as well as pitting, cracking, and chipping.

Oral pre-cancer and cancer have increased and are associated with some environmental determinants, such as solar radiation. The most common sites of occurrence are the tongue, the lower lip, and the lining of the cheeks and the back of the lip inside where it touches the teeth (Khanna 2010b).

Stress, physical and mental abuse, nutrition and diet, exposure to toxins, and determinants of growth and body composition can contribute to the risk of some human cancers, such as oral cancer. About 90% of the people with oral cancer and some types of throat cancer have at one time or another used tobacco. Higher incidences of lung cancer are found where there is much indoor air pollution or, specifically, radon as well as smoking. Also, it is noteworthy that environmental pollution causes trace elements in human teeth. Thus, the content of heavy metals in teeth indicates environmental pollution (Sandhu 2017).

Noma, an orofacial gangrene, contributes significantly to the disease burden. It strikes, for the most part, children between 1 and 4 years of age. Late stages of this disease occur in adolescents and adults. There are certain environments that attract Noma. These are ones characterized by malnutrition, lack of safe drinking water, deplorable sanitary practices, and a superior rate of infectious disease (Sandhu 2017).

A study surveyed the impact of air pollution, especially due to ozone, on the development of oral clefts in children. It influences the condition in animals. Researchers concluded that exposure to polluted outdoor air during the first 2 months of pregnancy may increase the hazard of this condition (Hwang and Jaakkola 2008).

Climate can also lead to oxidative stress in allergic reactions. It comes about as a result of inflammation, but also it is due to exposure to air pollution. Hyposalivation or dry mouth, increased dental caries, periodontal disease, and salivary gland disorder are stimulated. These can lead to tooth loss and nutritional defects. Oral diseases, like others, share a wide range of risk factors, some of which can be modified or eliminated.

It is claimed that children are the most impacted by climate change because of the swift modifications to their growth and development cycles. Furthermore, the air is permeated by greenhouse gases. Carbon dioxide emissions have increased greatly due to human activities related to the use of fossil fuels, solid waste management, and trees and wood products. Also, related to the emissions is methane from oils, coal, natural gas, and municipal waste that have accounted for a larger emission of carbon dioxide as well.

Children's health, and, specifically, their oral health, is greatly affected by climate change. Their water, air, and food undergo change. Moreover, the economy of their caregivers could change as well. Such modifications influence their quality of life. Also, they are imperiled by diseases, some of which are new and some of which cause discontinuity to their growth and development, as well as dental developmental defects and changes in the pattern of dental maladies. The approach of DCPs now emphasizes prevention rather than restoration (Kemoli 2019; Khanna 2010a).

In terms of dentistry, environmental hazards result from patients' travel; staff commuting; staff travel work; waste, including water and nitrous oxide; electricity; and procurement (Duane et al. 2019). The severity of climate change and its consequences was recognized in 2018, with the formation of the Health, Environment and Climate Change Coalition through the efforts of the World Health Organization, the United Nations Environment Assembly, and the World Meteorological Organization. Immediate objectives were to focus on air pollution and to attempt to decrease the number of deaths and diseases related to environmental hazards. It also desired and still wants to pool expertise and to produce more collaboration in efforts to mitigate the effects of climate change.

In addition, it desires to promote coherent health and environmental governance and policies, to enhance awareness and decision-making about environmental hazards impacting health, to make the community aware of the challenge, and to support collaborative activities that promote human and oral health and protect the environment. Given these objectives, it performs policy, scientific, communication, and capacity strengthening and country action functions.

In confronting the challenge of climate change and its hazards to oral health, team work is required. Collaboration and communication are essential between DCPs; patients; international, national, and sub-national policy-makers; and other healthcare professionals. The climate challenge will require an army of actors, many options, and a variety of interventions in the right places, at the right time (World Resources Institute n.d.).

DCPs have to recognize the impact of climate change on patients as individuals and also on their practice. It has been suggested that the impact will be negative on all types of healthcare services. It is foreseen that extreme weather could bring supply and transport problems creating a scarcity of resources. Dentistry professionals must bear this in mind and plan for a possible reduction of resources and an increase in the cost of their practice. On the other hand, financial benefits could result from the efficient and environmentally safe use of resources and rationalization of waste. In a research project on practice staff, the principal issue related to the amount of waste. The personnel wanted to change procedures, but were concerned about standing up to present guidelines on infection control (Grose et al. 2016). One must be optimistic. As aforementioned hazards also present opportunities.

Sustainable Development Goals (SDGs)

Closely related to general and oral health are the Sustainable Development Goals (SDGs) affiliated with obtaining a more sustainable future for everybody with nobody left behind. The agenda, approved in 2015 by the 193 members of the United Nations, consists of 17 ambitious goals and 169 targets that are to be met by 2030. Their purpose is to address global social needs and, at the same time, fortify local economies.

The goals relate to defeating poverty, overcoming hunger, achieving good health and all forms of well-being, quality education, gender equality, clean water and sanitation, affordable and clean energy, decent work, and economic development. The goals also include industry, innovation, and infrastructure; reduced inequalities; sustainable cities and communities; responsible consumption and production; action related to climate change; life below water; life on land; peace, justice, and strong institutions; and partnerships (United Nations n.d.). The last-mentioned subject relates to implementation of the agenda. It is to be fulfilled by each member of the United Nations assuming responsibility for its implementation and by the formation of partnerships among them and with other stakeholders.

Some areas, such as the United Kingdom and Japan, felt too many goals were enunciated in the agenda. They would have appreciated fewer. In addition, it was believed by other countries that the goals were too numerous to easily communicate to the public and that some, especially those related to environmental matters, would be difficult to achieve (Ford 2015).

All of the goals are globally interrelated. Also, they encompass the three dimensions of sustainable development: the economic, the social, and the environmental. The challenge for achievement is monumental. Hopefully, the agenda can be achieved by the 2030 deadline (Kroll et al. 2019; United Nations 2019, n.d.).

Individual countries have incorporated many provisions of the goals into their national development plans. Although progress related to many goals has been achieved, the latest report on the 2030 agenda raises some questions (United Nations 2019). However, in spite of progress in some sectors, immediate activities are called for in climate change and augmented inequality between and within nations. Suffering of various types exists within them. Some populations are fragile and vulnerable and lack basic necessities of life. Not only are the goals of the agenda interrelated, but the solutions are as well. A solution to one problem will aid in a response to another. Data should be collected regularly. It is noted, however, that most nations do not do so. Thus, severe gaps in data exist (United Nations 2019).

Unfortunately, poverty in all its forms has not ended, and according to the cited 2019 report, the world is not on track to eliminate it by 2030. As aforementioned, food insecurity, instead of decreasing, has increased. Millions more people are living in hunger and are undernourished, and, of course, well-being and health do not exist for all. Many poor are left behind. Inclusive and quality education, including lifelong learning, has not been totally developed because many younger folk are not proficient in reading and mathematics. Moreover, 750 million adults, two-thirds of which are female, are illiterate. Gender equality has definitely not been achieved. In many of its facets, the same holds for the availability and sustainable management of water and sanitation for all. In terms of access to affordable, sustainable, and modern energy for all, it is noteworthy that 90% of the global population benefit from access to electricity. As far as employment is concerned, the global unemployment rate stood at 5% in 2019. Industrialization is another critical area. In lesser developed countries, its growth is not fast enough to meet the 2030 agenda standard (United Nations 2019). Unfortunately, employment is even less due to the pandemic.

Many countries have developed national urban platforms, but many areas have residents (one of four) that live in slum-like conditions and with polluted air. A large amount of nations is adopting measures to ensure sustainable production and consumption. The true picture will develop with the implementation of these measures. Ocean, seas, and marine resources are to be utilized for sustainable development. It is noteworthy that ocean acidity has experienced an increase of 26% and is expected within the next year to augment further by 100% to 150% (United Nations 2019). Such a forecast causes anxiety because acidification threatens marine life and climate change.

In terms of the promotion of ecosystems and stopping biodiversity, its loss is taking place with land degradation at an accelerated pace. Peaceful, inclusive, and just societies with the same characteristics pervading their institutions would be ideal. Unfortunately, human trafficking and violence pervade many populations and seem to be augmenting. Just as unfortunate are the big gaps in social protection coverage (United Nations 2019).

The goals included in the agenda portray a utopian society in which all citizens would enjoy good health and all forms of well-being. Oral health would not be a major public health problem as it is today. Although progress has been made in reaching the goals, still much remains to be accomplished, and 2030 is around the corner. Critical and successful activities must be forthcoming. Time is of the essence. Successful measures would positively affect health in general and, specifically, oral health. Perhaps, on the other hand, those that thought the goals were too numerous were correct.

Tobacco

In addition to factors already mentioned, one's oral health status is also influenced by smoking and alcohol use. Tobacco use in one form or another is the single largest avoidable health hazard in the EU. It accounts for approximately 700,000 deaths annually. Moreover, it has a significant detrimental impact on oral health. It can cause oral cancer, and pre-cancer, halitosis, discoloration of teeth and fillings, smoker's palate, smoker's melanosis, the reduction of the ability to smell and taste, coated tongue, oral candidiasis, dental caries, periodontal disease, the failure of dental implants, as well as the impairment of the aesthetic outcome of dental implant treatment. In addition, typical indicators for periodontal maladies tend to have significantly increased values in smokers compared to non-smokers. Also, smoking is associated with a larger amount of tooth loss (Csilla et al. 2012; Dietrich et al. 2015; Sandhu 2017; Sheiham and Watt 2000; Stassen and Hammarfjord 2015).

Furthermore, smokers note more often that their teeth are sensitive to hot or cold. Also, they claim toothaches and mouth or face pain, whereas many fewer non-smokers do so. Smokers, as opposed to non-smokers, tend to wear dentures and claim social restrictions due to their teeth. In addition, smokers exhibit more crown and root surfaces with decay, and the extent and severity of periodontal disease tend to be more marked in them. Also noteworthy is the fact that tobacco chewing in a research project was found to be the strongest risk factor for oral cancer (Locker 1992; Millar and Locker 2007; Znaor et al. 2003). Tobacco use definitely causes damage to one's mouth, gums, and teeth.

The number of smokers in the Member States is quite large. Twenty-eight percent of the EU population smokes and 29% of those aged 15 to 24 do so as well. The highest proportion of adult daily smokers is found in France (24.1%), and Sweden has claimed the lowest proportion (10.7%) (Mossialos et al. 2016). The percentages were much higher at one time. In 2005, the highest proportion of smokers was found in Austria (45.1%) and Slovakia (44.5%). Portugal claimed the highest majority of non-smokers (81.3%) (Eurostat 2009).

Tobacco use in Europe was previously mostly identified with males, but this holds no longer. The gap in smoking prevalence between male and female adults is much smaller, especially in Austria, Denmark, the Netherlands, and the United Kingdom. In Sweden, more women smoke daily than men. In Bulgaria, Croatia, Poland, and Slovenia, more young females make use of tobacco products than young males (Bertollini et al. 2016).

A relatively recent phenomenon is the use of electronic or e-cigarettes. Use of this product has augmented, especially among younger smokers in middle and secondary education. These cigarettes are extremely popular in France. Those that experiment with them tend to be of the younger generation. Many people turned to this product hoping to alleviate their tobacco dependence and to decrease hazards to their health (Lermenier and Palle 2014). Hazards have been have been made known with this product as well.

Surveys of dental students and those studying dental hygiene have been undertaken concerning tobacco-use cessation. Smoking among the two groups was more or less similar: 37.78% (dental students) and 32.5% (dental hygiene students). A majority of both groups understood the negative impact of smoking on health. Unfortunately, both groups demonstrated poor knowledge of tobacco-use cessation activities. In addition, they were aware of their role in future professional practice as a counselor on the matter. Dental hygiene students were more comfortable with it. However, it is noteworthy that almost a majority of both groups expressed concerns in reference to the effectiveness of tobacco cessation activities. Given their lack of knowledge of tobacco-use cessation interventions, perhaps integration of this subject matter into their curricula and CPD activities would aid in their future practice (Pizzo et al. 2010).

A Romanian study of dental students, 43% of whom smoked, produced similar results. A majority, amounting to 62%, attempted to drop the habit. Although they themselves were not successful in quitting smoking, 88% were willing to advise future patients to stop smoking. The conclusion of the survey was similar to the one cited above. Students needed more knowledge on smoking prevention and cessation activities. The same result has been found regarding Croatian dental students and even dentists (Komar et al. 2018; Szekely et al. 2010).

It is interesting that in many surveys dental students demonstrated a willingness to counsel future individual patients to erase the smoking habit. Yet, far fewer of them were prompted to participate in anti-tobacco programs based in the community. Unfortunately, they held negative perceptions as to the effectiveness of professional guidance on the subject in both settings (Vanobbergen et al. 2007).

Member States have undertaken efforts in the sector of anti-tobacco use. Many of these activities are collaborative efforts, as they should be, involving educational, sports, health, and community structures, as well as other types of institutions. Examples of anti-tobacco use policies in the Member States include placement of health-related warnings on packages of cigarettes, prohibition of selling tobacco to people under a certain age, a tax on tobacco products, information campaigns, creation of smoke-free environments, public consultations, tobacco advertising restrictions, and a price increase of tobacco products. Furthermore, in some nations, tobacco firms are not to be considered as event sponsors. Also, some countries have met the requirements of international agreements related to the use of tobacco products. The existence of many of these policies in the Member States has decreased the use of tobacco products. Further reductions must take place.

The EU has been quite active in the anti-tobacco campaign. The Commission and the Member States have assented to the World Health Organization's Framework Convention on Tobacco Control aimed at ameliorating the health and economic consequences of tobacco use. At the recommendation of the Commission, the European Parliament (EP) and the Council passed Directive 2014/40/EU concerned with enhancement of tobacco operations in the internal market and the guarantee of the EU citizenry's health and safety. Rules relating to the packaging, labeling, and ingredients of tobacco products were prescribed. Flavoring of cigarettes was restricted as to types of flavors and their quantity. The new rules also affected e-cigarettes. Safety, packaging, and quality requisites were set forth, and e-cigarette manufacturers were required to alert Member States before placing new products on the market and to report annually to Member States their sales volume, user types, and preferences. In addition, e-cigarette manufacturers were required to enforce publicity restrictions. The new Directive was expected to decrease the consumption of tobacco by 2% within 5 years. Thus, public health would experience an improvement. It was thought that many youth would cease tobacco use or not undertake it.

The Directive also envisioned traceability and security features for tobacco products (Directive 2014/24/EU, Articles 15, 16). Such were to lessen opportunities for their illicit trade. In addition, the EU has agreements with the four principal transnational tobacco companies in order to avoid illicit trade practices. However, these accords have not received a favorable evaluation (Joossens et al. 2016).

The EU has also led campaigns across the Member States against tobacco consumption. One was known as Help. It involved experts, communication agencies, and youth. The major objectives of the effort were to encourage youth not to engage in smoking, to help smokers quit, and to make youth aware of the dangers of secondhand smoke. To communicate throughout the EU, the program had to contain diverse cultural and social ingredients. Thus, youth, governmental, and organizational participation were a necessity. The important ingredients to the pan-European message were use of common symbols, creation of a unifying media strategy, and working closely with institutions (European Commission n.d.). The Help campaign and others have met with success throughout the Member States. However, since 2016, EU focus has transformed. It has been on national initiatives.

Cross-border advertising of tobacco products is restricted on the radio and the Internet, in the press and other publications, and in information society services by Directive 2003/33/EC, the Tobacco Advertising Directive. The same document also bans tobacco firms from sponsoring activities involving several Member States, such as the Olympics. As for the print media, tobacco advertising is limited to those publications not intended to reach the general public, such as those meant for persons in the tobacco trade, and to those published outside the EU and not aimed at its market (Directive 2003/33/EC Article 3, Recital 4). As in other circumstances, responsibility for designing sanctions applicable to infringements of the named restrictions is assigned once again to the individual Member States. These prohibitions were extended to all types of audiovisual media by Directive 2010/13/EU. Other EU actions in its anti-tobacco activities include the framing of Council Directive 2011/64/EU which related to excise taxes placed on tobacco products. Most recently, the Scientific Committee on Health, Environmental and Emerging Risks agreed to a request for an opinion on the health effects, cessation, and initiation of e-cigarette use (Compte rendu de la réunion 2019).

These efforts on the part of the EU were directed at improving the oral health status of its citizenry. More specifically, its activities have been focused on youth, given that 93% of smokers have had the habit before they were 26 years old. The goal has been to encourage cessation or at least reduction of tobacco use or to stimulate this population not to engage in it. Such efforts are definitely worthwhile and valuable in terms of oral and systemic health. The EU citizenry is definitely better off.

Alcohol

After coffee and tea, alcohol is the most commonly consumed item in the United Kingdom and probably in other Member States as well. Europe has been labeled "the heaviest drinking region in the world" (Wuyts et al. 2016) because of its high amount of alcohol drinkers and episodic drinking, also known as binge drinking. All in all, its residents consume approximately 25% of alcohol consumption around the globe. Like tobacco, alcohol is also a health hazard and has an impact on both oral and systemic health. It has also been known to influence dental treatment.

Chronic diseases have been identified with persons consuming large quantities of alcohol. In terms of oral health, there is a linkage between alcohol and oral cancer, dental and maxilla-facial trauma, halitosis, tooth staining, periodontal maladies, tooth wear, caries, and tooth loss. Non-carious damage to teeth, such as dental erosion, has also been related to long-term alcohol use. It can cause irritation and infection of oral soft tissues, including the tongue. To use the words linkage and related does not necessarily indicate cause of these difficulties. These words merely refer to an association between alcohol and the ailment. Many of these indicators have been found among alcohol-dependent persons. They have featured a higher number of them (Grocock 2018; Khairnar et al. 2017; Priyanka et al. 2017).

It has been noted that under 25% of the EU population does not imbibe alcohol. In addition, statistics demonstrate that across the Member States among people aged 15 and over, drinking habits have tended to be diverse. In Belgium, Luxembourg, Germany, and Denmark, a large part of the population drinks at least every month, and a comparable amount of people are involved in episodic or binge drinking in the same time period. On the other hand, in Romania binge drinking is frequent, and the quantity of alcohol consumed at least monthly is low. In Spain, Italy, and Portugal, daily consumption of alcohol is part of the culture, and episodic single-occasion drinking does not take place often. Men, for the most part, tend to participate in binge drinking more frequently than women as do individuals with middle and higher educational achievements and financial gains.

Data indicates that a general decrease in the quantity of alcohol consumed by adolescents across the EU has taken place. This decline occurred between 2002 and 2010 in 15 of 21 EU Member States. Decreases were similar across genders and for those between 11 and 13 years of age and 15 years old. However, an increase in binge drinking took place in seven countries. In Lithuania, the Czech Republic, and Finland, adolescents are less likely to participate in binge drinking (Wuyts et al. 2016).

Changes in alcohol use for adolescents have been attributed to enforcement of age restrictions to purchase alcohol, price increases, an augment in young immigrants who are less likely to imbibe alcohol, transformation in cultural and social values, and enhanced knowledge of alcohol hazards (Health Equity Pilot Project (HEPP) 2018). It is noteworthy that presently the trend of lesser consumption of alcoholic beverages has stalled.

Frequency of alcohol consumption also varies across the EU. In the population aged 15 or older, daily alcohol consumers, accounted for 9.2% compared to weekly alcohol drinkers of 29.6% and 23.1% of those who imbibed monthly. And then 23.9% of Europeans do not engage in drinking alcoholic beverages. Member States having the most people who do not drink include Cyprus (46.4%), Croatia (43.9%), and Romania (42.1%). Those nations with the lowest number in this category include Denmark (8.7%), Germany (13.1%), the Czech Republic (14.1%), and Finland (15%). It is noteworthy that Denmark experienced a sharp decline in alcohol consumption, but it continues to feature one of the highest drinking rates of a most hazardous nature—episodic drinking (European Commission 2018a).

Studies have found that adolescents from families with greater socioeconomic resources drink more alcoholic beverages. Socioeconomic diversities have been related to all adults' drinking habits as well. For youth, these variables were found to vary. In some Member States, such as Great Britain, Germany, and Scotland, a decline in alcohol consumption occurred across all socioeconomic groups. The opposite took place in Finland and the Netherlands where lower socioeconomic groups realized a weaker decrease or an eventual augment. A target group for a public health intervention emerged (Health Equity Pilot Project (HPP) 2018).

Alcohol is costly. Its affordability is a significant factor in its consumption. In 2017, people in the Baltic Member States spent a greater part of household expenditures on alcohol than others in the EU. Estonians spent the largest share (5.2%). They were followed by Latvians (4.9%) and Lithuanians (4%). Next in the progression were the Polish (3.5%), Czechs (3.3%), and Hungarians (3%). Spanish people claimed the lowest proportion of household spending on alcohol (0.8%), while Italians and Greeks both spent 0.9%.

As in other cases, DCPs are in a unique position to counsel persons in reference to alcohol use. Even a brief encounter with a risky drinker has resulted in a reduction in the amount of alcohol consumed and the frequency of consumption. Even though dentists, for the most part, are enthusiastic about such counseling, lack of funding and time pressures stand in their way. As a result, only 11.6% of these professionals frequently undertake counseling related to alcohol. A team strategy should be adopted (Grocock 2018).

All Member States have legal documents whose goal is to reduce the harmful consumption of alcohol. The majority happen to have a general national policy document that can be used to design alcohol policies. However, Austria, Bulgaria, Denmark, Estonia, Hungary, Luxembourg, and Malta do not feature such a national alcohol action plan. Mechanisms for controlling alcohol distribution and sales include the establishment of a state monopoly on retail sales, licensing, limiting hours and days of the week for selling these products, and regulating the density of establishments. The need for a license in order to sell alcohol products is found in a majority of the Member States, and in 16 of them, business hours are not regulated in alcohol selling establishments. Only Finland and Sweden have a state monopoly on retail sale outlets of alcoholic beverages. In Finland, it applies to wine and liquor, but not to beer, and in Sweden, it relates to all beverages containing alcohol above a certain level (Eurocare: European Alcohol Policy Alliance 2016).

In many Member States, there are rules against selling alcohol to drunk people and those under an established age. Often, the set age differs according to the type of alcoholic beverage: beer, wine, and liquor. There is a diversity between Member States concerning the set minimum age. Regulations also relate to off- and on-premise selling. In general, they have proven to be quite effective in controlling underage drinking.

In addition, some Member States have posted an excise tax on all alcoholic beverages, and some have no tax on wine, but only on beer and liquor. Most of the EU associates have selected the general tax. However, the rate varies from country to country. It so happens that if the nation is a producer of wine, the excise tax on that product will be close to zero (Österberg and Karlsson n.d.).

Educational programs, both in schools and in the community, are important to creating public awareness of responsible consumption of alcoholic beverages. Advertising restrictions are numerous throughout the Member States. As in other matters, they relate to different groups of alcoholic products: beer, wine, and liquor. In some cases, there are no restrictions, and in others, they are partial and self-imposed, or advertising is prohibited. Primarily, advertising regulations relate to publicity on all types of media and to sponsorship of sports and youth events. More specifically, they relate to national television, printed media, cinemas, billboards, the Internet, and social media. Of the Member States, Belgium, Greece, Luxembourg, and Slovakia stand out because there are no restrictions on alcohol marketing in the noted media types (Eurocare: European Alcohol Policy Alliance 2016).

With this limited presentation on the regulation of alcoholic beverages, it is clear that the Member States have created legal documents pertaining to several facets of the alcohol sector. The EU, as will be seen, has done somewhat the same, but has assumed a diverse role.

In terms of alcohol regulation, the Member States are primarily responsible for their individual policies related to alcohol. The EU developed an Alcohol Strategy in 2006 in which its envisioned role was as coordinator of activities undertaken at the national level. It was to complement national initiatives. Its Strategy focused on five themes: protection of young people, children, and the unborn child, reduction of injuries and deaths from alcohol-related traffic accidents, prevention of alcohol-related harm among adults and reduction of its influence on the place of employment, enhancement of awareness of the risks related to alcohol use and appropriate drinking patterns, and, lastly, establishment of a data system on the subject matter of alcohol (Commission of the European Communities 2006b).

An evaluation of the Strategy, partially based on surveys, indicated that the document contained items of concern to the individual Member States. Moreover, the announced Strategy contributed to the formulation of national policies. In addition, the EU effort not only contributed to policies, actions, and strategies in individual Member States, but it had a weighty impact across most of them. It provided a basis for activity. The evaluation assigned a lesser grade to the availability of comparable, EU-wide data (DG Health and Consumers 2012).

A follow-up to the Strategy requested by the Commission was the *Action Plan on youth drinking and on heavy drinking (binge drinking) (2014–2016)* (2014) designed by the Committee on National Alcohol Policy and Action, a structure to ensure that national and EU policies are congruent. The purpose of the follow-up was to complement existing activities for the realization of the Strategy's objective of reducing alcohol-related harm. This new document addressed such harm among youth up to the age of 25. The Commission was assigned responsibility for facilitating the implementation and follow-up of the Action Plan. Also, it was to smoothly manage the exchange of information and best practice. The Plan listed several measures available to Member States for use in their attempts to reduce alcohol-related harm. The Commission was to provide support and the aforementioned coordination and to use instruments and tools at its hand, such as the Health Programme and Horizon 2020, the largest EU research and innovation project. The Health Programme of the Commission finances projects and several initiatives focused on alcohol. They have been most successful. In addition, in the Action Plan, the Commission was urged to continue to implement health aspects of other EU policies, such as those concerning transportation, education, and agriculture as well as others. These fields relate to alcohol use and oral and systemic health (Action Plan on youth drinking and on heavy episodic drinking (binge drinking) (2014–2016) (2014).

In a resolution on alcohol strategy, the EP (2015) urged the Commission to consider alcohol bottle labeling. Also, it stressed that treatment must be accessible and affordable to those suffering from maladies associated with alcohol use. It also issued a call for reliable data and educational and counseling programs. It declared support for the EU Alcohol Strategy and its multi-stakeholder approach, and it praised the Commission and its valuable role in nurturing good research and sharing evidence, hoping that it would continue to do so in the same manner.

The World Health Organization, in addition to the EU, has worked with the Member States as well. It too has an action plan to decrease the harms of alcohol that was endorsed by the 53 Member States of its European Region. The two associations with their strategies and action plans provide valuable guidance and advice to Member States on alcohol-related harm and responsible consumption. The EU has been active in the alcohol sector, but it has allowed the Member States to be the prime movers. Its principal legal documents have set forth problems to be solved, and, for the most part, it has been up to the individual Member States to design solutions to existing difficulties. As noted, progress has been accomplished, but given alcohol's association with oral health status, unfortunately, more remains to be done.

Conclusion

These issues cover different sectors related to oral health care, and they created discussion. All are of importance to diverse DCPs and the practice of their professions. The EU has been active in all sectors and has related to a multitude of these issues in different manners. All of its decisions, as noted, were not enthusiastically received.

References

Action Plan on youth drinking and on heavy episodic drinking (binge drinking) (2014–2016). (2014). http://www.ec.europa.eu. Accessed 10 May 2019.

An Roinn Sláinte (Irish Department of Health). (2016). *A healthy weight for Ireland: Obesity policy and action plan*. Dublin: The Stationary Office.

Anttila, J., Rytkönen, T., Kankaanpää, R., Tolvanen, M., & Lahti, S. (2015). Effect of national recommendation on sweet selling as an intervention for a healthier school environment. *Scandinavian Journal of Public Health, 43*(1), 27–34.

Baker, T. (2018, June 18). *The state of sugar and health taxes around the world*. http://www.kerry.com. Accessed 28 Apr 2019.

Bertollini, R., Ribeiro, S., Mauer-Stender, K., & Galea, G. (2016). Tobacco control in Europe: A policy review. *European Respiratory Review, 25*(140), 151–157.

BIO Intelligence Service. (2012). *Study on the potential for reducing mercury pollution from dental amalgam and batteries: Final report prepared for the European Commission–DG ENV (Directorate-General Environment)*. http://www.ec.europa.eu. Accessed 16 Apr 2019.

Bosello, F., Roson, R., & Toi, R. S. J. (2005). *Economy-wide estimates of the implications of climate change: Human health* (Nota di Lavoro (Work Note), No. 97). Milano: Fondazione £ni Enrico Mattei (FEEM).

Brattabø, I. V., Iversen, A. C., Åstrøm, A. N., & Bjørknes, R. (2016). Experience with suspecting child maltreatment in the Norwegian public dental health services, a national survey. *Acta Odontologica Scandinavica, 74*(8), 626–632.

Breda, J., Jakovljevic, J., Rathmes, G., Mendes, R., Fontaine, O., Hollmann, S., et al. (2018). Promoting health-enhancing physical activity in Europe: Current state of surveillance, policy development and implementation. *Health Policy, 122*(5), 519–527.

British Dental Association. (2016, May 10). *Sugar and children's oral health*. http://www.bda.org. Accessed 25 June 2016.

Commission of the European Communities. (2005, January 28). *Communication from the Commission to the Council and the European Parliament: Community Strategy concerning mercury.(SEC(*2005*) 101)*.

Commission of the European Communities. (2006a, July 4). *Communication from the commission: Towards an EU strategy on the rights of the child*. COM(2006) 367 final.

Commission of the European Communities. (2006b, October 24). *Communication from the commission to the council, the European Parliament, the European economic and social committee and the Committee of the Regions: An EU strategy to support member states in reducing alcohol related harm*. (COM (2006) 625 final).

Compte rendu de la réunion du groupe d'experts sur la politique du tabac (21 mars 2019) (Outcome of the meeting of the group of experts on tobacco policy (21 March 2019). (2019, May 13). *Bulletin d'Information Santé* (Health-EU Newsletter). Received May 13, 2019, From Sante-Health-EU-Newsletter@ec.europa.eu.

Council Directive 2011/64/EU of 21 June 2011 on the structure and rates of excise levy applied to manufactured tobacco.

Council Directive 2011/84/EU of 20 September 2011 amending Directive 76/768/EEC, concerning cosmetic products, for the purpose of adapting Annex III thereto to technical progress.

Council Directive 76/768/EEC of 27 July 1976 on the approximation of the laws of the Member States relating to cosmetic products (Cosmetics Directive).

Council of European Dentists (2015).Whitening lamps.

Council of European Dentists. (2016). CED Resolution: Sugar.

Council of European Dentists (2017) Use of tooth whitening products on persons under 18 years of age in the EU. http://www.cedentists.eu. Accessed 21 Jan. 2018.

Council Recommendation of 26 November 2013 on promoting health-enhancing physical activity across sectors, (2013/C 354/01).

Csilla, B. B., Mónika, K., Pop, M., Melinda, S., Hanga, D., & Zsuzsanna, M. (2012). A comparison of periodontal health status in smoker, former smoker and non-smoker patients. *Acta Medica Marisiensis, 58*(6), 367–370.

Cukovic-Bagic, I., Dumancic, J., Tiljak, M. K., Drvaric, I., Boric, B., Kopic, V., et al. (2014). Croatian dentists' knowledge, experience and attitudes in regard to child abuse and neglect. *International Journal of Pediatric Dentistry*. https://doi.org/10.1111/ipd.12151.

Curran, A. E., Caplan, D. J., Lee, J. Y., Paynter, L., Gizlice, Z., Champagne, C., et al. (2010). Dentists' attitudes about their role in addressing obesity in patients: A national survey. *The Journal of the American Dental Association, 141*(11), 1307–1316.

Dental Tribune. (2011, September 29). EU applies stricter rules to sale and use of teeth whitening products. *Dental Tribune*. http://www.eu.dental-tribune.com. Accessed 10 Dec 2018.

Deshpande, N. C., & Amrutiya, M. R. (2017). Obesity and oral health-is there a link? An observational study. *Journal of Indian Society of Periodontology, 21*(3), 229–233.

DG (Directorate-General) Health and Consumers. (2012, December). *Assessment of the added value of the EU strategy to support Member States in reducing alcohol-related harm*. http://www.ec.europa.eu. Accessed 9 May 2019.

Dietrich, T., Walter, C., Oluwegbemigun, K., Bergmann, M., Pischon, T., Pischon, N., et al. (2015). Smoking, smoking cessation, and risk of tooth loss: The EPIC-Potsdam study. *Journal of Dental Research, 94*(10), 1369–1375.

Dimitrova-Stull, A. (2014). *Violence towards children in the EU: Current situation*. n.p.: European Parliamentary Research Service.

Directive 2003/33/EC of the European Parliament and of the Council of 26 May 2003 on the approximation of the laws, regulations and administrative provisions of the Member States relating to the advertising and sponsorship of tobacco products.

Directive 2010/13/EU of the European Parliament and of the Council of 10 March 2010 on the coordination of certain provisions laid down by law, regulation or administrative action in Member States concerning the provision of audiovisual media services (Audiovisual Media Services Directive).

Directive 2011/36/EU of the European Parliament and of the Council of 5 April 2011 on preventing and combating trafficking in human beings and protecting its victims, and replacing Council Framework Decision 2002/629/JHA.

Directive 2011/92/EU of the European Parliament and of the Council of 13 December 2011 on combating the sexual abuse and sexual exploitation of children and child pornography, and replacing Council Framework Decision 2004/68/JHA.

Directive 2012/29/EU of the European Parliament and of the Council of 25 October 2012 establishing minimum standards on the rights, support and protection of victims of crime, and replacing Council Framework Decision 2001/220/JHA.

Directive 2014/40/EU of the European Parliament and of the Council of 3 April 2014 on the approximation of the laws, regulations and administrative provisions of the Member States concerning the manufacture, presentation and sale of tobacco and related products and repealing Directive 2001/37/EC.

Drigeard, C., Nicolas, E., Hansjacob, A., & Roger-Leroi, V. (2012). Educational needs in the field of detection of domestic violence and neglect: The opinion of a population of French dentists. *European Journal of Dental Education, 16*(3), 156–165.

Duane, B., Harford, S., Ramasubbu, D., Stancliffe, R., Pasdeki-Clewer, E., Lomax, R., et al. (2019). Environmentally sustainable dentistry: A brief introduction to sustainable concepts within the dental practice. *British Dental Journal, 226*(4), 292–295.

EA Editors. (n.d.). *How environmental changes can affect dental health: And what you can do to prevent it*. http://www.escapeartist.com. Accessed 12 Mar 2020.

Eurocare: European Alcohol Policy Alliance. (2016). *European report on alcohol policy: A review*. n.p.: Author.

European Commission. (2011, February 15). *Communication from the commission to the European Parliament, the council, the European economic and social committee and the Committee of the Regions: An EU agenda for the rights of the child COM(2011)60 final.*

European Commission. (2012, June 19). *Communication from the Commission to the European Parliament, the Council, the European Economic and Social Committee and the Committee of the Regions: The EU strategy towards the eradication of trafficking in human beings 2012–2016. COM(2012) 286 final.*

European Commission. (2015a, May 8). Are dental fillings safe? Safety of dental amalgam and alternative dental restoration materials. *European Union Commission E-mail Newsletter.*

European Commission. (2015b). *Report from the Commission to the European Parliament and the Council regarding trans fats in foods and in the overall diet of the Union population. COM(2015) 619 final.*

European Commission. (2017, May 18). *Questions and answers: EU mercury policy and the ratification of the Minamata Convention.*

European Commission. (2018a). *Alcohol consumption statistics.* http://www.ec.europa.eu/eurostat. Accessed 4 May 2019.

European Commission (2018b). *Initiatives on nutrition and physical activity.*

European Commission. (2018c). *Special Eurobarometer 472 report: Sport and physical activity.*

European Commission. (n.d.). *Help for a life without tobacco: A legacy.* http://www.ec.europa.eu. Accessed 8 May 2019.

European Commission and World Health Organization. (2018). *Promoting physical activity in the education sector: Current status and success stories from the Union Member European States of the WHO European Region.* http;//www.ec.europa.eu. Accessed 3 May 2019.

European Parliament Resolution of 29 April 2015 on alcohol strategy (2015/2543(RSP).

Eurostat. (2009). *Consumers in Europe.* http://www.europa.eu. Accessed 9 Nov 2015.

Ford, L. (2015, 14 January). Sustainable Development Goals: All you need to know. *The Guardian.* http://www.theguardian.com. Accessed 22 Mar 2020.

Green, T. (2019). *What we eat effects our teeth.* http://www.southcharlottedentistry.com. Accessed 3 Feb 2020.

Grocock, R. (2018). The relevance of alcohol to dental practice. *British Dental Journal,* Article number 18025. https://doi.org/10.1038/bdjteam.2018.25.

Grose, J., Richardson, J., Mills, I., Moles, D., & Nasser, M. (2016). Exploring attitudes and knowledge of climate change and sustainability in a dental practice: A feasibility study into resource management. *British Dental Journal, 220*(4), 187–191.

Gupta, P., Gupta, N., Pawar, A. P., Birajdar, S. S., Natt, A. S., & Singh, H. P. (2013). Role of sugar and sugar substitutes in dental caries: A review. *International Scholarly Research Notice's Dentistry.* https://doi.org/10.1155/2013/519421.

Harris, J. C., Elcock, C., Sidebotham, P. D., & Welbury, R. R. (2009). Safeguarding children in dentistry: 1. Child protection training, experience and practice of dental professionals with an interest in paediatric dentistry. *British Dental Journal, 206*(8), 409–414.

Harvard T. H. Chan School of Public Health (2016, November 4). Spotlight on soda. Internet newsletter received from Harvard T. H. Chan School of Public Health on 4 November 2016.

Hayden, C., Bowler, J. O., Chambers, S., Freeman, R., Humphris, G., Richards, D., et al. (2012). Obesity and dental caries in children: A systematic review and meta-analysis. *Community Dentistry and Oral Epidemiology, 41*(4), 289–308.

Health Equity Pilot Project (HEPP). (2018). *Analysis of youth alcohol trends in EU countries..* http://www.ec.europa.eu. Accessed 2 May 2019.

Hooley, M., Skouteris, H., Boganin, C., Satur, J., & Kilpatrick, N. (2012). Body mass index and dental caries in children and adolescents: A systematic review of literature published 2004 to 2011. *Systematic Reviews.* https://doi.org/10.1186/2046-4053-1-57.

Hwang, B.-F., & Jaakkola, J. J. K. (2008). Ozone and other air pollutants and the risk of oral clefts. *Environmental Health Perspectives, 116*(10), 1411–1415.

Improved child protection training needed. (2009). *British Dental Journal, 206*(8), 399.

International Academy of Oral Medicine and Toxicology. (2016, March 2). *Position statement against dental mercury amalgam fillings for medical and dental practitioners, dental students, dental patients, and policy makers*. http://www.iaomt.org. Accessed 17 Apr. 2019.

Joossens, L., Gilmore, A. B., Stoklosa, M., & Ross, H. (2016). Assessment of the European Union's illicit trade agreements with the four major transnational tobacco companies. *Tobacco Control, 25*(3), 254–260.

Jordan, A., Welbury, R. R., Tiljak, M. K., & Cukovic-Bagic, I. (2012). Croatian dental students' educational experiences and knowledge in regard to child abuse and neglect. *Journal of Dental Education, 75*(11), 1512–1519.

Kantovitz, K. R., Pascon, F. M., Rontani, R. M. P., & Gavião, M. B. D. (2006). Obesity and dental caries-A systematic review. *Oral Health and Preventive Dentistry, 4*(2), 137–144.

Kemoli, A. M. (2019). Paediatric oral health and climate change. *Edorium Journal of Dentistry, 7*, 100034DO1AK2019.

Khairnar, M. R., Wadgave, U., & Khairnar, S. M. (2017). Effect of alcoholism on oral health: A review. *Journal of Alcoholism & Drug Dependence, 5*(3), 266. https://doi.org/10.4172/2329-6488.1000266.

Khanna, S. (2010a). Climate change & oral health: Current challenges & future scope. *International Journal of Environmental Science and Development, 1*(2), 190–192.

Khanna, S. (2010b). *Potential impact of climate change on oral health & disabilities: A grass roots study.* Paper presented at the Seventh International Symposium on Recent Advances in Environmental Health Research, Jackson, Mississippi, September 12–15, 2010.

Komar, K., Glavina, A., Boras, V. V., Verzak, Z., & Brailo, V. (2018). Impact of smoking on oral health: Knowledge and attitudes of Croatian dentists and dental students. *Acta Stomatologica Croatica, 52*(2), 148–155.

Kroll, C., Warchold, A., & Pradhan, P. (2019). Sustainable Development Goals (SDGs): Are we successful in turning trade-offs into synergies? *Palgrave Communications*, *5*, Article number 140.

Lazarou, C., & Soteriades, E. S. (2010). Children's physical activity, TV watching and obesity in Cyprus: The CYKIDS study. *European Journal of Public Health, 20*(1), 70–77.

Lermenier, A., & Palle, C. (2014). *Résultats de l'enquête ETINCEL-OFDT sur la cigarette électronique(c* (Results of the OFDT survey on electronic cigarettes). n.p.: Observatoire Français des Drogues et des Toxicomanies (French Observatory of Drugs and Drug Addicts).

Levine, R. (2012). Obesity and oral disease: A challenge for dentistry. *British Dental Journal, 213*(9), 453–456.

Li, L.-W., Wong, H. M., & McGrath, C. P. (2017). Longitudinal association between obesity and dental caries in adolescents. *The Journal of Pediatrics, 189*, 149–154.

Locker, D. (1992). Smoking and oral health in older adults. *Canadian Journal of Public Health, 83*(6), 429–432.

Marshall, A., Eichenberger-Gilmore, J. M., Broffitt, B. A., Warren, J. J., & Levy, S. M. (2007). Dental caries and childhood obesity: Roles of diet and socioeconomic status. *Community Dentistry and Oral Epidemiology, 35*(6), 449. https://doi.org/10.1111/j.1600-0528.2006.00353.x.

Millar, W. J., & Locker, D. (2007). Smoking and oral health status. *Journal of the Canadian Dental Association, 73*(2), 155–155g.

Minamata Convention on Mercury: Text and annexes. (2013). http://www.unenvironment.org. Accessed 21 May 2019.

Mossialos, E., Wenzl, M., Osborn, R., & Sornak, D. (Eds.). (2016). *2015 international profiles of health care systems*. New York: The Commonwealth Fund.

Moynihan, P. J. (2005). The role of diet and nutrition in the etiology and prevention of oral diseases. *Bulletin of the World Health Organization, 83*(9), 694–699.

Muhamedagic, B., Muhamedagic, L., & Masic, I. (2009). Dental office waste- public health and ecological risk. *Materia Sociomedica, 21*(1), 35–38.

Nicholson, J. W. (2017). Emerging ethical issues in restorative dentistry. *The New Bioethics, 23*(3), 236–248.

Nihtila, A., West, N., Lussi, A., Bouchard, P., Ottolenghi, L., Senekola, E., et al. (2016). Oral health behavior and lifestyle factors among overweight and non-overweight young adults in Europe: A cross-sectional questionnaire study. *Healthcare, 4*, 21. https://doi.org/10.3390/healthcare4020021.

Nouvelles du rendez-vous de midi de la Direction-Générale Communication. (News from the Communication Directorate-General's midday briefing). (2011, September 20). *Midday Express*. http://www.ec.europa.eu. Accessed 20 Jan 2017.

Nuzzolese, E., Lepore, M. M., Montagna, F., Marcario, V., De Rosa, S., & Solarine, B. (2009). Child abuse and dental neglect: The dental team's role in identification and prevention. *International Journal of Dental Hygiene, 7*(2), 96–101.

Österberg, E., & Karlsson, T. (Eds). (n.d.). *Alcohol policies in EU Member States and Norway: A collection of country reports*. http://ec.europa.eu. Accessed 2 May 2019.

Paisi, M., Kay, E., Kaimi, I., Witton, R., Nelder, R., Potterton, R., et al. (2018). Obesity and caries in four-to-six year old English children: A cross-sectional study. *BMC Public Health, 18*, 267. https://doi.org/10.1186/s12889-018-5156-8.

Palle, A. R., Reddy, C. M., Shanker, B. S., Gelli, V., Sudhakar, J., & Reddy, K. K. (2013). Association between obesity and chronic periodontitis: A cross-sectional study. *The Journal of Contemporary Dental Practice, 14*(2), 168–173.

Peres, M. A., Sheiham, A., Liu, P., Demarco, F. F., Silva, A. E. R., Assunção, M. C., et al. (2016). Sugar consumption and changes in dental caries from childhood to adolescence. *Journal of Dental Research, 95*(4), 388–394.

Pizzo, M., Licata, M. E., Piscopo, M. R., Coniglio, M. A., Pignato, S., & Davis, J. M. (2010). Attitudes of Italian dental and dental hygiene students toward tobacco-use cessation. *European Journal of Dental Education, 14*(1), 17–25.

Priyanka, K., Sudhir, K. M., Reddy, V. C. S., Kumar, R. V. S. K., & Srinivasulu, G. (2017). Impact of alcohol dependency on oral health--a cross-sectional comparative study. *Journal of Clinical & Diagnostic Research, 11*(6), ZC43–ZC46.

Regulation (EU) 2017/852 of the European Parliament and of the Council of 17 May 2017 on mercury and repealing Regulation (EC) No 1102/2008.

Regulation No 1223/2009 of the European Parliament and of the Council of 30 November 2009 on cosmetic products.

Report on laws and recommendations on dental mercury management in the EU (2018). http://www.praktikertjanst.se. Accessed 31 Jan 2018.

Roadmap for action on food product improvement. (2016). http://www.europa.cu. Accessed 11 May 2019.

Saito, T., Shimazaki, Y., Koga, T., Tsuzuki, M., & Ohshima, A. (2001). Relationship between upper body obesity and periodontitis. *Journal of Dental Research, 80*(7), 1631–1636.

Sandhu, S. K. (2017). *Environmental factors in oral health*. n.p.: World Health Organization.

Scheraga, J. D., Ebi, K. L., Furlow, J., & Moreno, A. R. (2003). From science to policy: Developing responses to climate change. In A. J. McMichael, D. H. Campbell-Lendrum, C. F. Corvalan, K. L. Ebi, A. Githeko, J. D. Scheraga, et al. (Eds.), *Climate change and human health-Risks and responses* (pp. 237–266). Geneva: World Health Organization.

Scientific Committee on Consumer Products. (2007, December 18). *Opinion on hydrogen peroxide, in its free form or when released, in oral hygiene products and tooth whitening products*. http://www.ec.europa.eu. Accessed 12 May 2009.

Scientific Committee on Emerging and Newly Identified Health Risks. (2015). *Opinion on the safety of dental amalgam and alternative dental restoration materials for patients and users*. https://ec.europa.eu/health/scientific_committees/emerging/docs/scenihr_o_046.pdf. Accessed 23 Mar 2018.

Sheiham, A., & James, W. P. T. (2015). Diet and dental caries: The pivotal role of free sugars reemphasized. *Journal of Dental Research, 94*(10), 1341–1347.

Sheiham, A., & Watt, R. G. (2000). The common risk factor approach: A rational basis for promoting oral health. *Community Dentistry and Oral Epidemiology, 28*(6), 399–406.

Sheiham, A., Steele, J. G., Marcenes, W., Finch, S., & Walls, A. W. G. (2002). The relationship between oral health status and body mass index among older people: A national survey of older people in Great Britain. *British Dental Journal, 192*(12), 703–706.

Silva, A. E. R., Menezes, A. M. B., Demarco, F. F., Vargas-Ferreira, F., & Peres, M. A. (2013). Obesidade e cárie dentária: revisão sistemática (Obesity and dental caries: Systematic review). *Revista de Saude Publica, 47*(4), 799–812.

Stassen, L. F. A., & Hammarfjord, O. (2015). Smoking cessation and the role of the dental practitioner. *Journal of the Irish Dental Association, 61*(2), 90–92.

Szekely, M., Benedek, C., Carsteanu-Dombi, A., Camarasan, A.C., & Virtanen, J.I. (2010). *Smoking habits among Romanian dental students: A pilot study*. Paper delivered at the European Association of Dental Public Health Meeting, September 10–11, 2010, Constanta, Romania.

Taut, C. (2013). Dental amalgam: Is this the end? *Journal of the Irish Dental Association, 59*(6), 311–317.

Tripathi, S., Kiran, K., & Kamala, B. K. (2010). Relationship between obesity and dental caries in children--a preliminary study. *Journal of International Oral Health, 2*(4), 65–72.

Uldum, B., Christensen, H. N., Welbury, R., & Haubek, D. (2017). How Danish dentists and dental hygienists handle their role in child abuse and neglect matters. *Acta Odontologica Scandinavica, 75*(5), 332–337.

United Nations. (2019), *The Sustainable Development Goals report 2019.* http://www.un.org. Accessed 21 Mar 2020.

United Nations. (n.d.). *Transforming our world: The 2030 agenda for sustainable development.* n.p.: Author.

Vallgårda, S. (2016). Ethics dilemmas of early detection of obesity. *Scandinavian Journal of Public Health, 44*(6), 543–545.

Vallogini, G., Nobili, V., Rongo, R., De Rosa, S., Magliarditi, F., D'Antò, V., et al. (2017). Evaluation of the relationship between obesity, dental caries and periodontal disease in adolescents. *European Journal of Paediatric Dentistry, 18*(4). https://doi.org/10.23804/ejpd.2017.18.04.02.

van Dam, B. A. F. M., van der Sanden, W. J. M., & Bruers, J. J. M. (2015). Recognizing and reporting domestic violence: Attitudes, experiences and behavior of Dutch dentists. *BMC Oral Health, 15*, 159. https://doi.org/10.1186/s12903-015-0141-4.

Vanobbergen, J., Nuytens, P., Van Herk, M., & De Visschere, L. (2007). Dental students' attitude towards anti-smoking programmes: A study in Flanders, Belgium. *European Journal of Dental Education, 11*(3), 177–183.

Vesna, A. (2016). The role of dentists in recognition of child abuse. *Journal of Dental and Oral Health.* http://www.scientonline.org. Accessed 21 Nov. 2016.

Wechsler, H., Devereaux, R. S., Davis, M., & Collins, J. (2000). Using the school environment to promote physical activity and healthy eating. *Preventive Medicine, 31*(2), S121–S137.

World Resources Institute. (n.d.) *Climate: Advancing transformative climate solutions.* https://www.wri.org/our-work/topics/climate. Accessed 29 Jan 2021.

Wuyts, C., Barbier, S., & Loosveldt, G. (2016). *Comparison of alcohol consumption in European countries, and some methodological thoughts.* Paper prepared for presentation at the 3rd International ESS (European Social Survey) Conference, 13-15 July 2016, Lausanne, Switzerland. http://www.europeansocialsurvey.org. Accessed 2 May 2019.

Znaor, A., Brennan, P., Gajalakshmi, V., Mathew, A., Shanta, V., Varghese, C., et al. (2003). Independent and combined effects of tobacco smoking, chewing and alcohol drinking on the risk of oral, pharyngeal and esophageal cancers in Indian men. *International Journal of Cancer, 105*(5), 681–686.

Chapter 8
The European Union and the Dental Team

The EU, Oral Healthcare Providers, and Patients

Globalization and Europeanization have transformed the professions of dental care professionals (DCPs). The European Union (EU) has exerted a great impact on many of these professionals as they prepare for and practice their professions, even though it has no formal competence in the healthcare arena. Given its decisions, it has had significant and widespread effects on the oral health systems of the Member States and has played different roles. These repercussions have influenced practices related to some DCPs' education, recognition of professional qualifications, and freedom of movement, as well as several facets of the place of employment, such as working time, annual leave, equality, stipend, social rights, the right to information and consultation, health protection issues, safety, liability for defective products, medical devices, medicinal products, cross-border care, and work-life balance, among other elements. Furthermore, EU legislation also has effected advertising of practices and the use of certain materials affiliated with specific treatments. As noted, in addition to the service providers, the EU has also been concerned with consumers' or patients' safety and their rights, such as health protection, and their freedom of movement and from injury. As aforementioned, much of the EU's influence in the healthcare arena has resulted from the so-called spillover effect. In other words, actions in one field carry implications for another, in this case, oral health care.

The EU and Group Consultation

In its activities, the EU has injected transparency into many policies and has played different roles, ranging from initiator to coordinator. In addition, it holds public consultations and also consults with other associations, as aforementioned.

S. Z. Koff, *The Dental Team in the European Union*,
https://doi.org/10.1007/978-3-030-72232-6_8

Sometimes these organizations meet with each other individually or as groups. For example, the President of the Standing Committee of European Doctors met with his counterpart of the Council of European Dentists. The two leaders discussed common challenges faced by both professions. They agreed on the significance of professional autonomy for the maintenance of care quality and patient safety. Agreement between both leaders was extended to concerns related to the EU. They were troubled that the organization inserted standards into medicine and dentistry developed by groups lacking a public mandate and sufficient ethical and professional capacities. Both agreed to discuss this matter with other professional healthcare groups. Another concern with the EU on which the two leaders concurred was that its agendas were economically based and tended to challenge professional regulations. They were mystified that the EU failed to recognize that healthcare services are diverse from others. Leaders of both associations agreed to continue to collaborate and to discuss further issues of concern (Council of European Dentists 2016).

The Dental-Medical Divide and Its Integration

In spite of the noted fact that systemic and oral health are associated, unfortunately, their systems are rarely co-managed (Metcalf et al. 2011). Dentistry and medicine are separated, and thus, one speaks of the dental-medical divide that, in many cases, commences with both professions' separate educational systems. The divide is quite large, and it bears important consequences for providers of care, citizens, and patients in the Member States (Weil 2016). Mertz claims that "the importance of oral health for overall well-being cannot be overstated" (Mertz 2016, p. 2168). Yet, the divide exists.

In an effort to narrow it, somewhat or ideally to eradicate it, it has been advocated that oral health care become a formal part of general primary health care with an important role. It should be. This makes a lot of sense. It was noted in this work that oral health care in several Member States is sparse. In this new format, according to many advocates, some medical screenings would be undertaken in dental care structures. These should relate to matters that influence oral health, such as diabetes, hypertension, obstructive sleep apnea, smoking, osteoporosis, and weight management (Lamster and Eaves 2011). If the change becomes standard, DCPs' scope of practice would be somewhat modified.

The problem of unmet healthcare needs, especially those concerning oral health care, has been noted. This is a formidable challenge. People included in groups experiencing these needs, such as the poverty stricken, differently abled, aged, and geographically isolated, might be somewhat better off, if general and oral healthcare systems were truly integrated, if some medical screenings became standard in oral healthcare structures, and if the so-called divide no longer existed. The noted medical procedures have been viewed positively by patients and DCPs where implemented. They have proven to be cost-effective and to benefit health status. Authorities and organizations have held affirmative evaluations of medical screenings in dental structures (Friman et al. 2015). It must be remembered that DCPs have an ethical commitment and an obligation to foster the well-being of their patients (Sultan et al. 2014).

The Future

Integration of general and oral health care in order to narrow the so-called divide requires a somewhat different preparation of the dental squad. It has been suggested that two new members join the dental team: an oral healthcare provider and an oral clinical specialist. The former would be a practitioner who comprehends the relationship of oral health to general health and is a specialist in diagnosis and control of oral maladies. The latter, an oral clinical specialist, would provide advanced oral rehabilitation. In addition, the professional would be capable of treating patients having complex chronic illnesses and consuming several medications (Fejerskov et al. 2013). The capabilities of both professionals cross the aforementioned divide.

Also noteworthy is the fact that the digital modification of health care has invaded the workplace. Organized by Erasmus University Medical Center and the EU Commission, a meeting was held to discuss how future and current medical practitioners might integrate digital health care into their practice and also into professional training (Training future-proof doctors for a digital society: How smart health is changing the profession of our doctors 2019). Such encounters would be beneficial for all healthcare professionals, including DCPs.

A major problem that needs to be solved for the immediate future is the decrease in healthcare personnel of all types. Not only are populations living longer, but disease patterns are transforming as well. The healthcare workforce in the EU Member States is undergoing modification. It is aging, and, as noted, it includes more females who tend to have limited careers time-wise and also work fewer hours. A scarcity of all healthcare personnel is on the horizon (Data and statistics n.d.).

Noting that oral maladies are the most significant challenge facing socictics, the Council of European Dentists (2017) has developed a profile of the future professional so that contemporary challenges can be adequately confronted. Skills required are those of an oral health expert in a broader medical context, a communicator, an interprofessional and intraprofessional collaborator, a manager/administrator/organizer, a health advocate, a scholar, a researcher/teacher, and a professional. To produce an oral health practitioner to fulfill these roles is not an easy task. Training of DCPs must feature a more interprofessional and medical orientation (CED 2017).

The professions of DCPs have been shaped by politics of one type or another. Now, as is evident from this work, they are impacted by the EU and its decisions and policies. It would behoove all DCPs to be informed of EU operations. On current situations, at this level and at lower ones as well, they can make their voices heard. Policy choices do not just happen. All DCPs, making an effort, can help design them and they should.

References

CED (Council of European Dentists). (2017, May). *CED Resolution: Profile of the dentist of the future--Key driving forces in dentistry*. http://www.cedentists.eu. Accessed 21 Jan 2018.

Council of European Dentists. (2016). *Joint press release: Doctors and dentists in Europe face common challenges*. http://www.cedentists.eu. Accessed 18 Nov 2016.

Council of European Dentists (2017). *CED Resolution: Profile of the dentist of the future--Key driving forces in dentistry*. http://www.cedentists.eu. Accessed 18 Nov 2017.

Data and statistics. (n.d.). http://www.euro.who.int. Accessed 3 Apr 2018.

Fejerskov, O., Escobar, G., Jøssing, M., & Baelum, V. (2013). A functional natural dentition for all–And for life? The oral healthcare system needs revision. *Journal of Oral Rehabilitation, 40*(9), 707–722.

Friman, G., Hultin, M., Nilsson, G. H., & Wårdh, I. (2015). Medical screening in dental settings: A qualitative study of the views of authorities and organizations. *BMC Research Notes, 8*, 580. https://doi.org/10.1186/s13104-015-1543-8.

Lamster, I. B., & Eaves, K. (2011). A model for dental practice in the 21st century. *American Journal of Public Health, 101*(10), 1825–1830.

Mertz, E. A. (2016). The dental-medical divide. *Health Affairs, 35*(12), 2168–2175.

Metcalf, S. S., Northridge, M. E., & Lamster, I. B. (2011). A systems perspective for dental health in older adults. *American Journal of Public Health, 101*(10), 1820–1823.

Sultan, A., Warreth, A., Fleming, P., & MacCarthy, D. (2014). Does the dentist have a role in identifying patients with undiagnosed diabetes mellitus? *Journal of the Irish Dental Association, 60*(6), 298–303.

Training future-proof doctors for a digital society: How smart health is changing the profession of our doctors. (2019, April 7). http://www.eu.europa.eu. Accessed 21 May 2019.

Weil, A. R. (2016). Oral health. *Health Affairs, 35*(12), 2163.

Index

A
Academic programs, 11
Admission requirements, 35, 38
Adolescents, 176
Adverse pregnancy, 2
Alcohol
  Action Plan, 194
  beer, wine, and liquor, 193
  daily alcohol consumers, 192
  excise tax, 193
  socioeconomic diversities, 192
  in Spain, Italy, and Portugal, 191
Amçhi Programme, 45
Antimicrobial resistance (AMR), 148
Association for Dental Education, 10, 51

B
Binge drinking, 191
Bologna Declaration, 12
Bologna Process, 11
British Association of Dental Nurses, 145

C
Chamber model, 62
Chemical hazards, 141
Child maltreatment, 176
Children's rights, 177
Climate change
  foods and livestock production, 184
  human cancers, 184
  malnutrition, 184
  oxidative stress in allergic reactions, 185
  quality of life, 185
Clinical dental technicians, 117, 118
Clinical health promotion, 112
Compulsory membership, 64
Compulsory programs, 69
Compulsory registration, 67
Computer-aided design, 154
Continuing education, 68
Continuing professional development (CPD), 12, 64, 111, 144, 177
  amount, 73
  compulsory core, 70
  in Denmark, 71
  dental faculties, 69
  harmonization, 75
  knowledge, 69
  obligatory, 74
  quality, 69
  regulatory mechanisms, 75
  relevance, 74
  in Romania, 73
Cosmetic products
  EU's involvement, 157
  market surveillance systems, 156
  oral care products, 156
  stress, 156
Cost-sharing, 95, 96
Council Directive 2013/59/EURATOM, 144
Council Directive 78/686/EEC, 9
Council Directive 78/687/EEC, 10
Council Directives 86/378/EEC and 96/97/EC, 7
Council model, 67
Council of European Chief Dental Officers, 33, 100

S. Z. Koff, *The Dental Team in the European Union*,
https://doi.org/10.1007/978-3-030-72232-6

Council of European Dentists (CED), 27, 33, 47, 51
Council of Ministers, 23
Cross-border health care, 120
Cross-border mobility, 14
Cultural sensitivity, 45
Czech Dental Chamber, 71

D
Danish Dental Association, 70, 71
Dental amalgam
  mercury products, 173
  mercury supply and trade, 175
  patient's medical condition, 175
  role of mercury, 174
Dental assistants, 66
Dental care professionals (DCPs), 2, 22, 61, 133, 201
  curricula, 143
  development, 72
  diverse structures, 62
  environment, 68
  hazards, 140
  healthcare professionals, 62
  hospitals and clinics, 146
  infectious respiratory diseases, 140
  legislation, 66
  licensing, 82
  licensure, 61
  musculoskeletal difficulties, 142
  occupational hazards, 144
  physical hazards, 141
  psychological hazards, 141
  public sector, 151
  registration, 67
  regulation, 61
  risks, 140, 141
  structures, 69
  workplaces, 151
Dental chair-side assistant/dental nurse, 116
Dental education, 9
Dental Foundation Training, 28
Dental hygienists, 65, 66
  admission requirements, 35
  competence, 113
  corrective dental care, 34
  curricula and CPD programs, 114
  dental disease, 36
  development of legislation, 36
  diverse duration, 34
  employment and assessments, 36
  entry requirements, 36
  formal school system, 34
  healthcare professionals, 35
  Italy, 36
  Member States, 34
  Netherlands, 35, 114
  oral care, 36
  oral health education, 34
  oral health prevention, 34
  oral prophylaxis services, 34
  present-day education, 34
  professional groups, 36
  professional qualification, 35
  qualifications, 36
  role of, 113
  specific technical and professional skills, 34
  State examination, 35
  therapists, 36
  training and qualification, 34
  training courses, 35
  training program, 34
  training schools, 36
Dental squad members, 123
Dental tasks, 122
Dental team, 203
Dental technicians, 37–39, 67, 73, 117, 142, 152
Dental therapists
  in Netherlands, 115
  oral healthcare services, 116
  in United Kingdom, 115
DentCPD Project, 70
DentEd Thematic Network Project, 10
Dentistry, 119, 141
Dentists
  dental consultations and oral healthcare treatments, 109
  dental practitioner's performance, 111
  dentist-to-population ratio, 106, 107
  direct access, 121
  employment situation, 110
  females, role of, 108
  gender differences, 111
  gender factor, 110
  insufficient remuneration, 111
  lifestyle, 178–181
  oral health care, 105
  part-time employment, 108
  patient-dentist relationship, 111
  public and private sectors, 106
  research funds and pressures, 109
  skills and human resource planning, 122
Denturists, 142
Diploma in Dental Hygiene and Dental Therapy, 37

Directive (EU) 2018/958, 16
Directive 2005/36/EC, 12, 13, 23, 81
Directive 2006/54/EC, 7, 136
Directive 2013/55/EU, 13, 26, 33
Directive's implementation, 156
Discrimination, 124, 136
Domestic violence, 176
  in patients, 176

E

Earlier Council Directive 2000/78/EC, 136
e-Commerce Directive, 134
Education
  academic achievements, 23
  academic performance, 25
  admissions process, 23, 25
  aesthetics, 33
  associational membership, 30
  behavior, 42
  biology and genetics, 27
  clinical dental technicians, 39, 40
  Commission, 30
  communities, 21, 31
  competence domains, 51
  cost efficiency, 22
  curricula, 45, 46
  dental assistants, 40, 41
  dental nurses, 40, 41
  dental practitioners, 26
  dental public health, 31
  dental sector, 24
  dental specialty, 30
  dental students, 21
  dental technicians, 37–39
  dental training, 26, 27, 51
  dentistry, 21, 26, 29
  dentistry students, 22
  Directive 2005/36/EC, 26
  Directive 2013/55/EU, 29, 30
  diverse programs, 24
  diverse types, 24
  equity and diversity, 29
  EU program, 29
  European higher education systems, 26
  extrinsic factors, 21
  factors, 32
  faculty, 44, 45
  federal law, 22
  financial support, 25
  forensic and legal knowledge, 31
  forensic dentistry, 31
  graduate courses, 31
  graduate-entry dental programs, 25
  group of courses, 27
  health professional education programs, 51
  healthcare, 22, 25, 31
  higher education students, 26
  human service element, 21
  institutions, 29
  integration, 22
  interpersonal factors, 22
  interprofessional education, 46–48
  intrinsic factors, 21
  learning environment, 43, 44
  learning outcomes approach, 51
  legal dentistry, 31
  manual dexterity, 24
  medical program, 24
  Member States, 24, 28, 29
  minority ethnic group, 25
  multi-faceted knowledge, 31
  need-based and merit-based, 25
  number of students, 22
  opportunity, 21
  oral and maxillofacial surgery, 32
  organization, 29
  orthodontic therapist, 41
  outcome, 25
  Outreach, 48, 49
  performance, 23
  post-qualification experience, 28
  principal influences, 22
  public institutions, 25
  public/private sector, 21
  requirement, 33
  requirements, 32
  sector, 30
  significant relationship, 24
  social class, 25
  socio-demographic factors, 22
  special care dentistry, 31
  specialist training programs, 32, 33
  specializations, 31
  spectrum of variables, 24
  student attitudes, 42
  supervised clinical experience, 26
  supervised clinical training, 23
  teaching methods, 49, 50
  techniques and instruments, 33
  training institution, 30
  transition, 28
  treatment coordinators, 42
  types of students, 22
  United Kingdom, 25
  value of characteristics, 30
  vocational training, 28
Ergonomics and stress, 142

Ethical decision-making, 77
Ethical professional code, 75
EU AMR One-Health Network, 149
EU Cosmetic Products Notification Portal, 156
EU Daphne Programme, 178
EU legislation, 139
EU medical device regulatory, 155
  manufacturers, 155
  Member States, 155
  post-market surveillance, 155
EU's internal market, 6
EU-marketed medicines, 160
European collaboration, 11
European Community, 5
European Credit Transfer System (ECTS), 11
European Economic Area (EEA), 7
European Economic Community, 3
European healthcare, 15
European Labour Authority, 138
European Medicines Agency, 157, 159
European Ministers of Education, 11
European nation, 3
European Professional Card, 13
European Qualification Framework, 13, 14
European Union (EU), 22
  community responsibilities, 4
  directive, 6
  economic and social advancement, 3
  economic integration, 3
  group consultations, 201
  healthcare practitioners, 5
  healthcare services, 202
  membership, 3
  public health objectives, 5
  service providers, 201
  social security coordination, 4
  supranational and intergovernmental features, 4
  transparency, 201
  Treaty of Rome, 3
  voting system, 4
Europeanization
  DCPs, 3
  European landscape, 2
  result, 2
EU-wide assessment mechanism, 15
Evidenced-based elements, 46
Executive Committee of the Association for Dental Education, 27

F

Falsified Medicines Directive, 160
Females, in dentistry, 108
Finnish research project, 80
Framework Agreement, 145
Framework Directive, 143
Free trade agreements, 7
Free-pricing Member States, 159

G

General Dental Council, 76
Globalization, 160, 201

H

Health Care Quality Expert Commission, 78
Healthcare coverage
  Cyprus, 97
  dental procedures, 99
  duplicate coverage, 96
  expenditure and clinical relationships, 97
  Finland, 99
  Flanders, 97
  function, 98
  Germany, 97, 98
  hotel and hospital accommodations, 98
  insurance, 96
  Latvia, 97
  Member States, 96, 99
  Netherlands, 99
  Poland, 97
  population, 98
  private health insurance, 96
  voluntary health insurance, 96, 98
Healthcare delivery system
  Belgium, 90
  Cyprus, 91
  Denmark, 91
  diverse, 89
  employees, 93
  European Union (EU), 89
  finances, 90
  financial pressures, 92
  Germany, 92
  Greek, 92
  Hungary, 92
  insurance, 91
  Luxembourg, 92
  Member States, 89
  national, 90
  national health insurance fund, 90
  operation, 89
  payments, 90
  Poland, 93
  private healthcare services, 89
  public health insurance, 89

self-employed, 93
self-employed and unemployed, 90
Slovenia, 94
social health, 89
State health insurance, 93
support services, 89
Swedish, 90
tax-based revenues, 91
taxes, 89
Healthcare Quality, Complaints and Disputes Act (WKKGZ), 78
Hellenic Dental Association, 32
Help campaign, 190
Horror dentist, 81

I
Infection control
AMR, 148
EU document, 150
Member States, 150
optional and obligatory, 151
transmission, 148
Infringement proceedings, 121
Internal Market Information System, 13, 81
International Federation of Dental Hygienists, 35
Interprofessional communication, 123
Irective and Framework Agreement, 145
Irish study, 147

L
Learning environment, 43, 44
Legal instruments
curriculum, 10
dentistry, 9
EU/EEA, 9
healthcare professions, 9
higher education, 12
Liability insurance, 112
Licensing, 61
Lisbon Treaty, 177
Local anesthesia, 113

M
Maastricht Treaty (1992), 4
Maltese health system, 93
Maltreatment, 176
Mandatory CPD system, 70
Market authorization, 159
Medical Devices Regulations, 39
Medicinal products, 157
Directive 2012/26/EU, 160
EU legislation, 161
human use, 158
legal framework, 157
multi-faceted groups, 160
operations, 157
Regulation (EU) No 536/2014, 157
Member States, 22
Microbial contamination, 146
Minamata Convention, 174
Ministry of Health, 23
Modern dental education, 9
Musculoskeletal disorders, 141
Mutual-recognition procedure, 159

N
National dental associations (NDAs), 62, 111
National educational systems, 12
National Health Fund's, 93
National Health Service, 28, 90, 94, 99
National regulations and recommendations, 147
Netherlands, 114

O
One Health approach, 149
Online case-based discussions, 50
Online consultation, 147
Online discussion boards, 50
Open Method of Coordination (OMC), 7
disadvantage, 7
support and assistance, 7
Oral and systemic health, 4, 6
Oral cavity, 1
Oral health, 1, 2, 151, 202, 203
Oral healthcare delivery, 9
Oral maladies, 2, 203
Orthodontic auxiliary, 41
Orthodontic therapist, 41
Outreach, 48, 49

P
Panoramic radiographs, 113
Parental leave, 140
Parents concerning childcare, 140
Peer-assisted learning, 50
Personal protective equipment, 144
Pharmacovigilance, 160

Physical activity
  productivity enhance, 182
  public awareness, 182
Problem-based learning, 50
Product Liability Directive, 154
Product Liability Directive, Council Directive 85/374/EEC, 154
Professional healthcare groups, 202
Professionalism, 77
Professionalization, 7
  community, 8
  knowledge, 8
  process, 8
  professional standards and training, 8
  skill and training, 8
  training procedures, 8
Protective devices, 141
Public healthcare programs, 94–96

R
Registration, 68
Regulatory Fitness and Performance program, 147
Regulatory mechanisms, 68, 82
Regulatory model, 63
Revalidation/relicensure, 72
Risk assessments, 145
Risk-based approach, 147
Romanian Collegium of Dental Physicians, 63

S
Secondary sources of coverage, 96
Sectoral directives, 9
Self-regulation, 63, 67
Single European Act (1986), 4
Social Fairness Package, 138
Social health inequalities, 124
Social rights
  consultations, 139
  employment, 138
  European Pillar, 137
  responsibility, 137
Spanish Dental Association, 23, 28, 30
Special care dentistry, 124
Spillover effect, 201
Staff health precautions, 119, 120
Students' backgrounds, 24
Subsidiarity, 4–6
Supplements, 91, 92, 96
Sustainable Development Goals (SDGs)
  social needs, 186
  sustainable production and consumption, 187
Swedish Dental Association, 76
Systemic health, 1

T
Tallinn Health Care College, 41
Tanzanian Dental Students' Association, 45
Taxation, 89–93, 99
Team's performance, 123
Teeth whitening
  bleaching products, 171
  dentist's direct supervision, 172
  hydrogen peroxide and habitual use, 171
Therapeutic education, 112
Tobacco usage
  anti-tobacco use, 189
  cross-border advertising, 190
  e-cigarettes, 190
  tobacco-use cessation, 189
Transparency, 201
Treatment Coordinator Trainer, 42
Treaty of Amsterdam (1997), 5
Treaty of Rome, 9, 136

U
United Nations Environment Programme, 174

V
Violence against children, 176
Voluntary CPD system, 69, 70

W
Waste management
  circular economy, 153
  Council of European Dentists, 153
  dental practices, 152
  hazardous waste, 153
  policy-makers, 154
  practices, 153
Water quality, 147
Work-life balance
  EU citizens, 139
  EU legislative system, 139
  maternity leave, 139

paternity leave and parental leave, 140
principal elements, 139
Workplace, 138
dental office, 133
equal treatment, 136
equality goals, 137
EU legislation, 134
European consumers, 134
evidence and economic theory, 133
health and safety
consultation and participation, 143
equipment, 143
EU agenda, 143
inequality, 137
life and working conditions, 136
regulations, 133
severance pay, 137
statements and EU legal documents, 136
Work time
Commission, 135
Directive, 135
EU law, 134
financial payment, 135
guidance, 134
management executives, 135
World Dental Federation, 34

Z
Zero Waste, 152

Printed in the United States
by Baker & Taylor Publisher Services